Desperately Seeking the Aud

Desperately Seeking
the Audience

Ien Ang

ROUTLEDGE

London and New York

First published 1991
by Routledge
11 New Fetter Lane, London EC4P 4EE

Simultaneously published in the USA and Canada
by Routledge
a division of Routledge, Chapman and Hall, Inc.
29 West 35th Street, New York, NY 10001

© 1991 Ien Ang

Typeset in 10/12pt Times by
Columns Ltd, Reading
Printed in Great Britain by
TJ Press (Padstow) Ltd, Padstow, Cornwall

British Library Cataloguing in Publication Data
Ang, Ien
  Desperately seeking the audience.
  1. Television programmes. Audiences
  I. Title
  302.2345

Library of Congress Cataloging in Publication Data
Ang, Ien
  Desperately seeking the audience/Ien Ang.
  p. cm.
  Includes bibliographical references.
  1. Television audiences–United States.
  2. Television audiences–Europe. I. Title.
  HE8700.66.U6A54 1991
  384.55'1–dc20

ISBN 0 415 05269 6
      0 415 05270 X pbk

For my father and my mother,
Ang Khoen Ie and Oey Sioe Ing

Contents

Preface and acknowledgements

In the autumn of 1986 in New York, I had an informal lunch meeting with Jo Holz, then a researcher for the News Department of National Broadcasting Company (NBC), one of the three major networks of American commercial television. I was interested in how people inside the television industry look at the television audience, and we were talking about the kind of research in which she and her colleagues were engaged. She said earnestly and straightforwardly that, without doubt, all the research they do is in the interest of 'delivering audiences to the advertisers'. I was accustomed to hearing this expression being used in an ironical, if not cynical fashion by critical scholars and journalists who wanted to stress the perversity of the objectifying, commodifying logic that governs commercial television. But Holz made it clear that there's nothing ironical about it within the industry. Irony is an unfit attitude in an enterprise whose very economic base depends upon its success in 'delivering audiences to advertisers'. Industry people take this task very seriously – and for granted. This illustrates the importance of institutional setting in shaping the way in which the audience is perceived and assessed, problematized and conceived. 'In fact', Holz continued, giving a new twist to our conversation, 'industry people are much more inclined to see the audience as active than critics who worry so much about the effects of television from an outside perspective. We just can't afford to sit back and think of the audience as a passive bunch that takes anything they're served.' I found her remarks to be an insightful account of institutional self-consciousness. Her observations point to the argument that I will make in this book: that despite television's apparently steady success in absorbing people's attention, television audiences remain extremely difficult to define, attract and keep. The institutions must forever 'desperately seek the audience'.

This book's main purpose is to deconstruct this process of 'desperately seeking the audience' by rearticulating and contextualizing institutional discourses on the television audience so that they are robbed of their naturalness – so that the irony is put back in, as it were. It turns out that the audience so desperately sought does not exist, at least not in the unified and controllable mode in which it is generally envisioned.

But there were also other reasons for writing this book. First, having been interested as a researcher into the cultural details of how people deal with popular television in the realm of everyday life – details that generally remain private and discreet – I wanted to examine how this realm was accounted for, or rather accounted away, by those 'on the other side': the television professionals. Furthermore, I wanted to compare different, ostensibly contradictory institutional arrangements of television broadcasting – American style commercial television and West-European style public service broadcasting – because I believe that such a juxtaposition can highlight some general strategies of 'desperately seeking the audience' that remain unexplored when the systems are considered separately. It is in the common practice of audience measurement that those strategies are most clearly revealed. The comparative perspective offered here can hopefully contribute to a rethinking of the pervasive 'commercialization' and 'Americanization', real and perceived, that European public service broadcasting is undergoing in the present period.

Finally, this book aims to encourage the further development of an ethnographic understanding of television audiences. I argue that ethnography, conceived not just as a research method but as – within the academic field – a discursive practice *par excellence* that foregrounds the diverse, the particular and the unpredictable in everyday life, is especially suitable to free us from the desperate search for totalizing accounts of 'the audience' that characterizes much official knowledge about this overwhelmingly massive category. Only then, I suggest, can we arrive at understandings of the predicaments of our television-saturated culture that overcome unhelpful sweeping generalizations and meaningless abstractions.

The scope of this book then is both historical and theoretical, both political and epistemological, both institutional and cultural. If anything, what I have tried to unravel is the complex and contradictory operations of the power/knowledge connection in the context of an entrenched institutional practice – television broadcasting – which is undergoing rapid change in the era of the new communication technologies. In this situation, new forms of knowledge are demanded, but are often one-sidedly oriented towards the strengthening of vested commercial and bureaucratic interests. It is in order to challenge this bias that I squarely put 'the audience' at the centre of this book – not as an unproblematic object of study, not as an empirical point of departure, but as an uncertain discursive construct, a moving resultant of the power-laden ways in which it is known.

Many people have, in one way or another, played a supportive role in the creation of this book. I became familiar with the contradictory workings of American commercial television particularly during my stay as a Fulbright scholar at the Department of Communication of Hunter

College, City University of New York in 1986. I am indebted to many people who made my stay in New York worthwhile, both professionally and personally. I would like to specifically mention John Downing, then chairman of the Department, and members of the Salon for Media and Culture at the Graduate Center of the City University. Furthermore, the Television Information Office, the Museum of Broadcasting and the New York Public Library made resources accessible to me for getting acquainted with the history of American television.

Material about the Dutch Socialist Broadcasting Organization (VARA) was kindly made accessible to me by the management. I am especially thankful to VARA chairman Marcel van Dam for his co-operation, and to Paul Pennings, former teaching assistant at the Department of Political Science of the University of Amsterdam, for his judicious help in going through the VARA archives. I also thank researchers Wim Bekkers (Netherlands Broadcasting Foundation) and Dick Wensink (VARA) for the information they gave me about the role of research in public service broadcasting in general, and Dutch broadcasting in particular. Furthermore, the staffs of the libraries of the Netherlands Press Institute and the Netherlands Broadcasting Foundation have always been pleasantly co-operative, for which I am grateful.

Most of all I am indebted to my supervisor Denis McQuail, who has never failed to support me and has given valauble advice throughout this project. Especial thanks also go to Simon Frith for his good-humoured encouragement and stimulating comments on my ongoing work. Furthermore, I wish to thank a great number of people who have in one way or another given me intellectual or emotional feedback during the years that I was working on this book. In alphabetical order: Mieke Aerts, Tjitske Akkerman, Hans Boutellier, Charlotte Brunsdon, Jane Gaines, Larry Grossberg, Saskia Grotenhuis, John Hartley, Vera Keur, Ben Manschot, Uta Meier, Peter Neijens, David Paletz Anil Ramdas, Agnes Sommer, Louise Spence, Antoine Verbij and Ido Weijers. There were many others, and I hope I have not offended them by not mentioning them here.

Last but not least, four people deserve to be mentioned for special reasons. First, I am extremely grateful to my friend Dave Morley, who pairs a modest and open-minded critical intellectualism with a delight in exploring the boundaries of politically sensitive, non-dogmatic cultural studies, and was a careful reader of earlier drafts of this manuscript. With my colleagues and friends Liesbet van Zoonen and Joke Hermes I had the opportunity to explore the pleasures and frustrations of feminine and feminist professionalism, and to share intellectual interests that were sometimes not easily pursued. Their reliability and warm solidarity made the combination of writing a book like this with the day-to-day requirements of being an overloaded university teacher into a more than gratifying task. Finally, my thanks go to James Lull for his invaluable contribution to the development of this book, and especially for his love and camaraderie, for the joy and fun, for the wild enthusiasm and curiosity that we have shared about everything having to do with media and culture. Our arguments were sometimes *muy picante,* but always inspiring and passionate.

I.A.
January 1990

Introduction
(Not) knowing the television audience

> A certain fragility has been discovered in the very bedrock of existence
> – even, and perhaps above all, in those aspects of it that are most
> familiar, most solid and most intimately related to our bodies and to
> our everyday behaviour.
>
> Michel Foucault (1980b: 80)

A QUESTION OF PERSPECTIVE

In 1976, a group of friends from Los Angeles who often gathered
together in order to indulge in hour-long sessions of television viewing,
decided to call themselves 'couch potatoes'. With tongue-in-cheek
publications such as *The Official Couch Potato Handbook* (Mingo 1983)
and *The Couch Potato Guide to Life* (Mingo *et al.* 1985), they started a
mock-serious grassroots viewers' movement that promoted the view that
watching television is at least as good as, and perhaps even better than,
many other ways of spending leisure time. In their view, people should
stop considering television viewing as bad and harmful, something they
should be ashamed or secretive about. At least television viewing does
not cause air pollution![1] A few years later, the term 'couch potato' has
become so popular in America and other English-speaking countries that
it has come to denote television audiencehood as such. Now there is at
least a standard catch-phrase people can use to refer to that activity which
is so mundane and familiar and yet so little understood.

The rapid integration of 'couch potato' in everyday speech illustrates a
rather simple observation: namely, that although television has become
an integral part of our everyday lives, there is no sophisticated public
discourse that does justice to the complexity of the multiple practices and
experiences that television audiencehood involves. Instead, we are stuck
with a poor vocabulary full of unhelpful stereotypes, such as that because
we 'telly addicts' are 'glued to the box' we are now living in a 'global
village' and 'amusing ourselves to death'. In less than fifty years,
television has become a massive cultural institution whose impact can be

felt in almost all aspects of public and private life. With the coming of cable, satellite and video, television's presence has become even more ubiquitous, and as a consequence so it has its prominence as an object of social and political concern. However, whether television is considered as a profitable economic venture, a powerful educational apparatus or a symbol of cultural decline, the ordinary viewers' perspective is almost always ignored. Instead, the television audience is spoken for or about from a position of distance – by critics, scientists, journalists, teachers, politicians, law makers, advertisers, television producers.

There is, in other words, a profound disparity between everyday practice and official or professional discourse. This book is intended as a contribution to redress this imbalance, so that we can begin to improve our understanding of the everyday realities of television audiencehood. In general, I claim this understanding to be lacking because our knowledge about television audiencehood has been colonized by what I want to call the institutional point of view. In the everyday realm, living with television involves a heterogeneous range of informal activities, uses, interpretations, pleasures, disappointments, conflicts, struggles, compromises. But in the considerations of the institutions that possess the official power to define, exploit and regulate the space in which television is inserted into the fabric of culture and society, these subjective, complex and dynamic forms of audiencehood are generally absent; they disappear in favour of a mute and abstract construct of 'television audience' onto which large-scale economic and cultural aspirations and expectations, policies and planning schemes are projected, allowing these institutions to realize their ambitions to govern and control the formal frameworks of television's place in contemporary life. As a result, this institutional point of view silences actual audiences who nevertheless 'get along' with television in a myriad of creative yet tacit ways, whose details elude and escape the formal structures set up by the institutions.[2]

The purpose of this book is to disentangle the process of this symbolic silencing by examining the pragmatic logic of the institutional point of view from which the television audience is known. To put it bluntly, the basic problem with the institutional point of view is that it leads us to treat 'television audience' as a definite category whose conceptual status need not be problematized. The television audience is taken-for-grantedly defined as an unknown but knowable set of people, not more, not less. In this way of thinking, the television audience becomes an object of discourse whose status is analogous to that of 'population', 'nation' or 'the masses'. However, as Raymond Williams (1961: 289) has noted, masses are illusory totalities: there are no masses, 'only ways of seeing people as masses'. In a similar vein, 'television audience' only exists as an imaginary entity, an abstraction constructed from the vantage point of the institutions, in the interest of the institutions. This is the central argument that I will try to clarify and substantiate in the course of this book.

Alternative understandings of television audiencehood, developed from a perspective that displays sensitivity to the everyday practices and experiences of actual audiences themselves, can only be successful if we manage to radically dissociate ourselves from the assumptions and procedures which determine the way in which the television audience is known from the institutional point of view. The institutional point of view is a hindrance to such understandings because, as I will describe in this book, from this point of view actual audiences are constantly objectified, othered, and – if only symbolically – controlled.

THE INSTITUTIONAL POINT OF VIEW

The institutional point of view is pre-eminently embodied within the institutions that are directly responsible for planning, producing and transmitting television programming (television industry, broadcasting organizations, but also, in a more indirect way, the state institutions that shape and regulate national media policies). These institutions depend on the actual existence of the audience in very material terms. As John Hartley (1987: 127) has put it, television institutions 'are obliged not only to speak *about* an audience but – crucially, for them – to talk *to* one as well: they need not only to represent audiences but to enter into *relations* with them' (emphasis in original). But it is not easy for these institutions to assess and control these relations. For them, the television audience is an 'invisible mass', as it were, hidden behind the millions of dispersed closed doors of private homes, virtually unmanageable and inaccessible to the outsider. Therefore, the institutions concerned must produce what Hartley has called 'invisible fictions' of the audience, more or less well-circumscribed discursive figures of 'television audience', which allow the institutions to know, or at least get a sense of whom they must enter into relations with. How the television audience is known within television institutions, then, articulates the way in which they attempt to weave actual audiences into the mechanisms of their own reproduction. Various forms of institutional knowledge about the audience are by definition interested knowledge, inextricably linked with various forms of institutional power.

We can also put it differently. Quite obviously, before there was television, there was no such thing as a television audience. The television audience then is not an ontological given, but a socially-constituted and institutionally-produced category. This means that the notion of television audience as such derives its primary relevance only in relation to the specific institutional arrangements within which television technology is socially exploited and used. In other words, 'television audience' refers first of all to a structural position in a network of institutionalized communicative relationships: a position located at the receiving end of a chain of practices of production and transmission of audiovisual material through TV channels. It is within the constraints of this structural position that concrete people become actual audiences, whatever this means further in social, cultural and psychological terms. And it is never beyond the epistemological limits set by this structural position that the institutional point of view conceptualizes 'television audience'.

In Part I, which forms the theoretical prelude to Parts II and III, I will sketch a general outline of how the institutional point of view gives rise to the production of knowledge in which 'television audience' is constructed as an objectified category of others to be controlled. At an epistemological level, this construction is made possible by aggregating all people supposedly belonging to the category into a distinct 'taxonomic collective', that can be known as such. This operation is clearest in the institutional context of commercial television, where the practice that has come to be called 'audience measurement' has served from the beginning as the central instrument to come to such a construction. Through audience measurement, the commercial television industry has equipped itself with a basic mechanism to get to know the audience in a way that suits the industry's interests – a development which, not surprisingly, originated in the United States. By the 1990s, audience measurement has become a technologically-advanced practice in which enormous amounts of money and energy are invested. In Part II, I will discuss audience measurement as a prime instance for the objectifying, othering, and controlling kind of knowledge that circulates within the institutional context of American commercial television.

But technologically-advanced audience measurement has also come to play an important role in West European attempts to supply public service television institutions with knowledge about the audience that they deem necessary. Broadcasters, policy makers, critics and communication scholars alike are used to emphasizing the profound differences between public service and commercial arrangements of television broadcasting, not just at the economic level, but more importantly regarding the cultural values and intentions that sustain both types of systems. These differences are important indeed, but it is at least remarkable, as I will clarify in Part III, that the institutions of West European public service broadcasting have gradually come to appropriate similar ways of knowing the television audience as their commercial rivals, including an increasing reliance on the kind of knowledge provided by audience measurement.

This convergence has been possible, I suggest, not just because public service broadcasting has somehow been contaminated by commercial thinking, but more fundamentally because in the end all television institutions, irrespective of their founding principles, are seeking their own survival and continuity in a complex and uncertain, highly competitive social environment. In other words, when it comes to constructing the institution/audience relationship, public service and commercial institutions share more than is commonly acknowledged. The very real differences between the two have been outweighed by a massive concordance in their adoption of a specifically institutional point of view from which 'television audience' is known as an objectified category of others to be controlled.

THE CHANGING TELEVISION LANDSCAPE

This is a particularly suitable time to disentangle the problematic nature of current knowledge about television audiencehood because television institutions on both sides of the Atlantic have been in major turmoil since the late-1970s. In the United States, the virtual hegemony of the three commercial networks ABC, CBS and NBC has gradually been subverted by the emergence of hundreds of independent stations, cable and satellite channels, a development that was instigated by the deregulation policies of the Reagan administration (cf. Gomery 1989). By 1988, the balance of power within the American television business had shifted considerably in favour of the cable companies at the expense of the networks. For example, CNN, the 24-hour Cable News Network owned by media mogul Ted Turner, made more profit in that year than the CBS and ABC networks together (*Broadcasting* 12 October 1987; Foges 1989). As a result, competition has intensified and is unlikely to slacken, at least in the near future. It is a competition that is ultimately fought out over and about the audience: as a market, it is now in ever greater demand.

The advent of new television transmission and distribution technologies such as cable and satellite has also transformed the landscape of West European television. The time-honoured public service tradition in Western Europe has been thrown into a severe crisis – a crisis which is articulated by the growing influence of commercially-run channels. For example, Turner's CNN is only one of the American cable channels that has already entered the European airwaves through satellite, while a host of other, mostly European-based national and transnational channels such as Sky Channel, Sky Television, Super Channel, Sat1, RTL Plus, RTL Veronique, TF1, Canal Plus, TV5 and VTM, have made their way into people's living rooms in diverse countries. In the European context too then increased competition is the direct consequence of these recent developments, but for the public service institutions the crisis is more fundamental than this: the very viability of organizing television as a non-commercial institution destined to 'serve' the public is under threat (Euromedia Research Group 1986; Garnham 1989; Collins 1989b).

The changes are largely taking place over the heads of those in whose benefit all these grand institutional endeavours are supposed to be enacted. The millions of ordinary television viewers do not generally take any active part in determining the structural frameworks of the television culture of which they are mobilized to partake. They remain the invisible audience in whose name or on whose behalf the institutions put forward their interests, claims, defences, policies, strategies. Thus, the defence of public service broadcasting is often articulated in terms of some a priori notion of 'the public interest' that it pretends to represent. It is not the legitimacy of such a defence that is at stake here (this is a political question that I do not want to address at this point); what I do want to note is how the discourse of such a defence is typically based upon some invention of 'the public', that does not necessarily coincide with what actual audiences are interested in. Similarly, the widely-held commercialist assertion that competition between channels is beneficial because it leads to more freedom for the audience implies just as self-interested a way of speaking in the name of the invisible audience. Of course, competition does increase the number of channels from which viewers can choose (although many opponents of commercial television claim that this does not represent a genuine choice because more channels does not necessarily lead to more diversity and better quality of programming [cf. Gitlin 1983; Blumler *et al.* 1986]), but to call this opportunity to choose 'freedom' – which is of course inherent to the ideological discourse of capitalism – is to ignore the fact that specific institutional arrangements engender powerful mechanisms that set limits to the way actual audiences can relate to the medium. Audiences can never be completely free, because they are ultimately subordinated to the image flows provided by the institutions.

This is not to say that audiences are totally defenceless in the face of the power of the television institutions; far from it. But the 'freedom' they have (to choose between programmes, to watch little or a lot, together or alone, with more or less attention, in short, to use and consume television in ways that suit them) can only be seized within the parameters of the system they had no choice but to accept. In this sense the television audience is not only an invisible audience; it is also, literally, a silent majority. Surprisingly seldom do television viewers represent and organize themselves as 'we, the audience', and on the rare occasions when that happens, they are generally not taken very seriously. The self-parodying couch potato movement in America is a perfect example of this. Other spontaneous audience self-representations are often so volatile, such as when fans express impromptu their collective enthusiasm for some television star or programme (Ang 1985a; Lewis 1990), or are so limited and disorganized (as in letters to TV companies and producers) that they are easily accommodated, belittled, or ignored. More organized forms of audience self-representations that occasionally spring up (for example, in pressure groups for 'better' television, less sex 'n' violence, more positive images of blacks, women and gays, and so on) may have a bigger chance to be heard, but they too generally only play a marginal role in the decisions made within the television institutions (Turow 1982).

This suggests that if television institutions need to know the audience in order to establish and maintain a relationship with it, they are generally not interested in getting to know what real people think and feel and do in their everyday dealings with television. Indeed, institutional knowledge about the television audience inevitably abstracts from the messy and confusing social world of actual audiences because this world is irritating for the institutions, whose first and foremost concern is to seize control over their own conditions of existence. As I hope to clarify throughout this book, a too-detailed familiarity with the everyday engagements of actual audiences – that is, knowledge that takes into account the full complexity of the everyday realities of television audiencehood – would only be counterproductive in this respect. Institutional knowledge is driven toward making the audience visible in such a way that it helps the institutions to increase their power to get their relationship with the audience under control, and this can only be done by symbolically constructing 'television audience' as an objectified category of others that can be controlled, that is, contained in the interest of a predetermined institutional goal.

CONTROL THROUGH KNOWLEDGE

The practice of audience measurement provides a clear example of what this process of control through knowledge entails. Like retail statistics, opinion surveys, box office figures and other types of market research, audience measurement is an instance of what James Beniger (1986) has called 'market feedback technologies', that were developed in the first decades of the twentieth century as a response to the increasing demand for rationalized control of mass consumption in the United States. Beniger's characterization of these forms of research as technologies of control is illuminating, because it refuses to see them as neutral instruments but situates them in a larger social arena in which relations of power are at stake. Following this perspective, audience measurement can be seen as a central site where the television industry enacts its power to gain control over the audience.

In his discussion of the rise of the technologies of control Beniger adopts a macro-sociological perspective that he calls the Control Revolution, which leads him to foreground their status as sure agents of a major historical transformation towards today's 'information society'. Important as this telescopic historical perspective is, however, it does not allow for an examination of exactly how control is exerted by these technologies. In this book, I take up a more microscopic stance and will try to highlight the process by which audience measurement performs its controlling task within television institutions. This emphasis on process will make clear that the control made possible by audience measurement is inevitably precarious and provisional. This is obvious, because the fundamental mechanism by which control through audience measurement is implemented is of a discursive rather than a material nature; it works through the production of knowledge rather than through direct domination. Audience measurement, after all, is a form of research, whose manifest aim is to accumulate information about the television audience. But ironically, as I will describe in Part II, the information provided by audience measurement, while intended to solve the American television industry's problem of control, has itself become a problem. The information is indispensible for the industry to operate, but there is constant agony in industry circles about the adequacy of the information they get from audience measurement – adequacy defined, of course, from an institutional point of view. In other words, the control sought after is never completely achieved, and has to be continuously pursued by accumulating ever more information.

It is in the work of Michel Foucault that the epistemological dimension of power has been most consistently explored.[3] According to Foucault (1972; 1979; 1980a; 1980b; 1981), knowledge is one of the defining components for the operation of power in the modern world. Knowledge is an essential condition for the formation and functioning of a society that relies on the coordination and orchestration of every field of human activity (labour, politics, education, religion, leisure, welfare and so on) in and through large-scale institutions. Administration, planning, policy, rules and regulations, discipline – these are institutional forms of power over the actions and lives of people that can only be exercised through a whole range of bureaucratic techniques and procedures that imply the production of knowledge (e.g. statistics, reports, records, documents, programmes, plans, manuals, directives, formulas and so on). In this sense, Foucault's perspective shares Beniger's (1986) account of the role of the technologies of control in the information society. In Foucault's work, however, we find a much more detailed emphasis upon the way in which power and knowledge are intertwined through concrete discursive practices – that is, situated practices of functional language use and meaning production. In these discursive practices, elusive fields of reality are transformed into discrete objects to be known and controlled at the same time. But this only happens in specific, power-laden institutional contexts, that delimit the boundaries of what can actually be said.[4] More concretely, it is only in and through the discourses that express the institutional point of view that the dispersed realities of television audiencehood come to be known through the single, unitary concept of 'television audience'.

In this context, knowledge can be defined broadly as discourse invested with truth value. At stake in the discursive construction of knowledge, as Foucault (1980b) has stated, is not a battle 'on behalf' of the truth, but a battle 'around' truth. Truth is not a universal absolute that exists outside certain historical conditions, but is an institutionally-produced category which refers to 'the ensemble of rules according to which the true and the false are separated'. In this separation process 'specific effects of power are attached to the true' (ibid., 132).

In modern societies, scientific discourse is the source of one of the most powerful modalities of knowledge. Empirical science's prestige as the privileged domain of objective, systematic, verified truth is an effect of its own power to extend itself to ever more corners of human life, not the result of the inherent quality of its claims (Latour 1987). Empirical science, and the authority of the knowledge produced by it, has become indispensible to manage and regulate institutional practices, although scientific discourse is not the only resource of knowledge to which institutions resort in order to govern and legitimize their own operations. They can also make use of other authoritative discourses such as legal discourse or ideological discourse – discourses that produce other modalities of knowledge than science but are in principle equally capable of imposing themselves as repositories of truth. Even so, we can see a growing reliance on empirical stocks of knowledge gathered through scientific methods within television institutions. The ever increasing importance of audience measurement in almost all television institutions in the world is only one indication for the heightened status of scientifically-based rhetoric in the pursuit of knowledge about the audience within media industries (cf. Tunstall 1977).

In Part III, I will describe how this development was triggered by the perceived ineffectiveness of other, more philosophically-based authoritative discourses in producing knowledge that is able to perform the task of control within public service institutions. In fact, for a long time research such as audience measurement was not at all seen as necessary in public service contexts; as we will see, there was enough confidence among public broadcasters in the truth value of the non-empirical knowledge engendered by the philosophical assumptions of public service broadcasting's purpose – a purpose that prescribed a normatively-defined relationship with the audience. In other words, to have control over the audience public service institutions in Europe did not always see the need to know the audience in empirical terms, because there was a strong a priori, normative conviction about how the audience should be addressed. It is the cracking of this conviction that led these institutions to embrace forms of knowledge modelled after the discourse of empirical science. Reliance on research, and particularly audience measurement, has now become an integral part of the way public service institutions try to get control over the audience. Again an ironical occurrence, given the imperfections that this form of knowledge proves to display as a tool of control in the American context, as I have already pointed out.

I do not want to imply here that research that familiarizes us with the audience in empirical terms is illusory and of no use. But what should be stressed is that the move towards more scientific ways of knowing the audience within television institutions is not simply a sign of progress from ignorance to knowledge, from speculation to fact, from belief to truth. Rather, what is at stake here is a politics of knowledge. In the way television institutions know the audience, epistemological issues are instrumental to political ones: empirical information about the audience such as delivered by audience measurement could become so important only because it produces a kind of truth that is more suitable to meet a basic need of the institutions: the need to control. Empirical science, or better, the knowledge emanating from it, brings about a regime of truth that is in principle more flexible and conditional – and thus more practical – than the absolutist truth characteristic for philosophical knowledge, precisely because it purports to incorporate elements of the social world of actual audiences into its discursive realm of visibility. It thus brings institution and audience closer together, as it were. However, this incorporation cannot go beyond the horizon of the institutional point of view, from which 'television audience' must be constructed as an objectified category of others to be controlled.

THE PREDICAMENT OF ACADEMIC KNOWLEDGE

The institutional point of view constrains and sets limits to the substance and modalities of knowledge that television institutions produce about the audience. But the influence of the institutional point of view stretches beyond the immediate discursive domain of the television institutions themselves. As I have suggested at the beginning of this introduction, our understanding of television audiencehood has been thoroughly colonized by the institutional point of view. This is also the case for large chunks of academic mass communication theory and research, where 'audience research' has traditionally been one of the most intensively explored areas – and since the 1950s, it is the television audience that has most preoccupied academic researchers, especially in the United States. But despite often-stated value-freeness and independence, this academic knowledge has been deeply complicit with the institutional point of view, in the sense that, in the words of Todd Gitlin (1978: 225), 'it poses questions from the vantage point of the command-posts of institutions that seek to improve or rationalize their control over social sectors in social functions'.

There were very concrete historical roots for this complicity, perhaps most obviously embodied in the career of Paul Lazarsfeld, who is generally seen as the man who almost single-handedly instituted American mass communication research in the 1930s. Lazarsfeld, founder of the influential Bureau of Applied Social Research at Columbia University, was an active proponent of the administrative use of social science. He managed to acquire, through the building-up of direct corporate connections, both funding resources and intellectual legitimacy from the media establishment, and was particularly interested in questions having to do with the prediction of audience reactions to particular media messages (including the issue of audience measurement) by using sample surveys – an essentially marketing-oriented interest that decisively channelled the work of entire generations of future researchers (Tunstall 1977; Gitlin 1978; Czitrom 1982; Peters 1986).[5] The result, as Gitlin has remarked, was that

> the dominant sociology of mass communication has been unable to grasp certain fundamental features of its subject. More than that: it has obscured them, scanted them, at times denied them out of existence, and therefore it has had the effect of justifying the existing system of mass media ownership, control, and purpose.
>
> (Gitlin 1978: 205)

Most important to highlight in this context is not the ideological liabilities of mainstream mass communication research, but the specific discursive scope that emerged from its inability 'to grasp certain fundamental features of its subject'. As I have said earlier, the basic problem with the institutional point of view is that it leads us to treat 'television audience' as a conceptually nonproblematic category, consisting of a definite, unknown but knowable set of people. It is exactly this assumption that is inadvertently taken for granted and reproduced in most branches of academic audience research. This is because the research projects have consistently proceeded by implicitly singling out the (television) audience as a separate domain, treating it as an aggregate of individuals whose characteristics can then presumably be operationalized, examined, categorized and accumulated into an ever more complete picture.[6] Some titles of works emanating directly or indirectly from the Lazarsfeld tradition clearly suggest the ambitiousness with which 'television audience' has been set out to be fully covered in empirical terms: *The People Look At Television* (Steiner 1963); *Television and the Public* (Bower 1973); *Television and Human Behavior* (Comstock *et al.* 1978); *Television and its Audience* (Barwise and Ehrenberg 1988).[7]

Let me not be misunderstood: I do not want to deny that these studies can deliver some useful knowledge, although that usefulness usually goes unreflected and is too easily taken for granted. What I do want to emphasize here is how the institutional point of view can be felt in the very grain of audience research that is presented as independent scholarship. Not only do such studies ignore the socio-cultural and institutional contexts in which audiences are constituted; more importantly, they establish a kind of knowledge that sheds light on 'television audience' from an exterior, objectifying perspective, just as the television institutions do. Such a perspective can only slight the insiders' dimensions of television audiencehood, as it were: the complex and contradictory ways in which television becomes meaningful in people's everyday lives.

Of course, there has always been criticism against mainstream mass communication research, particularly from those who have rejected its positivist, behaviourist and empiricist footing. Critical communications scholars, mostly inspired by Marxist or neo-Marxist analytical perspectives, have often consciously opposed the unwitting adoption of the institutional point of view; instead, they have mostly dedicated themselves to examine the broad historical and political context in which media institutions operate, and to deconstruct their role as mediators of economic and ideological power (for overviews, see e.g. Gurevitch *et al.* 1982; Grossberg 1984). However, this preoccupation with large-scale structural issues has led to a downplaying or even ignoring of the importance of understanding media from the audience's perspective, so much so that, according to Fred Feyes (1984), the critical tradition in communication studies tends to suffer from 'the problem of the disappearing audience'.[8] Ironically, then, along very different lines critical communication studies has contributed to the invisibility of the dynamic complexities of television audiencehood which ultimately characterizes knowledge produced from the institutional point of view.

Admittedly, this is a very schematic sketch of the state of the art in academic knowledge on television audiencehood.[9] Moreover, the field of communication studies has in recent years seen a growing number of initiatives, from both 'mainstream' and 'critical' sides, to develop new approaches to the study of the television audience. Often methodologically unconventional (qualitative rather than quantitative) and theoretically fresh (emphasizing the social and cultural engagements of audiences with the medium rather than the traditional interest in effects and effectiveness), these new studies have paid attention to such diverse topics as the ways in which people make sense of news and documentary programmes, the culturally-specific pleasures which underlie the popularity of television genres such as the soap opera, and the social uses of television in the structuring of family life (e.g. Morley 1980a; 1986; Lull 1980; 1988a; Ang 1985a; Jensen 1986; Liebes and Katz 1986; Gray 1987; Lindlof 1987; Seiter *et al.* 1989). So far, there has been little coherence in these dispersed research initiatives. What does seem to emerge, however, is a growing awareness of the necessity to develop forms of knowledge about television audiencehood that move away from those informed by the institutional point of view.

This book does not straightforwardly address this emerging trend in academic audience studies.[10] In deconstructing the institutional point of view, however, I hope to contribute to the trend by providing it with a clearer vision of the ways of thinking which the institutional point of view entails, and which we need to settle accounts with, both politically and epistemologically, in order to avoid reproducing them unawares.

TOWARDS ALTERNATIVE UNDERSTANDINGS

Several theorists have recently begun to radically untangle received conceptions of audience in order to create a discursive space for new understandings (Nightingale 1986; Chang 1987; Hartley 1987; Allor 1988; Grossberg 1988; Radway 1988; Silverstone 1990). For example, Martin Allor (1988: 228) has criticized the 'abstracted reification of the individual in front of the [television] machine' that marks the self-evident starting point of most research into the television audience.[11] In his view, this starting point involves a naive epistemological realism which is the direct antecedent of conceptualizing the audience as an unproblematic category, empirically equated with the sum of all individuals in front of the machine. To overcome this liability, he suggests that we do away with the concept of audience altogether. 'The audience exists nowhere; it inhabits no real space, only positions within analytic discourses', he states (ibid.).

As illuminating and provocative as Allor's radical epistemological solution is, however, it cannot account for the power of the institutional point of view, which is fundamentally predicated upon stating the valid existence of 'television audience' as a category of others to be controlled. In other words, rather than claiming that the audience inhabits no real space – which is an idealistic, ahistorical claim – we should say that it does inhabit a real space: a crucial, institutional space which was installed as soon as the exploit of broadcast television became an institutional practice. Television institutions must keep believing that there is such a thing as an audience that can be conquered!

Rather than simply rejecting the concept of audience, then, I prefer to put forward the theoretical distinction between two realities: between 'television audience' as discursive construct and the social world of actual audiences. I have made this distinction rather casually throughout this introduction; it is now time to make it more explicit. The distinction does not just refer to the gap between representation and reality, signifier and signified, discourse and referent.[12] By using the plural term actual audiences, I mean to do more than just asserting that the television audience should be differentiated and multiplied into several disparate, more or less coherent and fixed groups, more or less distinct empirical realities.[13] My claim is more radical than this. Whenever I refer to the social world of actual audiences throughout this book, I use the phrase nominalistically, as a provisional shorthand for the infinite, contradictory, dispersed and dynamic practices and experiences of television audience-hood enacted by people in their everyday lives – practices and experiences that are conventionally conceived as 'watching', 'using', 'receiving', 'consuming', 'decoding', and so on, although these terms too are already abstractions from the complexity and the dynamism of the social, cultural, psychological, political and historical activities that are

involved in people's engagements with television.[14] It is these heterogeneous practices and experiences of audiencehood that form the
elements to be articulated in discourses of 'television audience'.

But the social world of actual audiences consists of such a multifarious
and intractable, ever expanding myriad of elements that their conversion
into moments of a coherent discursive entity can never be complete. In
other words, the fixing of meanings of 'television audience' is always by
definition unfinished, because the world of actual audiences is too
polysemic and polymorphic to be completely articulated in a closed
discursive structure. There is thus always a 'surplus of meaning' which
subverts the permanent stability and final closure of 'television audience'
as a discursive construct (cf. Laclau and Mouffe 1985). Indeed, if
'television audience' exists nowhere, actual audiences are everywhere
(Lull 1988b: 242)!

The theoretical distinction between the social world of actual audiences
(as I define it) and discursive constructs of 'television audience' is an
extremely important one: as we will see, it is the tension between the two
that accounts for the basic precariousness of the institutional point of
view, which forms a red thread through the analyses in the pages to
come. The distinction also clarifies why in the end knowledge of
'television audience', constructed from the institutional point of view, will
only make us lose sight of the intricacies of the social world of actual
audiences, of what Edward Said (1985: 5) would call the 'brute reality' of
audiencehood in the modern, television-saturated world we all live in.

If we are to come to an understanding that does justice to the dynamic
complexities of the social world of actual audiences – an understanding
that is 'on their side', as it were (Nightingale 1986) – we must, to begin
with, recognize the fundamental irreducibility of this 'brute reality' to any
attempt to contain it in an objectified construct of 'television audience' as
a category of others to be controlled. Hayden White (1978: 5) has
characterized understanding as 'a process of rendering the unfamiliar . . .
familiar; of removing it from the domain of things felt to be "exotic" and
unclassified.' What it comes down to, I suggest, is to find new ways of
making the unfamiliar familiar, or more precisely, to make something
that is so familiar in our everyday lives but has retained an 'exotic' quality
nevertheless, also familiar at the level of understanding, knowledge,
discourse. This book is an attempt to chart the terrain for such a project
by removing the epistemological and political obstacles we are liable to
encounter along the road.

Part I

Conquering the audience: the institutional predicament

1 Institutional knowledge: the need to control

In 'The Imaginary Signifier', film theorist Christian Metz (1975) has identified an acute problem for the film industry. The problem will come as no surprise to those who run the industry, for they are daily confronted with its practical repercussions. But its theoretical repercussions have been less charted. Here is how Metz has characterized the problem:

> In a social system in which the spectator is not forced physically to go to the cinema but in which it is still important that he [sic] should go so that the money he pays for his admission makes it possible to shoot other films and thus ensures the auto-reproduction of the institution – and it is the specific characteristic of every true institution that it takes charge of the mechanisms of its own perpetuation – there is no other solution than to set up arrangements whose aim and effect is to give the spectator the 'spontaneous' desire to visit the cinema and pay for his ticket.
>
> (Metz 1975: 19)

Conjured up here is the problem of institutional reproduction. The cinema can only continue to exist if and when enough people are willing and prepared to be regular members of the film audience, but the film industry does not have the means to provide itself with a guarantee that people will not one day stop going to the movies. The problem seems to be a rather far-fetched one, because since the turn of the century, when the cinema first entered our cultural life, the world has obviously turned into a place full of filmgoing women, men and children. However, the principle of the problem is undeniable, and that it is not entirely hypothetical, is easily exemplified by the sharp and steady decline in cinema-going since the 1950s, when television made its entrance in people's homes (Docherty et al. 1987; Gomery 1985).[1] At stake, then, is the institution's control – or better, lack of control – over the conditions of its own reproduction.

Broadcast television faces similar institutional problems: it too cannot take its audience for granted. Contrary to other social institutions such as the school or the family, television (as well as all other mass media) does not have the means to coerce people into becoming members of its audience. Television audience membership is not a matter of compulsion or necessity, but is principally voluntary and optional. Therefore, the television institution is ultimately dependent upon people's unforced appetite to continue watching day after day. Again, the problem seems far-fetched given television's manifest success in securing huge audiences for its transmissions, but this still does not mean that that success comes naturally and effortlessly. On the contrary, numerous institutionally orchestrated activities such as the publication of TV guides, advertisements and press interviews with TV personalities, as well as previews of forthcoming programmes during an evening's flow, the use of teasing jingles, logos and so on, testify to the enormous amount of money and energy being spent to reinforce and update people's desire to watch television (Ellis 1982; Ang 1985b). The very fact that these strategic institutional activities are of a continuous, never-ending character indicates that television networks and broadcasting organizations know that they cannot take the existence of an audience for granted: they can try to influence potential audience members, but they cannot control them in any direct manner.

A constant sense of uncertainty thus haunts television's persistence and continuity as an institution. The audience, *sine qua non* for both television's economic viability and cultural legitimacy, forms its ultimate insecurity factor because in principle there is no way to know in advance whether the audience will tune in and stay tuned. It is not surprising then that a constant need is felt within the institution to 'catch', 'capture' or 'lay hold of' the audience. Audiences must constantly be seduced, attracted, lured. How-to-get-an-audience is, willy-nilly, the institution's key predicament, even though this is not always acknowledged as such.

The seriousness of this predicament is deeply ingrained in the very structure in which television as an institution is formally organized in our societies. Television's dominant institutional arrangement is embodied within the framework of broadcasting, a framework whose basic configuration has been extended, without any radical changes, to cable and satellite television. According to Raymond Williams (1974: 30), the broadcasting framework is characterized by a 'deep contradiction between centralized transmission and privatized reception'. This 'deep contradiction' refers to the circumstance that while television is generally seen as a form of 'mass communication', no true communication – in the 'ritual' sense of that word: exchange of meanings that is both collective and interactive (Carey 1989) – between the television institution and the television audience generally takes place. Broadcast television transmission is both adamantly intentional and resolutely non-interactive: the diffuse and dispersed television audience, locked in its condition of privatised reception, is an invisible and mysterious interlocutor.[2] This makes the task of how-to-get-an-audience a particularly difficult one for television institutions (Gans 1957; McQuail 1969; Hirsch 1972; Elliott 1972, 1977; Cantor 1980; Ettema *et al.* 1987).

Over the years, a range of risk-reducing techniques and strategies of regulating television programming such as serial production, usage of fixed formats and genres, spin-offs, horizontal scheduling, and so on, have been developed (Ellis 1982; Gitlin 1983). These strategies do not only serve as a way to facilitate the organization and co-ordination of the industry's production practices, but are also aimed at the codification, routinization and synchronization of the audiences' viewing practices, to make them less capricious and more predictable (cf. Rojek 1985: 154–5). But all these strategies can only help to manage, not remove the basic uncertainty with which the television institution has to live. There are no guarantees that actual audiences will comply to the codes, routines and synchronities of viewing behaviour as designed by the institutions. Ultimately, then, the problem of (lack of) control amounts to one thing: the impossibility of knowing the audience – in the sense of knowing ahead of time exactly how to 'get' it.

This does not mean that no knowledge about the audience is produced in the multi-layered organizational process of television broadcasting. On the contrary, both formal and informal knowledge about the audience is constantly operative in the complex decision-making procedures which determine the shape and content of television's daily output of programmes. 'Know the audience' is the first basic principle every handbook for commercial broadcasting teaches the would-be television programmer (e.g. Howard and Kievman 1983; Tyler Eastman *et al.* 1985). The production of this knowledge does not only take place in the specialized, knowledge-producing activity of 'audience research'; it also emerges and comes into circulation more or less spontaneously through a whole range of concrete discursive practices – board meetings, informal conversation and interviews, discussions about programme ideas, scheduling principles, policy statements, research reports, and so on; practices that, in one way or another, ultimately revolve around one main objective: to come to terms with television's invisible addressee.

One such discursive practice is the 'story conference', a key event, in American commercial television at least, in which producers, writers, and other creative personnel (story editors, directors and so on) gather together to come to a shared understanding of what the television programme they are creating should look like. Paul Espinosa's (1982) analysis of a number of typical story conferences indicates that their unfolding is governed by the implicit application of a number of rules of thumb that articulate institutional perceptions about the audience. In the course of such story conferences the participants tend to display an intense preoccupation with the need to engage the audience, to consider the audience's presumed knowledge of the world, to meet the audience's expectations for the programme, and not to 'divide' the audience. Statements made during a story conference such as 'America has to embrace your characters' and 'I think we have to keep this non-racial' evince the sense producers have of what viewers will or will not accept. According to Espinosa (ibid.: 84), such 'perceptions of the audience function as an internalized, restraining mechanism which [the producers] bring into play at appropriate moments in the story conference'. How these perceptions come into being, however, is a rather elusive question. As he notes,

> these images [of audience] are the subjective, intuitive beliefs of producers. These images are not empirically generated by market research or any formal quantitative method. Rather the 'audience' is a cultural category for producers, a category which they form from a number of sources, including their experiences with audiences from previous programs, their personal projections about who their audience is, and their knowledge of the industry they work in.
>
> (ibid.: 85)

Despite their 'unscientific' nature, however, these images and perceptions serve as true knowledge for the producers because they empower them to reduce the extreme complexity of the process which the making of a programme entails: they are discursive tools that enable them to make choices, evaluate proposals, and so on.

Espinosa's study refers to the central role of informal, if not speculative knowledges about the audience in the creative sector of institutional activity, where development of programmes is the main task (Pekurny 1982; Newcomb and Alley 1983). But producers do not have the power to decide whether their productions will be put on the air; that power – that is the power to select programmes for transmission – lies in the hands of those occupying the administrative and managerial echelons of the television institution (Ettema *et al*. 1987). At this level, the problem of how-to-get-an-audience is not primarily the craftman's one of how to steer or constrain creativity in order to come to a finished aesthetic product (the programme), but is related to the more encompassing problem of overall organizational policy, which is ultimately aimed at creating and securing the institutional conditions in which a relationship with the audience can be established and maintained. It is at this level that having (and keeping) an audience *tout court* forms the single most important goal, and here too knowledge about the audience, both formal and informal, is used to help managers to make the decisions needed to reach that goal.

Consider, for example, the perspective of network executive Brandon Tartikoff, president of NBC Entertainment and responsible for airing much-acclaimed series such as *Hill Street Blues, Cheers* and *Miami Vice*. As a result, he acquired the distinctive reputation of being a programmer with an eye for 'quality' – something which, in what has been called the 'vast wasteland' of American commercial television (Boddy 1990) is quite a feat indeed. But this does not hold him from setting his standards within a definite idea of 'what the audience wants'. He asserts: 'I probably have more esoteric tastes than the average television viewer. I'll go to see *Amadeus* and pay my five dollars and fifty cents, but when the salesman from Orion [a production company] comes and asks me to buy it for the networks, I'll say no, because it's going to get a twenty-two share', which is, he implies, not enough because 'as a programmer I had to ask myself if it was something that would get a thirty share or better' (in Levinson and Link 1986: 256–7).

Thus separating personal taste and market judgement, Tartikoff extemporaneously adheres to the principle of 'audience maximization', which reigns so supreme in the operations of American commercial television. The language in which this principle is expressed is the quantitative one of 'shares' – a language that is only made possible by the existence of a very formalized procedure of knowledge production: audience measurement.

As a form of systematic research in which empirical information is gathered through quantifying scientific methods, audience measurement supplies a technical and formal kind of knowledge whose mode and status differs fundamentally from the intuitive, all-but-immaterial knowledges about the audience put forward and used by programme creators during events such as the story conference. For one thing, knowledge gained through research is produced by experts, whom Harold Wilensky (1967) has called facts-and-figures men, while the subjective and informal forms of knowledge circulating within the creative community remain largely implicit in the creative process itself. The first kind of knowledge holds the official status of 'organizational intelligence' (ibid.) within the industry because it enables managers such as Tartikoff to speak about the audience in tangible, apparently objective terms, and as I will show in Part II, it is precisely this sense of objectivity that accounts for audience measurement's centrality as a power/knowledge device in the structural operations of commercial television. Even the creative community ultimately has to submit, often grudgingly, to the regime of truth established by audience measurement, the truth of 'shares' and 'ratings', because it is this regime of truth that has the final say over what counts as 'success' and 'failure' (Cantor 1980; Gitlin 1983). Thus, within the television industry a hierarchy of diverse forms of knowledge about the audience has been established: the contextualized and more or less instinctive knowledge that is inherent in the *savoir-faire* of programme creation is ultimately subordinated, *qua* knowledge about the audience, to the stipulated, official and generalized knowledge produced by the discourse of audience measurement.

In fact, not only audience measurement, but research in general, with its aura of scientific rationality, has acquired an entrenched position in the institution as a whole. The elevated status of research as a means of providing the institution with 'seemingly systematic, impersonal, reliable ways to predict success and failure' (Gitlin 1983: 31) is exemplified by the career of Frank Stanton, who was hired as a researcher by CBS in 1935 and subsequently rose to become president of the corporation for twenty-five years. As Todd Gitlin (ibid.: 43) has remarked, 'Stanton embodied the postwar legitimacy, indeed the necessity, of facts-and-figures research in the culture industry'. Stanton was a pioneer in the field of audience research; together with Paul Lazarsfeld, the father of American mass communication research, he developed the Lazarsfeld-Stanton Program Analyzer, the first device for measuring audience reactions to radio and still the basis for CBS's television pre-testing system – a system aimed at testing programmes before they get on the air (Levy 1982). The three national networks of American commercial television, ABC, CBS and NBC, all routinely engage in this practice of pre-testing which, in Gitlin's (1983: 32) cynical words, consists of the production of 'numbers to predict numbers', that is, the creation of 'artificial test markets in hothouse settings where audience reactions can be cheaply reduced to numerical measures that they hope might predict eventual ratings'.

Research is often motivated and legitimized for its role in rationalizing managerial decision-making procedures. Indeed, where uncertainty or disagreement about the chance of success is particularly marked, resort to a neutral, non-subjective, facts-and-figures discourse, which pretends to provide the most explicit and systematic knowledge about the audience, is preferred in order to manage intra-industry relationships and mobilize support for unpopular or controversial decisions. Thus, pre-testing results can be capitalized upon in negotiations between creators and managers – something which is especially useful when opinion is divided: 'Network executives find it convenient to tell producers that their shows aren't being picked up because of low test scores, thereby deflecting some of the supplier's anger onto the hapless research department' (ibid.: 45). Such use of the rhetoric of quantitative justification is a well-known phenomenon in modern complex organizations (Gephart 1988), and suggests that the aura of 'scientific rationality' that facts-and-figures knowledge possesses is primarily useful for its rhetorical aptness in institutional practices: more often than not, research is a tool for symbolic politics rather than for rational decision-making. Therefore, research itself does not go uncontested within the institutions. As Gitlin (1983: 45) has noted, 'Valued but scorned, cited but patronized, [the] ambiguous position [of research] represents the culture industry's uneasy attempt to accommodate its industrial reality'.

Yet the importance of research can only be understood precisely in the light of this institutional uneasiness. Against this background, we should not only look at the differences in modalities of knowledge about the audience that circulate within television institutions, but also at their common conditions of production, their shared institutional context and function. No matter whether they are formal or informal, explicit or implicit, scientific or intuitive, 'objective' or 'subjective', they are all forms of interested knowledge, aimed at inducing strategic know-how: their purpose is to clarify what one should do in order to sustain a hold over the audience. It is this goal-directed requirement that binds all forms of institutional knowledge (including research) together, and that determines their common discursive construction of 'television audience' as a category of others to be controlled.

The pragmatic logic of this construction is evocatively recited by Brandon Tartikoff. In 1970, when he first explored the possibility of starting a career within the television industry, the programme director of a local television station gave him some extraordinary advice. Tartikoff recalls:

> He asked me if I had an Instamatic camera and I said I did. He said, 'Why don't you go down to New York, go to the Port Authority Bus Terminal, and take pictures of the first hundred people who get off the buses? Take those pictures, blow them up to eight-by-ten glossies, and wherever you go down to work in television, put those photographs up on the wall somewhere. And every time you have to make a decision, look at those pictures and ask yourself, will they like it?' If I did that, he said, I'd be very successful in the business.
>
> (In Levinson and Link 1986: 247)

Tartikoff did not literally follow the rather unusual advice, but the anecdote is telling enough because it clearly illustrates the general discursive operation that underpins all institutional pursuits of knowing the audience. Central to this discursive operation is the construction of a set of binary oppositions: production versus consumption, 'sender' versus 'recipient', institution versus audience. As a consequence, a relationship of confrontation is constituted. From the point of view of the institution, the audience appears in this discursive structure as a distinct category of others that stands against itself: 'us' versus 'them'. As Tartikoff's adviser wondered: 'Will *they* like it?'

This subject/object dichotomy reveals the structural position assigned to the audience from the institutional point of view: the position of object to be conquered. The audience must, in one way or another, be imagined as addressable, attainable, winnable, in short, a manœuvrable 'thing'. In this respect, it is not for nothing that the audience is as often referred to as 'it' as it is as 'they'. It is through this discursive objectification that the nexus of power and knowledge exhibits its effectivity.

In his book *Orientalism*, Edward Said (1985) has demonstrated a similar intertwining of power and knowledge in what he calls the discourse of 'orientalism': a systematic discourse, inextricably linked to

European colonialism and neo-colonialism, in which the 'Orient' is imagined and represented in ways which always buttresses and nourishes the superiority and hegemony of the West. Western observers have, consistently and persistently, pursued the aim of gaining knowledge about the Orient. But this knowledge inevitably articulates a power relationship. As Said remarks,

> Knowledge means rising above immediacy, beyond self, into the foreign and distant. The object of such knowledge is inherently vulnerable to scrutiny; this object is a 'fact' which, if it develops, changes, or otherwise transforms itself in the way that civilizations frequently do, nevertheless is fundamentally, even ontologically stable. To have knowledge of such a thing is to dominate it, to have authority over it.
>
> (Said 1985: 32)

The television audience can be seen as similarly 'orientalized' from the institutional point of view (cf. Hartley 1987). Institutional knowledge is produced as a result of the symbolic travels that are initiated and orchestrated by the institutions into the obscure territory of the audience; they lead to a capturing of 'television audience' as object of knowledge, object of scrutiny, object of control. The trip to Port Authority that Tartikoff was advised to take in order to take some pictures of bus passengers which he should then hang full-blown in his office, is an almost too fitting metaphorical illustration of this process, a discursive process in which the television business aims to 'freeze' the audience into a durable and factual thing, an object consisting of manipulable people.

The aggressive connotations are purposefully invoked here: television institutions need to know the audience because the latter is, in a manner of speaking, the wild savage which the former want to tame and colonize. One could object to this metaphor by pointing to the evidently immense success of television to attract audiences: the wild savage seems so willing to surrender to the colonizer! This is true, of course, but this does not mean that the colonizer does not meet with any resistance. What the television institutions are confronted with, rather, is a form of 'passive aggressiveness' on the part of actual audiences. As Gitlin (1983: 31) has put it, 'however passive, deadened, habit-formed the hypothetical audience may be, the fact remains that they do not have to turn the dial to a certain spot at a certain hour on a certain evening'.

At stake, then, is an eternal battle between institution and audience, a battle in which institutional knowledge serves as powerful ammunition (Ang 1985b). It is this battle, or more precisely, the way in which the battle is articulated in the formalization and rationalization of institutional knowledge – pre-eminently symbolized by the privileged status of audience measurement – that will be laid out in the following parts of this book. First, however, I need to become more specific about the historical varieties in the economic and cultural institutionalization of television, in order to develop a more concrete sense of the battleground upon which the institution–audience relationship is fought out (Chapter 2). In Chapter 3 I will proceed to disentangle the basic epistemological assumptions by which institutional knowledge manages to objectify 'television audience' into a unified, controllable category. Finally, in Chapter 4 I will point to the inherent instability of this process of objectification: the control mustered by institutional knowledge is prone to be partial, imperfect, incomplete.

2 Audience-as-market and audience-as-public

So far, I have unproblematically described the operation of the television institution in commercial terms. But of course the institutional arrangement of television broadcasting is not always based upon commercial principles. While the United States is the home of the most full-fledged commercial system, the nation-states of Western Europe are the historical base of a range of public service broadcasting systems, embodied by state-regulated and collectively-financed organizations such as the British BBC, the Italian RAI, or the Dutch 'pillarized' system (see e.g. Kuhn 1985). The two systems are both formally built upon the communicative framework of broadcasting, but they differ fundamentally as regards assumptions about the cultural and political purpose of broadcasting, and this difference is inextricably linked to a marked distinction in how each system prefers to define the institution–audience relationship. In other words, although all broadcasting institutions must by definition imagine the audience as object to be conquered, the meaning, intent or import of the conquest is not construed in the same way in the two systems.

The pragmatic philosophy behind the commercial system is the easiest one to unravel, because its axioms are simple and straightforward. Commercial television can be characterized at several levels, but in its barest form it is based upon the intertwined double principle of the making of programmes for profit and the use of television channels for advertising. Thus, the driving force of the system is ultimately a purely economic matter: it is principally connected with the capitalist concern of making money. As Jay Blumler (1986: 1) has observed, 'individual broadcasters [in American commercial television] may be moved by aspirations of communication excellence, "love of television", social purpose or sheer creative autonomy. But in the end, all such aims must be subordinated to the overriding profit-maximising goal.'

In principle, the workings of the system are relatively simple. Programmes are transmitted by commercial television networks and stations in order to carry commercials, which are usually inserted between programmes or sections of programmes. The advertisers whose products are offered for sale in the commercials pay large sums of money to the broadcasters in exchange for the air time they acquire to disseminate the messages. The system operates according to the laws of the capitalist market economy, so that advertising time in the most popular programmes is generally the most expensive. Thus, in the autumn of 1985, a thirty-second time spot in NBC's *The Cosby Show*, then the programme on American prime time television that was measured as drawing the largest audience, cost $270,000 (ibid.: 5).

It is for this precise economic reason that audience maximization has become so paramount a principle in commercial television, and concordantly, why the production of ratings through audience measurement has become an absolutely crucial subsidiary industry in the institutional framework of commercial television. The discourse of ratings, dry and technical as it is, provides knowledge about the television audience that is indispensable for the economic functioning of the system. Good ratings results are the agreed-upon signifier of effective communication between advertiser and audience, and the commercial networks must try to achieve those good ratings results – that is, to maximize their audience – through shrewd and attractive programming. As CBS executive Arnold Becker told Todd Gitlin (1983: 31): 'I'm not interested in culture. I'm not interested in pro-social values. I have only one interest. That's whether people watch the program. That's my definition of good, that's my definition of bad.'

The television programme then is the main instrument in commercial television's constant quest for the maximum audience. As Nick Browne (1984: 178) has noted, 'the network is basically a relay in a process of textualizing the interaction of audience and advertiser'. This process of textualizing – the process of translating the goal of maximum ratings results into concrete decisions about the programmes to be scheduled – is the core of the networks' task: the day-to-day activities of network managers ultimately revolve around constantly finding ways of regulating this difficult and complex process along orderly and manageable lines.

Ratings play a central role in this process, but that role is a highly ambivalent one. On the one hand, it offers managers a sense of knowing how successful the textualizing has been (what is called 'feedback'), but on the other hand, it leaves them in profound ignorance, or at least in great doubt, about the precise ingredients of their success or failure. That is, although ratings produce some generalized information about who has watched which programmes, they do not give any clue about the more specific question of what made people watch the programmes, so that it is very difficult to use ratings to predict future success or failure (Pekurny 1982).

Nevertheless, in the political economy of commercial television audience measurement is an indispensable knowledge-producing instrument. In the commercial system, the imperative of conquering the audience ensues from the positioning of the audience as a market in which audience members are defined as potential consumers in a dual sense: not only of TV programmes, but also of the products being advertised through those programmes (McQuail 1987: 220–1). What is essential in this context is knowledge about the size of the market, and this is precisely what 'ratings' and 'shares' are purported to signify. However, determining the size of the market is a difficult and problematic task, as is evidenced by the ever-increasing technological sophistication of the methods being used for measuring the audience, that took an accelarated pace in the 1980s and reached a temporary climax with the introduction of the so-called 'people meter', an advanced and expensive measurement device that provoked intense controversy in circles of the American television industry. This controversy, which shows how epistemological and political issues, issues of knowledge and power, are inextricably linked in commercial television's institutional point of view, will be described extensively in Part II.

In the philosophy of public service broadcasting, an altogether different place is reserved for the audience. Of course, the idea of 'public service' as such can be and has been interpreted and concretized in a variety of ways in diverse national contexts, manifested in historical particularities in institutional structure and socio-political and ideological grounding. However despite such idiosyncracies it can be said that in classic terms public service broadcasting institutions constitute what Williams (1976: 131) has called a 'paternal system'. A paternal system, Williams states, is 'an authoritarian system with a conscience: that is to say, with values and purposes beyond the maintenance of its own power'. In this philosophy, the institution–audience relationship is primarily defined in cultural and ideological terms: 'the paternal system transmits values, habits, and tastes, which are its own justification as a ruling minority, and which it wishes to extend to the people as a whole' (ibid.). 'Serving the public' then means, as Anthony Smith has put it, 'forcing [the audience] to confront the frontiers of its own taste' (in Kumar 1986: 59), although it should be noted that this ideal does not necessarily have to be linked to a conservative form of cultural elitism, as was the case in the early days of public service broadcasting. As we will see in more detail in Part III, contemporary public service broadcasting has over the years developed a much more eclectic conception of its task, emphasizing the duty to offer a broad range of high quality programmes (Blumler *et al.* 1986; Manschot 1988). Nevertheless, the relationship of public service institution to its audience remains essentially characterized, not by economic profit-seeking, but by a pervasive sense of cultural responsibility and social accountability, which is emphatically opposed to the easy-going commercial dictum of 'giving the audience what it wants'.

As a result, a different positioning of audience is at stake here. Not the audience-as-market, but the audience-as-public is the central object of concern within public service institutions (McQuail 1987: 219–220). The audience-as-public consists not of consumers, but of citizens who must be reformed, educated, informed as well as entertained – in short, 'served' – presumably to enable them to better perform their democratic rights and duties. Within this context, broadcasting has nothing to do with the consumerist hedonism of (American) commercial television – it is a very dignified, serious business. Typically, popular entertainment, so conspicuously and self-evidently the prevailing fare on American television, tends to be considered a less important programme category in European public service broadcasting, even though in practice entertainment programmes, both domestic and foreign, are an established part of the daily schedules of most public service channels (cf. Ang 1985a; 1985b).

The difference between the two paradigms of audience is impressive and can be clarified by placing them in two diverse theoretical models of mass communication. The audience-as-public idea is in fact the more classic one of the two and fits in the so-called transmission model of communication: here, communication is defined by such terms as sending or transmitting messages to others. Implied in this model is the conception of audiences as 'receivers' of those messages, and a more or less 'ordered transference of meaning' as the intended consequence of the process as a whole forms its basic rationale (McQuail 1987: 43–4; Carey 1989). In the audience-as-market idea, however, such purposive transfer of meaning is only of secondary importance. As McQuail (1987: 45) has remarked, 'the essence of any market is to bring goods and services to the attention of potential consumers, to arouse and keep their interest'. Thus, the essence of what McQuail calls the attention model of communication is comprised by the mere gaining or attracting of attention: communication is considered effective as soon as attention is actually given by audiences, no matter its quality or impact. This is the model of communication that undergirds the institutional arrangement of commercial broadcasting, but it is clearly insufficient and inadequate from the institutional perspective of public service broadcasting, for whom attention would only make sense when connected with some meaningful communicative purpose.

Audience-as-market and audience-as-public then are two alternative configurations of audience, each connected with one of the two major institutional arrangements – commercial and public service – of broadcast television. These two configurations provide the founding paradigms for the production of knowledge about the audience within specific institutions. Thus, institutional knowledge produced in the context of American commercial television generally displays a vocabulary and a set of preoccupations which articulate and ultimately fit into the idea that the audience is a market to be won, while the repertoire of institutional knowledge circulating within public service institutions in Europe and elsewhere needs to enhance and sustain the idea that the audience is a public to be served with enlightened responsibility.

As we have seen, commercial television has equipped itself with a highly formalized procedure of knowledge production to buttress its audience-as-market paradigm, namely audience measurement. The audience-as-public paradigm however does not have such a readily-available and straightforward discursive instrument to assert itself. This is not surprising, for the desire to 'serve' the audience, the aim to transfer meaningful messages necessitates a much more intricate, multidimensional and qualitative discourse than one that capitalizes on numbers of people giving attention, as offered by audience measurement. Therefore, public service institutions tend to have more problems than their commercial counterparts in coming to a satisfying knowledge about their relationship to their audience: knowing the size of the audience alone is not sufficient to gauge the degree of success or failure of public service television's communicative efforts, not least because success and failure are a normative rather than a material issue here.

The recent changes in Western Europe's television landscape as a result of national and integrated European deregulation and privatization policies correlate closely with a crisis in the audience-as-public paradigm of public service broadcasting. With the proliferation of commercial television offerings in the European airwaves, the idea of audience-as-public comes more and more under pressure. Several observers have noted, generally in a tone not unaffected by a sense of nostalgia and regret, how European public service broadcasting is in practice gradually pervaded by a mass-marketing mentality to almost the same degree as in the United States (e.g. Gitlin 1983; Garnham 1983; Richeri 1985; Burgelman 1986). And indeed, the trend is unmistakable: more and more have public service organizations developed an explicit interest in ratings, 'audience maximization' and similar concerns that derive from the competitive commercial system. More and more have they implicitly adopted, if not wholeheartedly and not completely, a limited attention model of communication to judge their own performance. More and more, in other words, is the audience-as-public transformed, at least apparently, into an audience-as-market.

But this process of paradigmatic transformation should not be seen as a mechanical one; on the contrary, as will become clear in Part III, it is accompanied by many tensions and difficulties within the public service broadcasting organizations themselves, tensions and difficulties having to do with the need for these organizations to develop a new, acceptable way of thinking about the specificity of their relationship toward the audience. In short, what they need to do is to somehow reconcile the two contrasting paradigms of audience. I will examine how this formidable work of discursive reconstruction has been accomplished, by delving into the histories of two particularly interesting European embodiments of the public service ideal: the British BBC and the Dutch VARA.

The BBC derives its relevance from its exceptional international influence and prestige when it comes to defending the value and superiority of public service broadcasting – something which is evidenced by the fact that British television has over the years won by far the greatest number of awards at television festivals such as Montreux and the Prix Italia (Blumler *et al.* 1986). VARA is a much less well-known institution internationally, but its case is equally interesting because of its unique democratic socialist roots (Ang 1987). While both organizations can pride themselves upon a long and strong tradition of 'serving the public' through broadcasting, then, the contrast between the two is also illuminating: while the ideological origins of the BBC, particularly as voiced by its first Director General, John Reith, represent an outstanding case of 'authoritarian paternalism', in which the audience is positioned as the public to be reformed 'from above', the history of VARA, based upon its founding philosophy of social democracy, is a peculiar case of what can be called 'populist paternalism', in which the desire for cultural uplift came 'from below', from (a segment of) the audience-as-public itself as it were.

Despite this seemingly radical difference in origins, however, both organizations have evolved, in certain aspects at least, along remarkably similar lines. Briefly, both histories are marked by an increasing uncertainty about how a public service institution should establish and maintain its normatively-defined relationship to the television audience. This is expressed in a growing reliance within both organizations on the kind of knowledge about the audience that could be delivered by research, and by audience measurement in particular. In other words, the prevailing form of institutional knowledge employed within these organizations became less and less of a normative kind, and has taken more and more the form of factual information. However, this does not mean that the audience is now squarely conceived as a market; rather, as Part III will show, it is the intermingling of old public service commitments and market thinking that motivates the use of audience measurement and related forms of research in public service institutions. Ideally, the information delivered by audience research is assumed to aid public service institutions in their effort to better serve the audience in a time when their authority, so taken for granted in the past, has been eroded by the growth of commercial competition.

These developments point to the fact that while the philosophical assumptions of commercial and public service broadcasting are indeed radically different, there is also a fundamental commonality in the two institutional systems which tends to be obscured – a commonality which has everything to do with the fact that in practice both kinds of institutions inevitably foster an instrumental view of the audience as object to be conquered. Whether the primary intention is to transfer meaningful messages or to gain and attract attention, in both cases the audience is structurally placed at the reception end of a linear, one-way process. In other words, in both systems the audience is inevitably viewed either from 'above' or from 'outside': from an institutional point of view which sees 'television audience' as an objectified category of others to be controlled.

The paradigms of audience-as-public and audience-as-market are thus only relatively conflicting. As McQuail (1987: 221) has noted, 'We never conceive of ourselves as belonging to markets, rather we are placed in market categories or identified as part of a target group by others'. But in a similar vein we can state that when people watch television, they do not spontaneously conceive of themselves as members of an institutionally-defined public. To put it differently, if it is true that consumers must be made rather than found in order to create a market, so too are the citizens that form a public not naturally there, but must be produced and invented, made and made up, by the institution itself.

Both commercial and public service institutions then cannot, with their specific goals and interests in mind, stop struggling to conquer the audience, no matter whether audience members are identified as consumers or citizens. This brings me back to the more general discursive mechanisms of knowledge produced from the institutional point of view, based as it is upon the positing of a clearcut subject/object opposition and the construction of 'television audience' as a unitary, objectified category. We will now take a closer look at the assumptions and consequences, both epistemological and ontological, of this construction.

3 Television audience as taxonomic collective

In enabling television institutions to see their task as that of conquering the audience, institutional knowledge must first of all constitute 'television audience' as a manifest, nameable object. Apparently, this is not so difficult to do. In our everyday language we are used to saying that one can draw or attract an audience; one can move, grip, or stir an audience; an audience can be responsive, enthusiastic, unsympathetic and so on. In all these cases, the audience is implicitly granted an autonomous, supra-individual existence. In common sense language, then, the object-ive status of audience is treated as self-evident; audience is assumed to be a given category. However, our ability to speak so confidently and taken-for-grantedly about audience in this way does not come naturally; rather, it is a matter of discursive effectivity, conditioned by the taking up – as the etymology of the word 'audience' suggests – of the performer's perspective in a theatre. An exploration of some of the basic assumptions and consequences of the general tendency to speak about audience as a given category can illuminate the objectifying mechanisms and operations performed by institutional knowledge.

Due to the messy status of the notion of audience in everyday language, an audience is routinely defined in terms of its most obvious empirical manifestation, i.e. a collection of spectators, a group of individuals who are gathered together to attend a performance and 'receive' a message 'sent' by another. An audience would then be synonymous with the total sum of people that are part of it, pure and simple. In other words, it would be what Rom Harré (1981) has called a 'taxonomic collective': an entity of serialized, in principle unrelated individuals who form a group solely because each member has a characteristic – in our case, spectatorship – that is like that of each other member.

This straightforward, taxonomic definition of audience as aggregate of attenders can be readily applied to audiences for football matches in a sports stadium – to name but one obvious example. In this case spectators have to be bodily present at a central location at a certain time, in order to be part of the audience. Apparently it is perfectly clear here who the audience is: those who are inside the stadium are, those outside it are not part of it. One could, in a manner of speaking, take an air photograph of the stadium during a match, and so get a sense of direct knowledge about the actual audience of this match. The stadium audience, so it seems, is characterized by immediate visibility, and as such it furnishes the certainty of an empirical referent for knowledge about the football audience: its object is clear, and clearly there.

The stadium audience bears many characteristics of the prototypical, pre-media audience idea. Unfortunately, however, the audience for the mass media, starting with the historical rise of the reading public in relation with the mass production of print in the eighteenth century, is a much more elusive phenomenon, and this is certainly the case for the television audience (McQuail 1987). The television audience is typically characterized by geographical dispersedness: television spectatorship takes place in millions of private homes. Furthermore, as a cultural form television is typically a virtually ever-present, kaleidoscopic medium: television's 'unit of performance' is not clear, instead it is characterized by a constant flow of programmes, segments and items (Williams 1974; Ellis 1982).[1] In other words, as a provider of culture television is increasingly characterized by permanent presence, always available to whoever wants to watch, at any time. As a result, actual audiences can never be observed in a direct empirical overview. A photographic image of the total television audience is impossible to take. This literal invisibility results in a lack of a readily identifiable referent for knowledge about 'television audience'.

Statistical figures that give estimates of the size of the audience, as produced by audience measurement, offer a compensation for this lack of immediate visibility. I have already hinted at the economic necessity of such information for commercial television. But the general currency of such figures, also in public service contexts, points to a more general institutional desire to be able to speak about the television audience as a clearcut, empirically definable thing. What such figures do then is construct a unified representation of 'television audience' by taking its conceptualization as a taxonomic collective as a starting point. Such figures produce a sense of concreteness, a sense of ontological clarity about who or what the television audience is. Mobilized here is an inherently empiricist epistemology, in that it suggests the ultimate possibility of defining the audience in its totality, and to empirically delimitate its boundaries – if not directly (for instance, through photography) then at least indirectly (for instance, through statistics).

Epistemologically speaking, it is easy to criticize the empiricist dogma of immaculate perception which lies behind the illusory matter-of-factness of conceptualizing the television audience taxonomically as the total sum of all viewers. No representation of 'television audience', empirical or otherwise, gives us direct access to any actual audience. Instead, it evokes 'fictive' pictures of 'audience', fictive not in the sense of false or untrue, but of fabricated, both made and made up (Clifford 1986). Even our photographic representation of the football audience, apparently such a perfect imprint of empirical reality, only gives us an illusion of objective neutrality. In fact, it actively produces a way of looking at people watching the game as a unified audience, rather than simply reveals it. Similarly, counting the heads of people watching television and representing the results in neat and round figures, involves the construction of a certain way of objectifying a group of people we then call 'television audience'. In other words, 'audience' as it emerges from its taxonomic definition as aggregate of spectators is not the innocent reflection of a given reality, but a discursive construct which can only be known and encountered in and through discursive representations such as the air photograph or, more ubiquitously, the statistical figure.

The issue to explore here, however, is not just the epistemological liabilities of the taxonomic definition of 'television audience' as a body of spectators, but the specific advantages it provides to the institutions that want to conquer the audience. Put simply, the abstract and decontextualized definition of 'television audience' as a taxonomic collective may be epistemologically limited, but at the same time it is institutionally enabling! What should be emphasized, then, is not just that defining 'television audience' as a taxonomic collective is not a matter of pure description, but more importantly, that it occasions the production of strategically useful knowledge. Like every discursive construct, it introduces an element of symbolic abstraction, which directs our thinking and our imagination in some directions and not others.

Thus, lumping people together as so many members of a 'television audience' already stresses something that compounds and unifies them, i.e. a type of observable activity, usually labelled 'watching television'. Basically, it is people's shared orientation toward some focal point – a centre of transmission, a centre of attraction – that turns them into 'audience members'. In this context, the idiosyncracies of the individual people making up an audience, as well as the specific interrelations between these people, do not matter: audience as taxonomic collective is in principle a term of amassment ('We all watched the football game on television yesterday'). At the same time, representing audience as a collection of people also implies an act of demarcation, of categorization: some people are considered part of it, others not. In other words, in the discursive act of putting people into a single taxonomic collective 'television audience' becomes constructed as a distinct category.

Aggregating and clustering people as members of the distinct category of 'television audience' are discursive mechanisms which establish the very representability of 'television audience' as a thing-like, objective phenomenon. Fundamentally, then, the representation of 'television audience' as a taxonomic collective provides us with an exterior perspective from which it can be imagined as an isolatable empirical phenomenon, a factual entity 'out there' existing in and for itself, possessing unambiguously describable features.

Here then we have the bottom-line discursive operation of the institutional point of view on the audience. Whatever information, images or beliefs about the television audience are constructed within television institutions, they always draw upon the assumption that 'television audience' is a separate category of people, objectively distinguishable from the non-audience. Representing 'television audience' as a taxonomic collective enables those working within the institutions to imagine the audience as variable in specific features but nevertheless absolute in its given existence as object ready to be conquered, just as the 'Orient', as Said (1985) has shown, is constituted as an ontologically stable fact in the discourses of Orientalism. To put it differently, once the taxonomic conceptualization of 'television audience' as aggregate of people is used as an implicit, taken-for-granted starting point, a workable 'operationalization' of the category of audience has been created on the basis of which it becomes possible to gain more elaborate knowledge, empirical or non-empirical, about the constitutive parts of the category, i.e. the so-called audience members. All forms of knowledge about the audience produced within television institutions, including Tartikoff's fantasy trip to Port Authority, exemplify this procedure: knowing 'television audience' is equated with knowing a cluster of audience members as if they were exemplars of an alien species.

Not only the audience-as-market, but also the audience-as-public is essentially imagined as a taxonomic collective within commercial and public service institutions respectively. If a market consists of a set of anonymous consumers grouped together according to some objectified common characteristics (e.g. demographic variables), a public is generally made up of a collective of citizens who are seen as bounded together in an imagined community such as a nation, sharing a common 'national culture' (as in the case of the BBC), or a political community, sharing a common 'popular culture' (as in the case of the Dutch socialist broadcasting organization VARA) (Anderson 1983). The average citizen may have different imputed characteristics than the average consumer, but they are both merely exemplary, prototypical audience members constructed from the perspective of the institutions concerned.

As members of a taxonomic collective audience members – whether defined as consumers or as citizens – are extremely depersonalized. They are not seen as individual persons or social subjects with their own particularities, but are given the status of serialized parts of an objectified whole (market or public). As Aaron Cicourel (1981: 64) has noted, 'When we aggregate across individual responses . . . we are forced to restrict severely if not eliminate the local and larger contextual conditions that could clarify the respondent's perspective. The aggregation is a summarization process that obscures our thinking of the way local context and individual responses contributed to the larger picture.' Thus, conceiving 'television audience' as a taxonomic collective implies a denial of the messy social world of actual audiences: the fact that television viewing is done by living people, in concrete locations, in real times. But this denial is not to be seen as a failure. On the contrary, it should be regarded as an accomplishment for institutional knowledge. It is what it needs to achieve, in order to be able to construct 'television audience' as object to be conquered.

The predilection within television institutions, commercial or public service, to think about audiences in this way cannot be overestimated. For instance, it frames the experiences of John Ellis (1983), a critical television theorist who became a programme maker for the British Channel Four in the early 1980s.[2] Disenchanted with the promise that the newly-founded channel had posed as a place for 'innovation and experiment in form and content', he came to the conclusion that it is exactly the evacuation of concrete viewers from the institution's perceptual horizon, and its commitment to an abstracted, taxonomic idea of audience, that structurally impedes radical televisual innovation:

> For 'audience' is a profoundly ideological concept, that has very little to do with what viewers are doing or how they are interpellated. Broadcasting institutions are not concerned with 'viewers', but they are with 'audience'. Viewers are individuals, people who use TV within their domestic and group social contexts. Viewers are the few people who ring in to the duty officer, or write to the broadcasters or to newspapers, expressing their opinions. Viewers record programmes on VCRs and use them later, pausing or replaying when attention wanders, shuttling forward when interest fades. Audiences, however, do not have these irritating characteristics. Audiences are bulk agglomerations created by statistical research. They have no voices and the most basic of characteristics, they 'belong' to income groups and are endowed with a few broad educational and cultural features. Audiences do not use TV, they watch it and consume it. Broadcasting institutions do not seek viewers, they seek audiences.
>
> (Ellis 1983: 49)

Conceiving television audience as a taxonomic collective of amenable audience members, then, leads to ascribing stability to the category of 'television audience' by purging from it the unpredictable, the capricious, and the erratic that characterizes the social world of actual audiences (Ellis's 'viewers'). The resulting discursive solidity of the category is a precondition for television institutions in order to pursue their ambition to conquer 'it'. But how effective is the control so implemented?

4   The limits of discursive control

We can now return to the institutional predicament as outlined by Metz at the beginning of Chapter 1: the fact that there is no way for mass media institutions to secure the conditions of their own reproduction by exerting direct control over their audiences. In this situation, says Metz, the conquest of audiences can only be endeavoured by instilling a 'spontaneous' desire in people to be audience members. The principal way to do this, of course, is trying to convince people of the attractiveness or usefulness of the medium and its programming. Thus, eventually it is through the rhetorical assumptions of the programmes transmitted – their genres, their style, their subject matter, their place in the overall schedule – that actual audiences are affected by institutional control. This is applicable to both commercial and public service television institutions. As Williams (1976: 133) has noted, 'the control claimed as . . . a matter of principle by [public service] paternalists, is often achieved as a matter of practice in the operation of the commercial system'. For instance, commercial television programming is generally characterized by a regular and predictable flow of entertainment programmes, so as to secure the prolonged attention of the taxonomized audience member/consumer, while public service television puts a distinctive emphasis on programmatic comprehensiveness (i.e. a varied range of informative, educational, high cultural and entertainment programmes) so as to offer the taxonomized audience member/citizen a responsible, meaningful TV diet.

To a certain extent then programming of TV channels implies a programming of television viewers as well. A clear indication of this is evinced in the sense of alienation that European viewers usually experience when first confronted with American television. The late British cultural theorist Raymond Williams recalled the experience thus:

> One night in Miami, still dazed from a week on an Atlantic liner, I began watching a film and at first had some difficulty in adjusting to a much greater frequency of commercial 'breaks' [than on British commercial television]. Yet this was a minor problem compared to what eventually happened. Two other films, which were due to be

shown on the same channel on other nights, began to be inserted as trailers. A crime in San Francisco (the subject of the original film) began to operate in an extraordinary counterpoint not only with the deodorant and cereal commercials but with a romance in Paris and the eruption of a prehistoric monster who laid waste New York. . . . I can still not be sure what I took from that whole flow. I believe I registered some incidents as happening in the wrong film, and some characters in the commercials involved in the film episodes, in what came to seem – for all the occasional bizarre disparities – a single irresponsible flow of images and feelings.

(Williams 1974: 91–2)

On his part, American researcher Thomas McCain had no less severe problems with adjusting to the typically more irregular rhythm of European television programming:

We moved to Dublin and I watched British and Irish television for one month with no small amount of puzzlement, amazement and frustration. Television was not very convenient to watch; programmes changed at odd, rather than predictable hours. Series seemed to be only a few weeks long; just as we came to enjoy or understand a character or programme. . . it was gone from the schedule. The news was on in the middle of the evening rather than later and earlier. The schedule or sequencing of programmes was most peculiar; a movie early in the evening, the British programme *In Search of the Wild Asparagus*, followed by a situation comedy and then a late evening documentary on pigeons. . . . It was a change of routine we had not anticipated, though we liked it. Having left Columbus, Ohio and the Qube cable system with 30 channels of nearly round the clock programming available, television had become an almost magnetic part of our lives, the television set drawing us to its field of fancy and frivolity with regularity of embarrassing proportions. But this European television was different. My initial reaction was that it was rather pretentious, quite dull and occasionally brilliant. Our family stopped 'watching television' and started viewing programmes.

(McCain 1985: 74)

Williams's and McCain's stories indicate the very real effects of specific institutional arrangements of broadcasting, not only upon what kinds of television material audiences are enabled to watch, but also more generally upon the structuring of everyday television experience as such. This is a form of control, but a rather indirect one. It does not consist of overt coercion, of imposing explicit rules and regulations, of commanding obedience and submission, but is a matter of structuration discursively mediated by the assumptions made about which programmes are most appropriate to tie the audience to the specific institutional arrangement concerned: schematically, assumptions about 'what the audience wants' in the case of commercial television, and about 'what the audience needs' in the case of public service television.

However, despite the massive amount of available knowledge about 'television audience' on which the programming assumptions are based, the discursive control emanating from it is still not sufficient to efface the uncertainty faced by the institutions. Indeed, the large emphasis usually given to the figures and calculations of audience measurement only obscures the fact that television institutions remain, for all the information they have at their disposal, in constant wonder of the best ways in which to address the audience. What has to be stressed here then is the ultimate lack of control. Even the executives of American commercial television depend as much upon intuition as on science. Scott Siegler, formerly CBS vice-president for drama development, has put it this way:

Because it's a mass audience – it's an unimaginably large audience – the audience tastes are so diffused and so general that you've got to be guessing. You can work off precedents about what's worked on television before. You can work off whatever smattering of sociological information you gleaned from whatever sources. You can let your personal judgments enter into it to some extent. . . . But you never really know.

(In Gitlin 1983: 22–3)

For all the information available, then, the quest for conquering the audience remains, more often than not, a matter of trial and error: more often than not do programmes fail to attract the audiences they were intended to. There are so many variables at play in the art of television programming, Siegler says, that 'the whole thing [is] very precise and very empirical, and at the same time totally absurd and unpredictable' (in Gitlin 1983: 23).

The limits of discursive control are inevitable, because although the television institutions do have the power to determine the formal boundaries of television culture, they cannot get to grips with the social world of actual audiences. As Stuart Hall has remarked,

We are all, in our heads, several different audiences at once, and can be constituted as such by different programmes. We have the capacity to deploy different levels and modes of attention, to mobilise different competences in our viewing. At different times of the day, for different family members, different patterns of viewing have different 'saliences'.

(In Morley 1986: 10)

In other words, the identities of actual audiences are inherently unstable, they are dynamic and variable formations of people whose cultural and psychological boundaries are essentially uncertain. The social world of actual audiences is therefore a fundamentally fluid, fuzzy, and elusive reality, whose description can never be contained and exhausted by any totalizing, taxonomic definition of 'television audience': the latter is, as has been suggested, a fictional abstraction which necessarily involves disavowals of dynamic complexity, of contradiction, of the unforeseen and the accidental. In short, institutionally-produced discursive constructions of 'television audience' are strategic structurations which are under constant pressure of reconstruction whenever they turn out to be imperfect weapons in the quest for control.

We can conclude then that there can be no prefixed recipe for controlling the institution–audience relationship. The institutions are never totally in control, as it were. Control is always sought after, but never completely achieved. As a result, the conquest of the audience is never something absolute and definitive; it is always a temporary victory, perpetually in danger of being eroded, constantly contested, or simply evaded. Taxonomic definitions of 'television audience' are used by the institutions 'in a situation of confrontation to deprive the opponent of his means of combat and to reduce him to giving up the struggle' (Foucault 1982: 225), because they conveniently assign structure to an opponent which is perceived as threateningly unstructured: huge, dispersed, elusive, unseen. Unfortunately, however, the 'opponent' will never give up the struggle, which is merely to say that it will always eventually resist the structure assigned to it.

Writing about problems of cultural description and representation in anthropology, James Clifford (1986: 10) has noted, ' "Cultures" do not hold still for their portraits. Attempts to make them do so always involve simplification and exclusion, selection of a temporal focus, the construction of a self–other relationship, and the imposition or negotiation of a power relationship.' The same thing happens to the social world of actual audiences, I argue, when 'television audience' is conceptualized as a taxonomic collective, holding still for its portrait. How television institutions construct such portraits, and the difficulties they encounter in the process, is plotted in the next two parts of this book.

Part II

Marketing the audience:
American television

5 Commercial knowledge: measuring the audience

The phone rings on the bedside table in a richly furnished Beverly Hills home. The clock on the table registers 5.05 as a man's arm reaches the phone at the instant the second ring starts. Obviously he has anticipated the call, because he is immediately wide awake and has a pen and preprinted sheet of paper at hand. After a curt 'Good morning', he begins furiously writing numbers on a sheet. These are Nielsen rating numbers for the preceding Friday, Saturday, and Sunday nights being read to him by a research department employee in New York. The man in Beverly Hills is the network's program vice president preparing himself for today's possible repercussions from those rating figures. In somewhat different conditions, perhaps, two other network program heads are also getting numbers at about the same time.

(Beville 1985: 186)

This scene, with its efficient evocation of rising suspense and mystery, may remind the regular television viewer of the opening sequence of a run-of-the-mill television adventure show. In fact, it is a fictionalized description of the extremely pronounced place that 'ratings' take in the professional activities of American network executives - a place that, certainly to the sceptical outsider, has a mysterious edge indeed. Hugh Malcolm (Mal) Beville, writer of the scene, is one of the founding fathers of the American ratings industry and he assures his readers that the scene he has summoned up does not give an exaggerated picture at all. So, ratings are said to dominate the lives of the typical, and obviously typically workaholic, network president. As the *New York Times* once wrote about Robert Daly, then president of CBS Entertainment: '[Ratings] are the first thing he thinks about in the morning, . . . and one of the last things he thinks about at night' (quoted in ibid.: 187).

Ratings are the most conspicuous products of a large-scale enterprise called 'audience measurement'. They are generally produced by independent, commercially organized research firms, of which the A.C. Nielsen Company is the dominant one in the United States. The production and selling of ratings is big business![1] Ratings reports are offered as a regular service to the television industry and whoever else is interested enough to pay for it. The networks and stations, who are responsible for the scheduling and transmission of television programming, currently assume about 85 per cent of the total cost of the ratings services (ibid.). The eager use made of this information by media managers has already been dramatically evoked in Beville's opening scene. Other regular users of ratings are advertising agencies and advertisers, the financers of commercial television programming, and programme producers. Furthermore, ratings data have found their way to trade journals and the popular press, where lists of top-rated programmes are routinely published. For example, *TV Guide* magazine devotes considerable space to ratings trends every week, presumably because readers find the information interesting. The observation that *The Cosby Show* is 'the number one show', for instance, is a ratings' construction. It is also through ratings data that we acquire a sense of objective and generalizable certainty that prime time soap operas like *Dallas* and *Dynasty* are more popular among women than among men, although perhaps we already intuitively know this by putting out our feelers in our own social environment.

Ratings are collections of statistics, numerical summaries of the outcome of the rule-governed calculations involved in measuring the audience. In the American situation, two features of the audience are the main objects of measurement: its size and its composition. Size refers to the number of people tuned in to a certain programme or channel at a certain hour on a certain evening; composition refers to the sorts of people who are watching, defined in terms of demographic variables such as age, location, income, and sex. Measurements are taken in relation both to the total potential audience and to the actual audience at the moment of measurement. This leads to two essential types of figures: ratings and shares. Technically speaking, a rating is defined as the estimated percentage of all 'television households' (that is, households, usually families, who are in possession of one or more television sets), or of all people within a demographic group, within a certain survey area who view a specific programme or station.[2] A share, on the other hand, expresses the percentage of all households having the TV set on and tuned to a certain programme or channel at a particular time. Ratings and shares are part of standard language in industry discourse: for example, Hill Street Blues 15·7/26 means a rating of 15·7 (i.e. 15·7 percent of all households with television are tuned to the programme) and a share of 26 (i.e. 26 per cent of all households with a television set activated are tuned in).

These figures can be obtained in several ways, but historically two major methods to collect the basic data have been the most common until well into the 1980s: the diary and the setmeter.[3] In the diary method, a sample of households is selected whose members are requested to keep a (generally, weekly) diary of their viewing activities: when did who watch which programmes on which channels? At the end of the week the diaries must be mailed to the ratings firm.[4] They are then processed and put together in regularly appearing reports on who has watched which programmes, the delivery of which takes place several weeks after the end of the survey period. In the second case, an electronic meter is attached to the television sets of a sample of households. The setmeter gives a minute-by-minute automatic registration of the times that the television set is on or off, and to which channel it is tuned. The data are transmitted to a home storage unit, where they are stored until they are accessed by the central office computer during the night. These data yield an enormous amount of information on gross audience size, of which the national over-all Nielsen ratings for the three national networks, ABC, CBS, and NBC, are the most well known. These figures can be delivered to the desks of network executives the next morning.[5]

It is well-known that ratings play a tremendously important role within the commercial television industry, particularly the American one. Beville expresses the generally accepted understanding about the scope of ratings' role when he sums up:

> They *determine* the price that will be paid for programmes and the pay that performers will receive. They *govern* the rates that advertisers will pay for 60-second or 30-second or smaller units in and around a programme. Ratings *determine* stations' audience and rank order in their market, and to a large degree they *dictate* the profitability of broadcasting stations and their value when put up for sale. The salary and bonus compensation of key network and station officials are also *governed* by ratings success. Ratings results ultimately *determine* whether top management and programme and news management in television and radio broadcast organizations will retain their jobs, be promoted, or demoted.
>
> (Beville 1985: xi, emphasis added)

This all-importance of ratings, real and perceived, for operations of the television industry has always been accompanied by severe cultural criticism. One of the most general assumptions about the negative effects of ratings is their presumably detrimental influence on the quality of television programming – its contribution to what is often called the 'vast wasteland' of American television (Boddy 1990). For example, critic Harold Mehling, in an early book on television with the merciless title *The Great Time-Killer* (1962), sneers at the authority of ratings within the industry by evoking an anecdote in which the popular comedian Phil Silvers (Sergeant Bilko) comments on the epilogue to a rating triumph over Milton Berle, his great rival. Silvers: 'When I walked out of the CBS elevator the morning after, all the secretaries rose to their feet and applauded. There, in one dramatic nutshell, was an indication to me of the height of frenzy to which the rating race has climbed' (in Mehling 1962: 240). Mehling dismisses such instances of 'rating fever' by succinctly characterizing it as sheer 'foolishness', and it is safe to say that his view represents a widely shared position concerning ratings among cultural and media critics.[6] However, such simple dismissal, in its implied refusal - or inability - to take what seems so 'foolish' seriously as a situation that needs analysis rather than categorical rejection, has often prevented us from gaining insight into the structural and institutional reasons why ratings figure so prominently in the business of commercial television.

The industry itself, for its part, typically justifies the centrality of ratings by stating again and again that ratings, as estimates of audience size, are more or less direct reflections of audience taste. In a particularly self-serving leap of argument ratings are celebrated as guardians of the public interest, as instruments which require that the television industry 'give the audience what it wants'. The ideological bearings of this argument become crudely explicit in, for example, Mal Beville's (1985: 240) self-congratulatory statement that 'ratings are . . . an expression of democracy in action. . . . No other medium anywhere in the world can match the variety and quality of the total output of the programs that weather our ratings system to reach the American public'.

Established here is the reduction of popularity to a matter of numerical superiority, as well as the easy equating of numerical superiority with audience preference – as the term 'ratings' as such suggests. But such discursive simplifications are not 'ideological' in the sense that they are 'false'. Rather, they exemplify a representation of the relation between television and its audience which has been made possible by the very existence of ratings. As I will clarify, the power of ratings is productive not repressive: they exert influence primarily by enabling the putting together of a coherent, streamlined map of 'television audience' – a map that charts the ways in which the industry defines the audience as market.

Meanwhile, it is not surprising that Beville holds such a high-minded, legitimizing view of ratings. After all, he speaks from the partisan perspective of someone who has committed almost his whole professional life to industry-related broadcast research. Thus inhabiting the institutional point of view, he asserts that by providing information about the audience that is reached by a given programme or station, ratings give the industry a regulating device that is crucial for success: 'Programs are the heart of broadcasting, while sales provide the muscle. Ratings with their feedback element are the nerve system that largely controls what is broadcast' (ibid., xi). However, what remains unclear here is exactly how this 'nerve system' works. What falls beyond Beville's consideration is the mechanisms of all that determining, governing, and dictating that ratings seem to succeed in carrying out. What is it about ratings that gives them so much leverage? If they constitute a 'feedback element', in what sense do they perform that function?

Beville's optimistic account is based upon the common sense assumption, shared by ratings' proponents and opponents alike, that ratings are so important because they supply the industry with valid and reliable data about the audience, data which it needs in order to be able to operate and to evaluate its performance. Pure and simple, then, it is assumed that ratings represent more or less objective knowledge about the audience, obtained through methodologically sound procedures. Resulting from this 'epistemologically deterministic' assumption is the idea that ratings have a purely instrumental function in industry policy and practice. Ratings are highly appreciated because they are useful, and they are useful because they supply the broadcasters with pure information.

Strangely enough, much criticism of ratings tends to reproduce this instrumentalist view by uncritically acceding to the assumption that audience measurement is a question of science. Attacks on ratings, then, are typically levelled at its perceived methodological shortcomings: the samples are too small and biased, the measurement instruments are not accurate, and so on.[7] However, the very frenzy with which ratings are devoured day after day by industry people suggests that something more dramatic is at stake here. One network executive, NBC's William Rubens, has even spoken about a 'psychic need for ratings', which he relates to 'the very human need to know how well you are doing' (quoted in Beville 1985: 187). In other words, what ratings seem to satisfy is not just the need for practical and objective information, but a more generalized, diffuse need to know, which in turn is related to the wish 'to do well'. And 'how well you are doing' can apparently be known by looking at figures and statistics which are seen as mirroring audience behaviour - the ultimate yardstick for doing well in the commercial television industry. In this sense, ratings are a solution for the most fundamental problem that the industry is preoccupied with: the need to know the audience.

But in this complex circulation of corporate needs, wishes and preoccupations, ratings perform more than just a 'scientific', instrumental function. Todd Gitlin (1983: 53), for example, has dubbed the obsession of the networks with ratings 'the fetish of immediate numerical gratification'. Network managers, he observed, generally disregard the 'scientific', technical-methodological criteria by which ratings data should be evaluated:

In the tumult of everyday figuring and judging, network executives, even research specialists, often commit the standard occupational error of unwarranted precision. When Nielsen publishes its figures every two weeks, it reminds subscribers of the standard errors, but executives functionally forget what they were taught in elementary statistics: that all survey statistics are valid only within predictable margins of error. For example, the 1981–82 series rankings showed *Dynasty* in twentieth place with a 20.4 season rating and *Hill Street Blues* in twenty-ninth place with 18.6. But statistically there was a 10 percent chance the two shows actually drew the same size audience. Once managers agree to accept a measure, they act as if it is precise. They 'know' there are standard errors - but what a nuisance it would be to act on that knowledge. And so the number system has an impetus of its own.

(Gitlin 1983: 53)

This suggests that ratings do more than just offer hard, factual information. Rather, the recurrent and institutionalized use of ratings in industry circles has ritualistic and rhetorical dimensions. What ratings primarily seem to achieve is a sense of control over the audience, a control however that is not 'real', but symbolic. What audience measurement produces is a discursive framework – what I will call ratings discourse - which enables the industry to know its relationship to the audience in terms of frequencies, percentages and averages. But this discourse does not provide the industry with 'feedback' from actual audiences, as Beville and others would have it. Ratings discourse does not just consist of factual, objective, and more or less accurate descriptions about the audience; it should be considered, as has been suggested by Donald Hurwitz (1984: 207), as 'a symbolic form and activity with profound expressive and strategic components'. It is in this sense that Beville's (1985) characterization of ratings as the 'nerve system' of broadcasting bears some truth. Through the symbolic world created by ratings, a world inhabited not by actual audiences but by a discursively constructed 'television audience', the industry has armed itself with a guiding principle for solving the multiple dilemmas, problems and disputes which the gigantic enterprise of commercial broadcasting entails (Pekurny 1982; Gitlin 1983).

But this ingenious 'nerve system' is not exempt from any hitches and complications. On the contrary, rather than seeing audience measurement as a perfect machine that keeps the organism of the television industry running smoothly, as Beville's 'nerve system' metaphor insinuates, I would like to evoke, not only for drama's sake, a less polished and more agitated scenery. Here, ratings form a focal site of the inherently contentious relationship between industry and audience, a site in which a battle between television and its audiences is constantly being fought out, but never absolutely won or lost. I will expound upon this battle by tracing the constitutive role and significance of audience measurement in the American television industry - the pre-eminent commercial system. As I have already indicated in Part I, audience measurement has also come to occupy an important place in European public service broadcasting. In that context its history and role differ, however, as will become clear in Part III. While in Europe ratings have never lost a somewhat suspect reputation, even within the broadcasting organizations themselves who tend to consider too much reliance on ratings inappropriate, the almost shameless and completely taken for granted prominence of ratings in the operations of American commercial television offers a fascinating panorama on the multiple ramifications of audience measurement as a guiding practice in broadcast television – ramifications which, as we will see, do not only entail structural rewards, but also engender continuing discontent within the industry.

Throughout the history of commercial broadcasting, ratings firms have always been pressured to develop better measurement instruments, better sampling techniques, more advanced statistical analyses, and so on – an emphasis on 'progress' which in itself indicates that the current measurement system is perceived as less than perfect. Since the late 1970s, especially, the established ratings services are under severe pressure due to the changing television landscape – a terrain that has been invaded by new phenomena such as video cassette recorders, video rental stores, cable, satellites, videotex, teletext, computer games, and so on (e.g. Rubens 1984). In the United States, major changes in the ratings business have reached a momentary climax with the introduction of the 'people meter' in September 1987, marking a significant change in the technology of audience measurement. The debates and controversies around the people meter are particularly suitable for examining how the struggle over ratings represents a crisis of the relationship between industry and audience – a crisis which, as I will try to show, has to do with the increasing difficulty of constructing a coherent and encompassing discourse on 'television audience' in an increasingly multi-faceted and chaotic television environment (Chapters 8 and 9).

Before delving into these stirring contemporary developments, however, I will first explore in greater detail the historical and structural forces that have determined the importance of audience measurement in commercial television institutions (Chapter 6), in order to better understand the discursive process through which power and knowledge are intertwined in the construction of 'television audience' through ratings discourse. This process is a process of 'streamlining' (Chapter 7). The problems faced by audience measurement are in fact symptomatic of a more fundamental, and ultimately unsolvable, institutional problem: the profound, structural uncertainty about the audience which is the core predicament of the television industry. We will see that ratings discourse, while providing the industry with a comforting sense of knowing the audience, cannot proffer a definitive solution to this structural predicament, not only because of current shortcomings of the measurement technology, but more fundamentally because 'television audience' as such turns out to be a category that cannot be contained in ratings discourse, no matter how sophisticated and detailed the measurement procedures. In short, the television institutions are faced with the problem that 'television audience' is a fictional construct that will always refuse definitive representation (Chapter 10).

6 In search of the audience commodity

A short consideration of the corporate structure of American commercial broadcasting will make us comprehend more fully why the practice of audience measurement has acquired the central role it has been occupying almost from its inception. In economic terms, production for profit is the sole objective of the commercial broadcasting industry, which has for decades been dominated by the three national networks, NBC, CBS and ABC. To finance the whole system, the networks are dependent on advertisers as sponsors. The idea of advertising is principally based upon the assumption that it is possible to enlarge sales of products through communication.[1] It is the prospect of fusing selling and communicating that induces interest on the part of advertisers to make use of television or radio to disseminate their promotional messages. Therefore, a system has emerged in which advertisers buy air time from the broadcasters, either fifteen- or thirty- or sixty-second spots, to be inserted in programmes that are furnished by the networks.[2]

Important in this transaction is the need advertisers feel to have some kind of guarantee that they haven't spent their money for nothing. They need to be reassured that their messages actually reach those for whom they are intended: the potential consumers of the products advertised. Here, the audience enters the story. Advertisers see the audience as potential consumers, and thus it is the audience's attention that advertisers want to attract. From this perspective, then, what advertisers buy from the networks is not time but audience: commercial television is based on the principle that the networks 'deliver audiences to advertisers', as the slogan goes.[3] But how does one know that the exchange is a fair one? If 'chunks of audience' are the commodities that the networks sell to the advertisers, some measure has to be set to determine the price the latter must pay to the former.

At this point the idea of audience measurement acquires its relevance. Audience measurement bears an economical meaning in so far as it produces the necessary standard through which advertising rates can be set. That standard is fixed according to the number of people who watch the programmes in which the commercials appear,[4] resulting in the so-called 'cost-per-thousand' that the networks could demand and the advertisers would pay. The ratings firms occupy a key position in this corporate transaction, because it is their product, the ratings information, that forms the basis for the agreed-upon standard by which advertisers and networks buy and sell the audience commodity. Against this background, it is also only logical that the production of ratings should be carried out by an independent third party, because, as Eileen Meehan (1984: 222) has remarked, neither the networks nor the advertisers could trust the other for supplying the measure, even though some measure is needed to enable the transaction in the first place: 'While continuity [of interests] rests in the need for an official description of the audience, discontinuity arises from the connection between that description and pricing.' This analysis of the political economy of ratings production leads Meehan (ibid., 221) to conclude that 'ratings per se must no longer be treated as reports of human behavior, but rather as products – as commodities shaped by business exigencies and corporate strategies'.

However, ratings are not only products with an economic exchange value. In fact, they could only become saleable products in the first place, because they contain a certain productivity, a certain use value. In Meehan's (ibid., 222) words, what ratings do is provide the industry with 'an official description of the audience', that becomes the foundation upon which the economic negotiations of the industry are effectuated. The permanent institutional uncertainty about the audience which is inherent to the broadcasting situation makes such an official description necessary: in the commercial context of mutual dependency between networks and advertisers, that uncertainty is a catastrophic condition – a condition that would be lethal for the industry if it would not be surmounted. After all, the selling and buying of the audience commodity can only take place if and when one can define the object of the transaction. Uncertainty about the audience must therefore be combated at all costs. It must be converted into a situation in which there is at least agreement among the parties involved about what they are referring to when they speak about the audience commodity. In other words, an 'official description of the audience' is needed where such a description is not readily at hand, because the object of that description, the audience, is such an intangible referent. Audience measurement became the basis for that official description. With its invocation of the quantifying, objectivist and scientific imagination, audience measurement is a perfect instrument that could weld together the economic need for a common ground with the simultaneous provision of a workable definition of the audience. In short, ratings could become a saleable product precisely because they acquired the status of reliable and valid supplier of information about the audience.

In the early days of radio, when the economic foundation of

broadcasting in the United States was being established, advertisers were sceptical about the use of radio as a medium that could enhance sales of consumer products. What needed to be demonstrated was the very existence of an audience. Clues for radio's grip on people were available, for example, in the nationwide nightly suspension of 'normal life' during the broadcast of the comedy series *Amos 'n Andy* at 7.00 pm, and in the enormous amount of fan mail for radio stars and programmes (NBC received one million letters in 1929, and two million in 1930).[5] But these impressionistic cultural indications of radio's popularity were not satisfactory to the advertisers: they wanted systematic and objective evidence. It is not surprising then that it was the advertisers who financially supported Archibald Crossley, head of a market research firm, in setting up the first audience measurement service in March 1930.[6] It soon became clear that Crossley had created a lucrative market for a new business venture when he started experimenting with the idea of assembling factual information, through telephone interviews, about radio listening behaviour: when were sets used, who listened, what programmes and stations were heard, and so on. As Crossley recalls, the new, objectivist emphasis meant a true revolution at the audience research front:

> The thing that gave us the most publicity was the origination of radio ratings in 1929, which, having never been done before, created quite a stir. Dan Starch, about the same time, had done a survey, asking people what kind of programs they liked. But he didn't ask, 'What program did you just listen to or listen to in the past few hours?' We did that.
>
> (In Bartos 1986: 49)

The 'Crossley ratings' rapidly caused severe 'ratingitis' among industry people, and soon it was commonly accepted that ratings should be considered as the measure of performance which the radio stations previously lacked – a measure of performance that was able to create confidence among advertisers in the 'audience delivery' of radio. Finally a method was found, so it was thought, to supply tangible evidence for radio's viability as an advertising medium. A very ingenious method indeed: one that could command authority at a time when the emerging field of scientific, survey-based social research was gaining much prestige.[7] The broadcasting media needed such a method, not only to be able to convince advertisers, but also in a more elementary sense because, as Beville (1985: 234) claims, 'broadcasters have to make greater effort to "count the house" . . . because of the intangible character of the audience'. This reasoning makes it understandable why eventually it was the broadcasters and not the advertisers who would pay for most of the costs of the ratings services: in the commercial supply-and-demand logic of the market, it is the former's responsibility to furnish the evidence of existence and value of the audience commodity they offer for sale.

Ratings then deliver the very currency of the industry's economic transactions. But that currency does not exist in material form: the audience commodity is not a material object that can be readily exchanged such as a car or a pack of cigarettes. Therefore, an instrument is needed to object-ify the audience, as it were, and this is exactly the specific productivity of audience measurement. And while this practice originated in the commercial necessities of radio broadcasting, it is in the area of television that the production of ratings has become a truly prominent industry in itself. It is the specific achievement of audience measurement that it converts an elusive occurrence – the real occurrence of people actually using television in their everyday lives – into a hard substance, a calculable object, an object suitable for transaction.

This process of object-ification is established and maintained through the procedures of audience measurement as a discursive practice. Audience measurement is not just an innocent way of quantifying television's reach. The very act of 'head counting', which is the most basic operation of ratings production, is a very specific discursive intervention that results in moulding 'television audience' into a quantifiable aggregate object. Ratings discourse transforms the audience from a notion that loosely represents an unknown and unseen reality, a *terra incognita*, into a known and knowable taxonomic category, a discrete entity that can be empirically described in numerical terms. The audience commodity is thus a symbolic object which is constructed by, and is not pre-existent to the discursive procedures of audience measurement. It is this symbolic object – 'television audience' as it is constructed in and through ratings discourse – that is the target of the television industry's practices, advertisers and broadcasters alike.

The strategic role of ratings, then, is not fully described by pointing at their intermediary function in the business negotiations between advertisers and broadcasters. It is the manner in which they perform that function that should be emphasized. Ratings are neither simply an exemplar of scientifically-produced information and as such, a neutral tool for feedback, as is claimed by their official proponents and assumed by their main users. Nor should they be considered merely as a product of the economic and institutional exigencies of commercial industry arrangements, as is put forward by radical political economists. The latter are right in criticizing the former position as a rather self-serving and narrow-minded perspective that neglects the larger political context in which ratings could become a lucrative business venture. But a strictly political economic approach fails to account for the symbolic effectivity of the knowledge-producing endeavour that is implied in audience measurement as a discursive practice. Ratings are so important for the industry because they articulate the economic and the symbolic, the institutional and the discursive, power and knowledge.

It is through ratings discourse that the social world of actual audiences is incorporated in the complex system of production and exchange that keeps the industry going. The system performs a double objectification of actual audiences: by turning 'television audience' into an object of knowledge, ratings discourse simultaneously enables the making of 'television audience' as an object of economic exchange. This makes audience measurement a clear instance of what Foucault (1980b) has called a technology of power, in which the wish to exert control over people is connected to and articulated in the institutionalized production of knowledge about them.

Ratings proved to be so useful that the operation of commercial television without the intermediary role of audience measurement as a management tool would be unthinkable today. Its mechanism of permanent registration and delivery of audience information is attractive because it holds the promise of solving the industry's basic uncertainty about the audience. Therefore, ratings have become more than just a currency for transaction: they have become a central focus in the day-to-day concerns and problems facing the industry. The obsession with ratings among network managers has to do with the reassurance offered by ratings. As a CBS executive has put it: 'We get a daily report card. This is one of the few businesses in the world I know where a guy comes to work every morning and looks to see how he did the day before' (in Gitlin 1983: 48).

But unfortunately ratings do not give perfect and uncontested 'report cards'. On the contrary, since the days of its original conception, the practice of audience measurement has encountered many real and perceived imperfections. These imperfections have created tensions within the industry, which have not only led to continuing competition between ratings firms, but also, often enough, to skirmishes between advertisers and networks over the right measurement standards. Given the enormous financial consequences of every variation in the outcome of the measurements, such concern is not at all surprising. In fact, the desire to have a better and better measurement service in industry circles has spurred the development of ever more sophisticated measurement procedures, which are hoped to deliver more accurate, detailed and useful official descriptions of 'television audience'. The growing emphasis on demographic information, for example, was a direct consequence of the advertisers' wish to advertise their products to specific market segments (such as 'young urban adults') rather than to the general 'mass' audience – a development which had a major impact on American network television since the late 1960s (Brown 1971; Barnouw 1978; Feuer 1984). And, as I will show at length in Chapters 8, 9 and 10, the emergence of VCRs, cable and other new communication technologies have made the industry very nervous about the adequacy of the figures provided by the ratings services. In the industry's feverish attempts to adapt its official description of 'television audience' to the new television landscape, audience measurement becomes a prime focus of concern.

The concern is typically cast in terms of the need for more 'correct measurement', but it is generally motivated by divergences of interest within and among diverse branches in the television industrial complex. As we shall see, the present turmoil in the audience measurement enterprise is directly related to a growing lack of consensus within the industry as a whole about what represents correct measurement. At a more fundamental level, however, the continuing struggle over ratings also reveals a more structural and profound predicament of audience measurement – a predicament that forms the epistemological ground for the pragmatic and self-serving debates over correct measurement fought out within the industry. Mal Beville, the ratings expert, voices this predicament in stating that 'there is no perfect or ideal way to measure electronic media audiences, nor will there ever be' (1985: 128). But this impossibility is not just a matter of unsolvable technical insufficiencies, as Beville implicitly suggests. It is, in fact, implicated in the epistemological foundations of audience measurement as such.

To understand this, we have to remember that watching television is an ongoing, day-to-day cultural practice engaged in by millions of people. To capture and encompass the viewing practices of all these people in a singular, object-ified, streamlined construct of 'television audience' is a very ambitious project indeed, but exactly this is what ratings discourse basically sets out to do. I will go into the details of this streamlining process in the next chapter. For the moment, it is enough to say that although the streamlined 'television audience' is a source of control for the industry, it also carries the explanation of why in the end audience measurement, apparently such an ingenious technology of power, can never be the perfect and definitive solution to the industry's uncertainty about the audience: by definition, streamlining is a never-ending discursive process. In short, the streamlined audience is the utopian symbolic object that will never be realized, but which audience measurement perpetually strives to approximate.

This is the central predicament of audience measurement, the drama of its unfulfilled promise, as it were: the constant search for improvement of measurement technology is pursued in the belief that it will provide more and more 'correct' information about, and thus more control over, the audience. But unfortunately this only tends to aggravate the industry's problems. As Hurwitz (1984: 212) has argued, the growing technical sophistication of audience measurement 'only increased the abstractness of the broadcast situation that the introduction of reseach was intended to resolve in the first place'. In other words, the more information the ratings services try to accumulate in their measurement endeavours, the more problematic the object-ification of actual audiences into 'television audience' tends to become: the procedure of streamlining becomes more and more complicated. The stormy recent developments in audience measurement can be understood in this light. Before laying out the scenario of this contemporary drama, however, we must explore in greater detail the way in which ratings discourse constructs a streamlined 'television audience'.

7   Streamlining 'television audience'

Ratings discourse's object of knowledge, 'television audience', is not the transparent representation of pregiven actual audiences. In and through the descriptions made by ratings discourse a certain profile of 'television audience' takes shape – a profile that does not exist outside or beyond those descriptions but is produced by them. In this sense, 'television audience', as it is constructed in ratings discourse, is a fictive entity. This does not mean, of course, that ratings dream the audience into existence. They are based on actual data on how many and who are watching what. The knowledge produced by ratings is therefore neither false nor untrue. On the contrary, ratings are powerful precisely because of their ability to define a certain field of empirical truth. That regime of truth is fictive, however, because the very terms with which it covers empirical reality inevitably result in a description of the audience that foregrounds certain characteristics but suppresses others. As I have indicated in Chapter 3, the category of 'television audience' as such already implies a highly selective delineation of the real, and the very fact that we tend to regard 'television audience' as a taxonomic collective having a definite and defineable size and composition is a 'reality effect' of ratings discourse (Hall 1982).

For one thing, to perceive the audience as something that *can* be measured is already a rather peculiar move. It is an assumption originating in the general idea of the 'measurability of markets' quintessential to the parameters of marketing thought as it began to be developed in the early 1920s (Beniger 1986). The emphasis on size leads to a representation of the audience as a calculable entity, a taxonomic collective consisting of the sum of individual, serialized units, defined as households or persons. The attention given to demographic composition of the audience does not alter this in any essential sense: it only breaks down the total audience into separate slices of audience that are, each of them, in turn imagined as countable entities (often called segments). The units of those entities only matter insofar as they can be added up: in the imagination of ratings discourse, all households of the total audience are, by projection, principally the same; all people belonging to one demographic segment basically equivalent and equal.[1] In other words, in ratings discourse the individual units of the audience, the 'audience members', are ultimately devoid of personal identity and history, of idiosyncratic subjectivity.

But 'television audience' as constructed by ratings discourse is not only characterized by objective, thing-like figures such as size and composition. A subjective, human dimension is inevitably comprised in it, simply because ratings are assumed to measure something done by human beings. Awareness of this subjective dimension can be found in a certain ambivalence within everyday industry language: although the role of the audience in the institutional set-up of the television industry is structurally that of commodified object, it is often spoken about as if it were a huge, living subject. Industry people are often heard saying things like, 'the audience wants comedy', 'the audience won't understand this show', or 'they don't like soap ads'. Such attribution of preference or competence invests the concept of 'television audience' with human qualities, although strictly speaking 'television audience', being a category that owes its existence to its position as 'passive' target of corporate practices, cannot want or understand something. Only people, invested with subjectivity, can. The 'slip of the tongue' is not meaningless. It indicates that however object-ified 'television audience' as a categorical entity is, its construction is related to the subjective moment of actual people watching television.

The notion that the television audience is a taxonomic collective in which viewers are aggregated undergirds ratings discourse. This notion brings together the idea of the whole (television audience) and that of separate units (audience members) which make up that whole. Thus, 'television audience' as constructed in audience measurement is an object that is made up of subjects. This leads to a fundamental instability of the category. As an object made up of subjects, 'television audience' is not a static, stone-like object whose characteristics can be described once and for all, but is a continually changing, dynamic object that always seems to elude definitive description. The fact that the production of ratings is an ongoing, never-ending practice testifies to this slipperiness: even the most factual, objective characteristics of 'television audience', its size and its composition, cannot be assumed constant, and have to be re-established again and again, day after day. Ratings are very fleeting products: they become obsolete almost instantly.

As has been remarked before, individuals watching television (gathered in households) are taken to be the basic units of audience measurement data. But individuals are concrete social subjects and because they are situated in concrete everyday contexts and circumstances, the way they watch television will be subjective too, formed by and associated with those concrete contexts and circumstances. However, taking this into account would make the production of ratings, which seeks to arrive at a generalized construct of 'television audience', utterly unmanageable. Therefore audience measurement, as is the general rule in quantifying social science, tends to abstract from the detailed singularities in experience and practice. In other words, in order to construct an object-ive 'television audience', it has to mould the subject-ive into wieldy, measurable forms. As a result, the subjective practices and experiences of actual audiences are objectified in audience measurement in the easily identifiable and verifiable concept of 'viewing behaviour'.

Behaviourism marks the convenient marriage between the objective and the subjective in ratings discourse: individual television viewers are typically 'captured' and measured in ratings discourse in terms of their externally observable behaviour, excluding more intractable subjective dimensions such as the psychical (e.g. viewers' internal, mental states or orientations), or the cultural (e.g. the specific social uses people make of television in various contexts, or the various ways in which viewers interpret television material). In short, the subjective is 'domesticated' and 'purified' in ratings discourse by breaking it down to measurable behavioural variables.[2]

The technologies of audience measurement testify to this tendency toward reductionist behaviourism. For example, the electronic setmeter can register nothing more than whether the set is on or off. In this case, viewing behaviour is defined as a simple, one-dimensional, and purely mechanical act. As Gitlin (1983: 54) has rightly remarked, 'the numbers only sample sets tuned in, not necessarily shows watched, let alone grasped, remembered, loved, learned from, deeply anticipated, or mildly tolerated'. Thus, what audience measurement tends to erase from its field of discernment is any specific consideration of the meanings, saliences or impacts of television for people, the 'lived reality behind the ratings' (Jensen 1987: 25). In standard ratings discourse watching television is reduced to the observable behaviour of having the TV set on: it is done by subjects but is devoid of subjective dimensions. Human subjects here are thus merely relevant for their bodies: strictly speaking, they appear in the logic of ratings discourse only in so far as they are agents of the physical act of tuning-in. As a result, the problem for the industry facing the subjectivity of viewers is funneled into one simple but obsessive question: how do we get them tuned in?

It would make no sense to simply condemn this lack of sensitivity for the subjective dimension of viewer practices in audience measurement. Nor is it to the point to criticize it for its faulty epistemology, in terms of lack of conceptual validity or methodological adequacy. After all, audience measurement is not social science, but social technology: its purpose is the systematic accumulation of strategic knowledge. Knowledge about the audience is only interesting for the industry when it is useful for their commercial purposes, and too much awareness about the heterogeneous and contradictory responses of actual audiences to television is just not practical for the industry.[3] Industry people need a kind of knowledge that allows them to act, not paralyze them – a convenient kind of knowledge that enables the industry to concoct its relation to the audience in a simple, clear-cut, and manageable way. Ratings discourse offers this knowledge because it puts together a streamlined map of 'television audience'.

The streamlined audience is a 'disciplined' audience. It is constructed by ratings discourse through a smoothening out of problematic subjectivity and translating it into ordered and regular instances of viewing behaviour. This is achieved through the quantifying perspective of audience measurement, which inevitably leads to emphasizing averages, regularities and generalizable patterns rather than idiosyncracies and surprising exceptions (cf. Anderson 1987). As a result, a streamlined profile of 'television audience' comes into being that reduces the individual viewer to a 'typical' audience member who can be objectively classified. In the discursive map of the streamlined audience, each viewer can ideally be assigned an exact place in a comprehensive table of knowledge, formed by the central axes of size and demographic composition on the one hand, and the variables of 'viewing behaviour' on the other hand.

This procedure of streamlining can be clarified by having a closer look at the logic of demographics. The matching of factors such as age, sex, race, income, occupation, education and area of residence with viewing behaviour variables (e.g. amount of viewing and programme choice) results in the statistical determination of relatively stable 'viewing habits'– a set of imputed behavioural routines that form a perfect merger of the objective and the subjective. Thus, in an article aptly entitled 'The World According to Nielsen', it is observed that '[V]iewing may vary by age, sex, region, and income, but within those categories the vast TV audience has surprisingly predictable habits' (Traub 1985: 26). This, then, is the streamlined audience: an objectified category in which the stable is foregrounded over the erratic, the likely over the extraordinary, the consistent over the inconsistent. Through demographics 'television audience' is streamlined by neatly slicing it up in substantive 'segments', each of which consists of presumably well-organized, serialized viewers displaying dependable viewing behaviour. Sometimes, typical characteristics are assigned to each segment which conjure up nicely contained subjectivities, formalized in so-called 'psychographics'. For example, in 'The World According to Nielsen' the viewing habits of a typical member of the 'Men 55+' category, 'George', are described:

Over the years George's tastes have grown oddly similar to Ruth's [his wife]. He still likes sports (though now he prefers golf to football), but he can no longer watch without flinching those death 'n destruction shows like *A Team* . . . . Nowadays he sits around with Ruth to watch the likes of *Dallas*. . . . Perhaps he's surrendering his own fantasies for his wife's.

(Traub 1985: 71)

In this portrait, 'George' is a type, an exemplar of 'later-middle-aged, married men', not a personalized, situated individual. In such psychographic profiles ratings data are combined with projections about the category's typical 'life style', as a result of which it is possible to 'freeze' the viewing practices of later-middle-aged married men into some fixed habits, even comprising some peculiar psychological and behavioural inclinations. As Traub sums up, 'older men are in the living room more, but they get tired early'.

Of course, users of demographic and psychographic information know perfectly well that such descriptions are generalizations and that all statistical generalizations are conditional, but the patterns emerging from that information still enable broadcasters and advertisers to develop simple practical truths, such as that women 18 to 49 (one of the most desirable demographic segments for advertisers) are more changeable than over-50 viewers and thus more easily introduced to new programmes, that women aged 18 to 35 are in their early married years and like to try out all kinds of new products and make major purchasing decisions on home furnishings and appliances, and so on (Tyler Eastman *et al.* 1981). Such profiles provide an extreme example of what streamlining the audience amounts to: in the end, it conjures up the utopia of a neatly ordered world inhabited by perfectly predictable people.[4]

Again, the streamlined audience is not a false representation of people's concrete ways of relating to television, but rather a certain structuring mould imposed upon the multifaceted activities of television viewers. As a result, whatever contingent routines actual audiences create in their everyday engagements with television cannot be expected to coincide with the predictable 'viewing habits' invented by audience measurement. The latter are conceivable only because ratings discourse describes individual viewers, and the differences between and among them, exclusively in terms of a small number of generalized and standardized viewing behaviour variables. All other bases of identity and difference are considered irrelevant and are therefore deliberately ignored.

Streamlining, then, is a discursive procedure that results in the construction of a representation of 'television audience' consisting of a finite and limited set of parameters. This mapping of the virtual 'audience field' leads to the establishment of a more or less comprehensive classificatory system over which all viewers (as projected from the sample) can be distributed and arranged. However, this cannot be known once and for all: the mapping has to be repeated every day, because it is not certain how viewers will actually respond to the television programmes which are intended to attract them. That is, every day the viewing behaviour of each viewer (or his or her representative in the sample) needs to be regauged: this is the one element that ratings discourse cannot determine in advance, but must confirm and reconfirm empirically. After all, it is the relative success or failure of the broadcasters' efforts to attract audiences which is the ultimate rationale for audience measurement. What the streamlining procedure does, in fact, is the calculating of that success or failure (i.e. of 'audience response') in compliance with a prefabricated formal structure. As a result, all too big surprises are not likely to occur: uncertainty about audience response is reduced to uncertainty about the number of viewers in each parcel of the map. Empirically found variations within the streamlined audience are conveniently contained in 'types' and 'patterns'; developments over time are straightened out in terms of 'trends'. This is the core productivity of the streamlining procedure: it purifies, through a kind of filtering process, people's concrete viewing activities by representing them in a smooth, totalized but adaptable map.[5]

The map of the streamlined audience then is characterized by variation in regularity, regularity in variation – stable enough to guarantee continuity, malleable enough to allow for responsiveness to temporal fluctuations. The map is very handy indeed for the industry: it supplies both broadcasters and advertisers with neatly arranged and easily manageable information, a form of knowledge which almost cannot fail to provide a sense of provisional certainty, as maps generally do. For example, the ranking of programmes according to their ratings performance constitutes a weekly flow chart which is used as a reliable and agreed-upon indicator of 'popularity', and thus of the value of the audience commodity.

But such discursively constructed 'facts' are not only indispensible guidelines for both broadcasters and advertisers in their economic negotiations; they are also made to serve as cultural clues for the networks to develop and commission new programmes. This use of ratings is made possible by the construction of the 'hit show' for instance. It is a peculiar oddity indeed that while the networks know perfectly well, thanks to ratings discourse, which programmes have been 'successful', they do not know why they have been and which new ones will be. There is no way to foretell the ratings performance of a new programme.[6] Therefore, the use of past 'successes' in the constant search for future ones remains a gamble. As one network programmer, Donald Grant of CBS, has said: 'When I originally picked out *Dallas*, I didn't know it was going to be a hit – it was only after it was on that it sparked *Knot's Landing* and *Dynasty*. Hits create trends, not the other way around' (in Wilner 1987: 44). Even so, although ratings and demographics are estimates about audience size and composition for a past situation, the regularities highlighted by ratings discourse allow the industry to take decisions that do affect the future. These regularities furnish a sense of predictability and, as a consequence, the (imagined) power to anticipate and act upon it, in an attempt to bring the variable element in the streamlined audience under control.

The impact of this power to anticipate is reflected in the iron repetitiveness which characterizes television scheduling and programming in American network television. A programme that proves to be a ratings winner is likely to set the tone for a whole number of other programmes, either in the form of spin-offs or of copies. As a consequence, a kind of streamlining of television programming itself is achieved, a form of what Gitlin (1983) has called 'recombinant culture'. The construction of the streamlined audience then goes hand in hand with the streamlining of television's output: the categorization and structuring of programmes in terms of formulaic genres, the segmentation of time in regular units, the placing of programmes in fixed time slots, and their sequencing into a smooth flow – these are all strategies developed by the networks to match the streamlined audience with an equally streamlined television 'super-text' (Browne 1984).

The idea of 'prime time', for example, is essentially a construct of the regularity that was found in the fluctuations of audience size evening after evening: continuous audience measurement has demonstrated that as a rule it is between 8.00 p.m. and 11.00 pm that the number of households having their television sets on is the largest. Now the concept of prime time has acquired an entrenched, institutionalized status within the industry: programming and scheduling are geared to it; advertising rates are determined accordingly.

To sum up, we can conclude that audience measurement's discursive object-ification of 'television audience' necessarily involves the serialization of television viewers as 'audience members'. But actual television viewers are always more than just audience members; their identities as television viewers is more complex than their being part of the audience. In other words, when people watch television they of course inevitably occupy the position of audience members, but they also simultaneously inhabit a myriad of other subject positions such as parent, critic, fan, democrat, cook or whatever – culturally specific subject positions whose interdependent meanings elude the symbolic world constructed by ratings discourse.[7] As a consequence ratings discourse, and the audience facts mapped by it, always inevitably stand in a strained relationship with what actual audiences are up to. The mould never quite fits, as it were.

By itself, however, this epistemological gap between the map of the streamlined audience and the world of actual audiences does not constitute a problem for the industry. As long as the map works, the industry will not bother to look for more 'realistic' maps. In other words, the concrete practices and experiences of actual audiences are irrelevant for the industry so long as the information delivered by audience measurement is uncontested and perceived to be adequate. Therefore, the gap will only be problematized when the streamlining process tends to slacken; that is, when it no longer seems possible to establish fixed viewing habits, unambiguous behavioural variables, and so on, by which viewers can be unproblematically typified and classified. At such moments, the existing streamlining procedures themselves will be questioned, and a lack of validity or reliability in the ratings services will be perceived in industry circles. Suddenly, elements of the subjective world of actual audiences do matter and help to disturb the consensus over the existing map of the streamlined audience. Then, a reconstruction of the streamlining process is called for in order to come to a new, more satisfying map: a struggle over the very question of how to streamline the audience will be fought out. Then, audience measurement is in crisis. In fact, such a crisis has been unfolding in the American television industry throughout the 1980s. It is to this historical episode that I will turn in the remaining chapters of part II.

8 The streamlined audience disrupted: impact of the new technologies

Until the early 1980s, the practice of audience measurement for American television was a relatively stable and quiet business. For decades, Nielsen's setmeter, the Audimeter, measured household ratings, while demographic data were collected through a simple family diary in which each family member was supposed to record which programmes and channels he or she had been watching during a week. This two-track system was used to determine the audience for programming on the three commercial networks, ABC, CBS and NBC. The system generally worked, advertisers and networks were satisfied enough. So long as there was a sense of balanced interests, there was no reason to question the system as the fair and objective basis for negotiations and decision making. In these circumstances, the available map of the streamlined audience could be used unproblematically – much to the industry's peace of mind. In this uncertain business, at least one thing could be counted upon: that the regularities and patterns yielded by the Nielsen ratings give adequate information about the viewing behaviour of the audience at large. The ratings were the solid bedrock on which the industry lived: they told industry managers, or so it was the common belief, who their viewers were. Ratings discourse made the anonymous television audience visible in a neat and manageable way, and viewers seemed to be content and happy, or at least happy enough, with what they were offered. Otherwise, why should they keep on watching?

Since the beginning of the 1980s, however, all is not so quiet any more at the television front: unprecedented things occur in front of the small screen, in the millions of homes where the television set has conquered such a firm and central place. Gradually, the certainties in which the industry could permit itself to luxuriate have been eroded. One of the most obvious signs of that erosion is the steady decline of the three networks' combined share of the national prime-time audience, from over 90 per cent in their heyday in the mid-1970s to less than 75 per cent in the mid-1980s (Carman 1987).[1] What happened? Where have all those viewers, on whom the networks could so reliably count, gone? The answer is simple: the rise of new television-related technologies has provided people with new options, new choices.

In 1987, about half of all American homes has a video cassette recorder (VCR). Also 49 per cent has been connected to a basic cable system, while 27 per cent has chosen to subscribe to one or more pay cable channels, such as Home Box Office. All in all, thirty or more channels can be received in 20 per cent of American homes, while two per cent even have satellite dishes installed (*TV World* 1987). This means that viewers are no longer stuck with the fixed schedules of network programming; they can now rent a film from the local video store, or record a programme on their VCR and view it at a later, more suitable hour, or watch one of the independent stations (whose number has tripled to more than 300 in the 1980s) or the more specialized cable channels, such as the pop music channel MTV and CNN (Cable News Network). An entirely different television landscape unfolds before viewers' eyes these days, one characterized by abundance rather than scarcity. And viewers seem to have responded by eagerly altering their viewing habits, and multiplying the range of their viewing activities. 'After years of submitting passively to the tyranny of [network] television programmers, viewers are taking charge', comments Sally Bedell Smith (1985: H21) in the *New York Times*.

Are viewers really 'taking charge'? And if so, exactly what are they taking charge of, what does it mean, and what implications does it have? From the industry's perspective, what is going on is very confusing indeed. Both for the networks, who see their established, virtually monopolistic position threatened, and for the advertisers, who are now faced with doubts about the effectivity of their current strategies of communicating to their potential consumers, the old certainties have begun to crumble: they feel that they are losing their steady grip on the audience. The advertisers' basic worry, of course, is whether network television is still the best medium to reach their intended audience with their commercials, while the networks are confronted with a heightened necessity to develop ever more effective programming and marketing strategies in an increasingly competitive environment. And in this new and chaotic situation, audience measurement has become a central focus of concern, the site on which the uncertainties and worries are expressed and articulated. As the representative of a large advertiser, quoted by Bedell Smith (1985: H23), notes: 'There is no question that the new electronic media are rendering a lot of the traditional ways we measure audiences old-fashioned.'

The problematic nature of the new state of affairs is succinctly articulated in the title of Bedell Smith's article, 'Who's watching TV? It's getting hard to tell'. But why, and for whom, should it be a problem that it is getting hard to tell who's watching television? The fact that we tend to accept that we are naturally dealing with a problem here – a problem of want of knowledge – only brings to light the industry's power to impose its own institutional point of view on what is going on: the proliferation of viewing options presents a problem because they threaten to destroy the dependable overview of the audience that the industry presumably used to have. What we witness here then is the industry's anxiety and uneasiness about the growing unpredictability of viewing habits as a consequence of the fragmentation of the electronic media landscape. In short, what is at stake is a disruption of the map of the streamlined 'television audience'.

As a result, pressure on the ratings services to adjust their measurement procedures to the new situation became stronger and stronger: not only the advertisers and networks, but also the newcomers (such as the cable networks and the growing number of independent stations, who are in the business of snatching shares of audience away from the networks) were insistent on getting a more finely tuned map of the audience – so insistent, that the ratings services are said to be under greater pressure to innovate than they ever have been (*Broadcasting* 26 December 1988). The research firms feverishly began to search for technologically feasible answers to the new demands of the industry. And the expectations are high. Debates about the issue have been replete with dramatic terms such as 'revolutionary', 'sea change', and so on. As one industry official put it, 'It's possible that we may see more changes in the ratings in the next five years than we have seen in the previous twenty' (in Bedell Smith 1985: H23).

The emergence of cable television posed the first challenge to the existing order of things in the industry. Although cable was initially envisioned by its adherents as a medium greatly different from, and superior to, broadcast television (Streeter 1987), the dominant use of cable has become simply that of an extension of broadcast television. As a matter of course, the measurement of the cable audience appeared on the agenda of the ratings producers. However, audiences for cable channels proved to be very difficult to measure. The traditional techniques used to measure the broadcast television audience – setmeters and diaries – did not succeed in producing accurate and consistent figures for the size and composition of the cable audience (Livingston 1986). The diary method especially was blamed for having serious flaws. According to a large-scale methodology study performed by Nielsen in 1983, diaries tended to underestimate cable audiences up to a dramatic figure of 45 per cent (Beville 1985).[2] Thus, frustration abounded among cable industry managers: in their view, cable's position *vis-à-vis* the networks was done serious harm as a result of 'misrepresentations' (that is: underestimation) of their share of audience in the Nielsen data. So, insistent calls for 'correct measurement' and 'getting the methodology right' were the central tenets in the cable industry's 'love–hate relationship' with Nielsen (Livingston 1986).[3]

The shortcomings of the diary method as an audience measurement instrument were actually not exactly news for the industry. It has always been acknowledged that, because the gathering of data through diaries is dependent on the active participation of viewers in the sample, bias in the results is perfectly possible as a consequence of errors or inaccuracies in the diary keeping process. As early as 1962 for example, Harold Mehling, in his sweeping crusade against 'the rating game', ridiculed the method by gleefully making up the following scene behind the closed doors of a sample family home:

HUSBAND: While you're putting out the lights, dear, I'll fill out the diary for this evening – oh-oh, for the last two evenings. We didn't fill it out last night. Let's see, we watched *The Play of the Week* and *CBS Reports*, right?

WIFE: Yes, but the children saw the cartoon show. You'd better put that down. You don't want it all *that* kind of thing.

HUSBAND: You're right. [They] did say [their] ratings help them figure out what people want to see, and we shouldn't weight it with our high-brow stuff, should we?

WIFE: No, it wouldn't be fair. A lot of people get a kick out of the wrestling, you know.

HUSBAND: Well, what did we see tonight? There was *Eyewitness*, and that concert show they got from the educational station. That's all – well, now wait. I'm not going to impose my Beethoven on everybody. I *considered* watching *Rawhide* for once, so I think I'll just. . .'

(Mehling 1962: 225)[4]

Mehling's message is clear: the diary method is too subjective to be a reliable instrument for measuring even such a simple thing as 'who's watching what'. (In his view, the 'Nielsen family' is a 'subspecies of viewers' created by the practice of the ratings firms themselves.)

The industry has never been unaware of the problem of subjectivity in the diary technique. On the contrary, there has always been distrust of people's accuracy in filling out the diary. But possible inaccuracies, let alone such highly individualistic, willingly distorting twists in deciding what to write down in the diary as imagined in Mehling's absurd scene, fall beyond the grasp of the ratings producers: they are fundamentally context-bound cultural practices that are not translatable in figures and statistics. Therefore, they have to be suppressed from the measurement system. Ratings discourse, as we have seen, is not about the social world of actual audiences, but about 'viewing behaviour'. Nevertheless, the potential of distorted ratings as a consequence of strictly behavioural 'flaws' has been quite clearly documented in empirical terms. Evidence was mounted, for example, that certain groups, such as children, teenagers and young males, tend to underreport themselves in diary data.

Also, a tendency to report programmes that are usually seen rather than are actually watched in the particular week was discovered – a tendency which militates against less well-known and familiar programmes (such as those of the new cable channels) because people tend to forget about them more easily when they fill out their diaries at the end of the week.[5] Still, the diary was the most widely used technique in television audience measurement: for decades, its weaknesses were tolerated because it is a relatively simple and inexpensive method, even though, as Beville (1985: 112) admits, 'for all household members to keep an accurate record of viewing on several television sets is a challenging task indeed'.

The proliferation of cable channels, however, acutely dramatized the problems inherent in the diary technique. Suddenly its lack of accuracy mattered, because it tended to result in statistics disadvantageous for the cable companies. All of a sudden, then, the built-in subjective (and thus 'unreliable') element of the diary technique was perceived as an unacceptable deficiency. For example, officials of the pop music channel MTV complained that their target audience, young people between 12 and 24, consistently comes off badly in the demographic data produced through diaries, because 'younger viewers . . . tend not to be as diligent in filling out diaries as older household members' (Livingston 1986: 130). Ratings specialists have come to talk about this issue as the 'non-co-operation problem': the fact that some groups of the audience are not so easily mobilized to keep diaries. And there is no way to force them to do so. . .[6]

But the new multi-channel environment has also in a more general sense unsettled the relatively uncomplicated assumptions about watching television that have been the traditional basis for audience measurement. Now that viewers have so many channels to choose from, they have the opportunity to switch around from channel to channel more – a type of conduct which was greatly facilitated by the remote control device, enabling viewers to swiftly 'zap' through all the channels without having to leave their couch. This practice of 'channel switching' presumably makes for rather chaotic and erratic scenes in front of the TV sets. And in this situation the diary problem became so urgent that it could no longer be ignored. Agreement grew that the diary had now become an obsolete measurement tool. In the words of David Poltrack, CBS vice president of research:

> It used to be easy. You watched M*A*S*H on Monday night and you'd put that in the diary. Now, if you have 30 channels on cable you watch one channel, switch to a movie, watch a little MTV, then another program, and the next morning with all that switching all over the place you can't remember what you watched.
>
> (In Bedell Smith 1985: H23)

Some irony: the more 'freedom of movement' viewers have, the more intricate and perplexing the situation for the industry becomes. The map of the streamlined audience is under pressure! Behind the controversy over the diary technique lurks a great suspicion of the capriciousness of the new viewing behaviour brought about by the sheer increase of channels and encouraged by the remote control device. Viewers could no longer be trusted to report their viewing with sufficient accuracy: they lack perfect memory, they may be too careless. In short, their subjectivity has become too problematic!

In this situation, feeling thrived that a better method to obtain ratings data should be developed. And better means: more 'objective', that is, less dependent on the fallibilities of viewers in the sample – a method that erases all traces of unreliable subjectivity. The electronic setmeter, the other technique through which Nielsen produced its ratings figures, is such an objective method, but it only measures viewing per household and cannot capture viewing by individual audience members, for which the diary technique was used in the first place. Demographic data, which have become more and more important for the industry, could only be acquired through those wretched diaries.

Confronted with this predicament, the ratings business came up with a new, technologically advanced instrument to measure the television audience: the people meter. The people meter is supposed to combine the virtues of the traditional setmeter and the diary: it is an electronic device that measures individual viewing rather than household viewing. Although currently operative versions of the people meter are still vulnerable because they need the co-operation of the viewers at home, the instrument was welcomed by the industry as a first step in the direction of a more appropriate measurement technology – a possible solution to the problems haunting the industry (Stoddard 1988). But before continuing to go into the vicissitudes of the people meter, let us have a look at another 'new technology' that has thrown the audience measurement field into turmoil: the video cassette recorder.

The VCR has also played a major destabilizing role in disrupting the streamlined 'television audience'. By 1986 the new machine, which only became available for domestic use in 1975, could already be found as part of the household equipment in about half of all American homes, while optimistic estimates place VCRs in up to 85 per cent of households by 1995 (Potter *et al.* 1988). It is clear that the VCR has helped to enlarge the usage possibilities of the television set. All sorts of viewer practices have flourished as a consequence of the VCR. Rentals of prerecorded tapes, for example, have proven to be an increasingly significant use of the VCR (Potter *et al.* 1988; Henke and Donehue 1989).[7] When watching these tapes, however, viewers simply cease to be members of the broadcast (or cable) television audience. Confronted with this practice of what has been called 'source shifting' by actual audiences, the industry laments in nostalgia over the 'loss'.[8]

But the VCR also enables 'time shifting': a desired programme is recorded while the viewer is watching another channel or is out or is otherwise occupied, with the intention of playing it back at a later time. It is this application of the VCR which has caused the most commotion in industry circles.[9] Time shifting may be a welcome new option for viewers because it makes watching television a more flexible practice, but for the industry it brings about all sorts of troublesome complications. Time shifting is obviously changing the way in which people relate to television, although it remains to be seen exactly how, and to what extent.[10] But as the industry cannot live with too much uncertainty, demand for measurement of the VCR audience has been the not so surprising response to the problem. How often is the VCR used? How can the VCR audience be segmented? Which programmes are recorded most by which viewers? And when are they played back? Thus, VCR use is now being meticulously scrutinized with such questions in mind. Since 1986, for example, Nielsen has added a weekly VCR Special Analysis Report to its services package (Potter *et al.* 1988; Sims 1989).

The networks' interest in such information is dominated by the drive to know how time shifting affects the audience-maximizing effectiveness of their carefully arranged schedules. If, as one researcher has put it, 'VCR ownership heightens overall awareness of the TV schedule because owners are making decisions on whether to view or tape programmes' (Rosenthal 1987: 69), viewers will be able to interrupt the flow of programmes as dictated by the networks' schedules and construct their own schedules. This would make all sorts of tried and tested scheduling tricks, such as 'hammocking' (a strategy which is intended to boost the ratings of a programme by placing it in between two popular programmes) less effective: viewers can no longer be 'captured' so easily. Poltrack (in ibid,: 39) refers to this phenomenon by calling it 'schedule cannibalization', a voracious metaphor that indicates the apprehension, if not implicit regret, felt in network circles about the new freedoms viewers have acquired through the VCR. VCR users as wild savages!

But the networks are also creative in inventing effects of the VCR that they can bend to their advantage. For example, one survey found that 4 per cent of the audience for a series like *LA Law* comes through the VCR, as against only 2 per cent for *The Cosby Show* (ibid.). Thus, as recorded programmes are included in the Nielsen ratings, the VCR can be seen as enhancing, if only slightly, the ratings performance of *LA Law*. Such play with statistics has led NBC's Brandon Tartikoff to cheerfully remark that VCRs 'are actually helping our ratings rather than competing with them' (in *Broadcasting* 6 April 1987: 90). And Barry Cook, NBC's managing director of special media research, predicts: 'I don't see the VCR becoming a dominant force. It could allow the network to take more of risk in scheduling a new show against strong competition' (in Rosenthal 1987: 68). In other words, the networks furiously attempt to interpret the new situation caused by the VCR in manageable terms. They make every effort, at least rhetorically, to render the entrance of the VCR compatible with their own programming and scheduling strategies.

What is at stake in such strategies is the remapping of the audience in the VCR era. To illustrate the networks' ambition to incorporate VCR use in a streamlined map, just note some of the more daring suggestions made by Poltrack to regulate recording and playback practices. Drawing on survey findings that Saturday night is the night on which the VCR is used most (both for playbacking recorded tapes and for watching rented tapes), he noted that, where it used to be network strategy to discourage taping, now the time might have come to promote it: 'for example, [by] encouraging stay-at-homes to watch rented tapes early and then watch network programs, or tape shows from previous nights and watch them then, or night-outers to record Saturday night programming to watch later that night' (in ibid., 67). Exactly how Poltrack imagined such streamlined VCR viewing behaviour could be orchestrated is not mentioned, nor whether he should be taken entirely seriously. What is significant here however is the very emergence of such ideas from the networks' point of view.

Advertisers, for their part, are sceptical. Not surprisingly, they are most worried about the fate of their commercials in time shifting practices. What if recorded tapes are not played back at all? Then, not only the programmes, but also, more importantly, the commercials will remain unwatched! The concern is still aggravated by the VCR's fast-forward button. This button enables viewers to 'zip' through the tape at several times the normal rate, in some cases even with the screen going to black in the process. What if viewers practise this on the commercials when they play back their tapes? Then viewers would watch the programmes while skipping the commercials – a most undesirable state of affairs for the advertisers.

Here again, we see a cultural battle being acted out: while 'zipping' and 'zapping' enlarge the freedom of viewers to watch television as they feel like, they form a serious problem for the industry, a problem that unsettles the consensus between networks and advertisers about the 'right' measure of the audience. To counter the problem, research was summoned to bring about the relevant facts. But there is a lot of controversy about the frequency of zipping and zapping, as survey results tend to contradict each other. While some findings speak about a 'zipping rate' of 60 per cent, others lead to the conclusion that for all the zipping that is practiced, still 90 per cent of the commercials are seen on playback, because people do not seem to be zipping consistently (ibid.). Still less evident is the eventual impact of playback and zipping for commercial exposure. Thus, a network representative foregrounded the finding of one survey that the average tape is played back 1·6 times, which he cunningly interpreted as an advantage to the advertiser: 'We're providing a hard copy of a commercial, so there's the potential to watch a commercial more, if it's worth viewing.' And so he ventured to put the burden on the shoulders of the advertisers: 'We've never guaranteed the viewing of a commercial without the VCR. It's the agency's responsibility to make it appealing. [Zipping data] will educate the agencies on which commercials are being viewed and which aren't' (in ibid.: 70)

Clever logic, but not particularly appealing to the advertisers. In general, the latter are keen to emphasize that even without zipping, time shifting will inevitably lead to a loss of audience for commercials – according to one estimate, only 58 per cent of all recordings made for time shifting are ever replayed (Potter *et al.* 1988) – and that including recorded programmes in the ratings is unfair because it tends to benefit the networks at the expense of the advertisers. Similar concerns are expressed as to zapping. One study estimated that almost 20 per cent of homes is populated by 'heavy zappers' (switching channels more than once every two minutes), and such figures tend to reinforce advertisers' claim that they are paying for millions more viewers than the networks are actually delivering them (Kneale 1988). Advertisers became obsessed with the question 'how to grab viewers before they grab remote controls' (Marton 1989; see also Sepstrup 1986). On the other hand, an occasional voice could also be heard saying that 'maybe the valley of the shadow isn't so dark after all' (Greene 1988): in this case, a market researcher reasoned that the reach of commercials may be less impaired by active viewer strategies such as zapping and zipping than is feared, because 'a programme viewer who switches channels (or fast forwards or even erases commercials at recording or on VCR replay) has to really watch the set to see/know/perceive what she or he is doing and ends up with more commercial exposure value than we have been prone to grant' (ibid., 15). All in all, advertisers are clearly increasingly worried about the fact that viewers can actively avoid watching the commercials that are embedded in the programmes. Against this background, advertisers have begun to call for audience measurement based upon reach of commercials rather than reach of programmes – a development which is met with less than enthusiasm by the networks because they realize that such differentiation will probably lead to lower ratings (Cook 1988).

Such industry disputes may sound petty and tedious to the outsider, and as all too blatantly betraying self-serving positions. But the zeal with which industry managers seem to indulge in these discursive quarrels tells us a great deal about the nervousness with which the new situation has been encountered. The industry needed to adapt; advertisers and broadcasters clearly needed to define a new common ground, a formal agreement about the new technologies' consequences for the way in which 'viewing behaviour' should be measured. And in order to do so, they needed to know more than they used to. The knowledge offered by the traditional Nielsen ratings obviously no longer sufficed.

The new television landscape, then, has wiped out 'the good old days' when American commercial television was a relatively neat and ordered business, which could complacently believe in and rely on the premise of an easily streamlineable audience. That premise could no longer be taken for granted. Gone is the consensus over the information which Nielsen's ratings discourse had managed to supply, to the satisfaction of all, for so many years: as nobody was sure any more who is watching what and when and how, an agitated ferment in the field of audience measurement has sprung, fundamentally throwing into doubt the accepted map of the streamlined audience. The industry now insists on knowing not only who's watching what, but also what which viewers do with their remote control devices and their VCRs. In other words, what the industry was bracing for is an ever more meticulous monitoring of the television audience: more and more differentiations of viewing behaviour began to be considered relevant for coverage in the enterprise of audience measurement. In the midst of all this consternation and bewilderment, the people meter was introduced.

9 The people meter 'solution'

By the late 1980s, the people meter had undeniably become the industry's token of what has been called a ratings 'revolution'. The British research firm AGB introduced the instrument in the United States by announcing its plans to enter the American ratings market in 1983, and started testing its PeopleMeter (with Boston as test market) in 1985. AGB aggressively marketed the new measurement instrument by presenting it as the answer to the inadequacies of both the setmeter and the diary, thereby challenging Nielsen's monopoly in the national television audience measurement arena (Fierman 1985). Nielsen, of course, did not want to be outdone and followed suit by developing and testing its own version of the people meter, called the Homeunit.[1] Within a few years, people meters have achieved tremendously high acceptance in the industry, in the conviction that they are 'the technological cutting edge of the future' (Beville 1986a: 54). As a result both AGB and Nielsen, locked in deadly competition, officially inaugurated their people meter national ratings service in September 1987. Nielsen, who terminated his NTI Audimeter service a month later, succeeded in regaining its monopoly in the national ratings scene when AGB, who only managed to contract one network, CBS, had to close down its service about a year later (*Broadcasting* 20 June 1988; 1 August 1988). By that time, the people meter had established itself as the standard instrument for measuring the television audience, as succinctly proclaimed by the title of one *Broadcasting* feature, 'Television in the peoplemeter age' (7 September 1987).

The people meter has been presented as a highly sophisticated, technologically-advanced instrument to measure the various kinds of viewing behaviour in the complicated television landscape of the late twentieth century. Essentially, the basic idea is deceptively simple. A people meter is an electronic monitoring device that can record individual viewing rather than just sets tuned in, as the traditional setmeter does. When a viewer begins to watch a programme, he or she must press a numbered button on a portable keypad, which looks like the well-known television remote control device. When the viewer stops watching, the button must be pressed again. A monitor attached to the TV set lights up regularly to remind the viewer of the button pushing task. All members of a sample family have their own individual buttons, while there are also some extra buttons for guests. Linked to the home by telephone lines, the system's central computer correlates each viewer's number with demographic data about them stored in its memory. The AGB people meter for example was capable of continuously measuring the activity of up to four sets in each household, including VCRs, and monitors 97 channels.

This intricate measurement technology is attractive for the industry because it holds the promise of providing more detailed and precise data on the television audience, because it requires all household members to identify themselves when watching. The people meter has boosted the hope for better measurement of the wide spectre of cable and VCR viewing (including zipping and zapping), and has been praised for its capability of providing demographic information on a programme's audience composition overnight (which is several weeks faster than the now rejected paper-and-pencil diary method). Smaller audience segments may now be detected and described, allowing advertisers and broadcasters to create more precise demographic targets.[2] Furthermore, because the people meter provides continuous, on-line data, daily, all year long, it becomes possible to accumulate longitudinal data on an individual's viewing behaviour – which was not possible with the diary technique because the diaries were typically only filled out by a sample family every four weeks. As a result, people meter data are able to reveal, for example, what percentage of women between 25 and 54 watched the second episode of a programme, or what percentage of men between 18 and 34 watched both the first-run and repeat of a football game, or, during an advertising campaign, what percentage of any demographic category has seen one commercial break, a second, a third, and so on (*Broadcasting* 17 September 1984; 5 January 1987; Ehrenberg and Wakshlag 1987). In sum, the people meter yields such a dazzling array of data, that, in the words of Mal Beville (1986a: 53), 'the dramatic increase in volume of figures . . . will challenge the talent of the best number-crunchers in the business'.

The people meter can make hitherto hidden and unknown minutiae in aggregated viewing habits visible, and opens up the potential of drawing a new, more detailed map of the audience. In line with the cartographic metaphor, it could be said that the old map was no longer adequate as guide in the rocky terrain of the television business, because more traffic is now on the road, making careful driving more necessary. The new map should enable finding the correct signposts and avoiding the danger zones more efficiently. This, at least, is what the entire industry is in agreement about. The people meter was embraced by the industry at a time when changes in the television landscape had made the old, rather schematic map of the streamlined audience obsolete. The timing was perfect: the new situation called for new solutions, or at least new ways of satisfactorily smoothing out the escalating contradictions and disputes over 'television audience' which came with it. The people meter provided the promise of such a solution.

But the transition to the people meter did not take place without any resistance. As with many a new beginning, the introduction of the people meter was accompanied with excitement, controversy and ambivalence. The big three networks especially were less than happy with it. Not surprisingly so, because test results of the new instrument consistently produced over-all ratings that were 5 to 10 per cent lower than those arrived at with the old measurement system. For example, in August 1987, when Nielsen's old and new systems were temporarily operating simultaneously, there were 1.3 million fewer households watching the tube according to the people meter data (*San Francisco Chronicle* 17 August 1987). The most popular programmes seemed to suffer most. For example, the audience for NBC's *The Cosby Show* was estimated to be 10 to 15 per cent smaller by the people meter (*Broadcasting* 7 September 1987). Given the enormous financial reper-cussions of such declines, it is no wonder that the networks were quite reluctant in accepting the rewrite of the measurement standards (*Broadcasting* 6 April 1987).

Of course, the networks shared the view that the old diary method of acquiring demographic information was outdated. But they were also not very pleased with the people meter. In voicing their protest, however, they could not straightforwardly foreground self-interested arguments. Thus, they cast their position in technical terms, stressing the methodo-logical imperfections of the people meter. For example, NBC's vice president of research William Rubens complained in a speech that the changeover to people meters 'has brought home to me how far away the research business has drifted from sound methodology'. He went as far as condemning the fact that 'market pressures forced [Nielsen] to introduce a ratings service before its time', and argued that 'critics of the old system should be just as skeptical about people meters, for if we don't have the best media measurement money can buy, we will wind up with inaccurate ratings' (*Broadcasting* 21 March 1988: 27). CBS's head of research David Poltrack (1988), too, asserted that 'the industry's standard of living' has 'lowered' since the introduction of people meters. Thus, soon after the people meter's official inauguration, ABC, CBS and NBC took the initiative, together with the National Association of Broadcasters, in requesting Nielsen to co-operate with an independent evaluation of the people meter methodology (*Broadcasting* 21 March 1988).

In formulating criticisms of the people meter, strikingly similar arguments are reiterated as those once levelled against the old paper-and-pencil diary technique: they involve too much subjectivity. The term 'people meter', it is contended, is a misleading one because a meter is supposed to measure automatically, and should not require the co-operation of those being measured. Rubens has sneeringly dubbed the people meter an 'electronic diary', requiring 'people pushing buttons instead of pencils' (in Beville 1986a: 78). And indeed, it is this button-pushing chore that has become a focal concern among the critics. A general discourse of distrust has developed around it: how can one place reliance on people's veracity in handling the pushbutton gadget? Mal Beville, the doyen of ratings specialists, has cited many problems: 'Unlike the diary, where recording errors can be corrected after the fact, the people meter requires perfect instantaneous button-pushing performance. No second chance is available to correct a mistake.' (1986a: 78) And another professional observer wondered: 'Will the families in the sample really take the trouble? Will they always press the buttons as they begin watching? Will they always remember to press their buttons when they leave the room – as when the telephone rings, or the baby cries?' (Baker 1986: 95).

In an environment where so much depends on the figures, these worries are perfectly understandable and logical. Therefore, from the very beginning the ratings firms themselves have done their best to determine what they call the 'compliance rate' to the device, to see to what extent people can be motivated to co-operate with the system (Gardner 1984).[3] But doubts have not calmed down. Support for that doubt was delivered by a test with Nielsen's initial sample of 1,000 households, which according to Poltrack showed that 'half of the people aren't cooperating and only 75 per cent (of those) offer good information each day' (in Donlon 1987). Such low 'compliance rates', the network researchers were eager to emphasize, will inevitably lead to all sorts of bias in sampling and in the resulting data. For example, they were extremely taken aback by test results that indicated that the technology seemed to be more acceptable to larger families, to those with higher income and education levels, and to people familiar with 'high tech' items such as personal computers and VCRs, and less in blue collar families and among older people in rural areas. Furthermore, children, teenagers and women especially seemed to be less 'reliable' in their push-button behaviour. And lastly, they were sceptical about whether sample families will not get tired of pushing buttons day-in, day-out, for the whole period that they are part of the sample (which can be years), every time they start and stop watching . . .(*Broadcasting* 5 January 1987; 6 April 1987; 5 September 1988). Given all this, Rubens put his verdict in extremely militant terms:

People meters go against human nature. You can't expect people to work on data entry during their leisure activity of watching TV. Either they take a leisurely approach to data entry, or TV viewing becomes work – and they may ease the burden by watching less.

(*Broadcasting* 21 March 1988)

'Accuracy', then, has become a key term with which evaluations of the people meter are formulated.[4] The ratings firms try hard to solve the perceived problems. Thus, much attention is given to general methodological issues such as attaining a sample base which is as representative as possible, improving response rates, and developing incentive plans to get sample members to push buttons more diligently (e.g. Soong 1988). For example, Nielsen started a programme to coach younger viewers by letting them order from a merchandise catalogue as a reward for consistent button-pushing (*Broadcasting* 5 September 1988)! Such shrewd conditioning procedures notwithstanding, however, the bottom line remains that the people meter can only work if people are willing to submit themselves to it and co-operate properly. This subjective element is perceived as the fundamental 'weak link' in the current state of affairs in people meter technology. Again and again, one hears expressions of lack of confidence in 'button pushing'. This 'imperfection' of the people meter looms large in the consciousness of the audience measurement scene. Even Nielsen officials are convinced that 'the device isn't the ultimate ratings solution because it requires viewer co-operation' (*Broadcasting* 4 May 1987: 72). It should come as no surprise, therefore, that furious attempts are being undertaken to develop what is called a passive people meter: a meter that doesn't require any buttons at all, and senses automatically who and how many viewers are watching what in the living rooms (*Broadcasting* 26 December 1988).

Several proposals 'bizarre enough to boggle James Bond' had already started to circulate in the ratings firms (Waters and Uehling 1985). An article in *TV Guide* summed them up with an acute sense of incredulous amazement:

> One suggestion is to implant tiny electronic 'bugs' in the navels of all family members in a people-metered household. That way, the meter will automatically 'know' who's watching, with no action required of the viewer. Another solution is to give every family member a special bracelet or wristwatch that would transmit a signal identifying the wearer to the meter. Or how about an ultrasonic device (like those used for burglar alarms) in all the rooms with TV sets, so that family members would be recognized by the meter the instant they switched on the set. Another modest proposal is to build into the TV set a photoelectric eye that would watch *you*. And finally – the device audience-measurement theorists fondly call 'the whoopee sofa': a divan wired to detect tiny variations in the temperatures of household members' bottoms and thus identify them for the meter.
>
> (Hickey 1984: 10)

If most of these ideas seem as yet to be no more than the products of science fiction-like fantasizing, experiments on the technological feasability of a passive people meter are one of the top priorities in the audience measurement field. Initiatives abound (e.g. Lu and Kiewit 1987). Thus, one research firm, Seattle-based R. D. Percy & Co, has experimented with a local ratings service in New York since 1987, using a heat sensor that presumably can discern how many household members are watching television without them having to push any buttons, although apparently it has remained unclear how the sensor differentiates between a person and a large pet, such as a big dog (E. Jensen 1986; Kneale 1988).[5] And in June 1989 Nielsen disclosed a plan, developed together with the David Sarnoff Research Center at Princeton University, for a rather sophisticated passive people meter system, consisting of an image-recognition technique capable of identifying the faces of those in the room. The system then decides first if it is a face it recognizes, and then if that face is directed toward the set (unfamiliar faces and even possibly the dog will be recorded as 'visitors'). If tested successfully, this system could replace the imperfect, push-button people meter by the mid-1990s, so Nielsen executives expect (*San Francisco Chronicle* 1 June 1989; Friedman 1989).[6]

These dazzling developments indicate the sheer attractiveness of the idea of a perfect measurement technology in industry circles: so pressing is the felt need for a more precise map of 'television audience'. But at the same time the whole commotion about the people meter reveals the more general political issue involved in the audience measurement project as such. The frenzy around people meters clearly suggests that there is more at stake than just a desire for methodological improvement: at stake is the problem of control.

Now that the industry as a whole is confronted with a more competitive and hectic television landscape, a loss of manageability of 'television audience' – a streamlined audience, one that can be commodified and objectified, exchanged and acted upon – is threatening to take place, fuelling 'our worst fears', as one advertiser put it, 'that people aren't sitting as they did 25 years ago, eyes transfixed to the tube, watching everything that comes across' (in Kneale 1988: 27). The remedy, embodied in ever more sophisticated versions of the people meter, is being sought in more and faster finely-tuned information, allowing for more microscopic differentiations and characterizations in audience measurement data. More detailed ratings, so the implicit philosophy goes, will supply the industry with new symbolic means to regain its lost consensus over what constitutes the correct description of the audience. In other words, the people meter was welcomed because it promised to put the streamline back into the map of 'television audience'.

In practice, the people meter has now, for better or worse, become the new standard of empirical truth that the industry has to live by. But the general idea behind it can be seen to play an extended political role: it symbolizes the desire for having ever more complete, objective, accurate, in short, more 'realistic' knowledge on people's viewing behaviour, minute by minute, all year long – knowledge that is somehow expected to solve the industry's problem of control. In fact, the people meter would never have been developed had such a desire not been felt in the first place. The currently operative, push-button people meters are, from this perspective, only partial materializations of this desire. The vision of the perfect, passive, people meter measurement device may sound extravagant, but such an instrument is the ultimate dream of an industry continually in search of the perfectly streamlined 'television audience'.

10 Revolt of the viewer?
The elusive audience

In his seminal study of the birth of the prison, *Discipline and Punish*, Michel Foucault (1979) has carefully analysed the importance of the examination as a social procedure for the exercise of disciplinary power. The examination

> establishes over individuals a visibility through which one differentiates them and judges them. . . . In it are combined the ceremony of power and the form of the experiment, the deployment of force and the establishment of truth. At the heart of the procedures of discipline, it manifests the subjection of those who are perceived as objects and the objectification of those who are subjected.
>
> (Foucault 1979: 184)

The examination, so widely practised in social institutions such as the school, the hospital, the military, works through 'the fixing, at once ritual and "scientific", of individual differences, as the pinning down of each individual in his own particularity' (ibid.: 192). Those under examination get subjected to a sort of compulsory visibility, they become individuals to be looked at, observed, described in detail, monitored from day to day. Knowledge about them is accumulated through small and seemingly innocent techniques such as notation, registration, the constitution of files and dossiers, and the arrangement of facts in columns and tables; and the vast, meticulous, documentary apparatus thus acquired, constituting a comparative system in which it is possible to classify individuals, to form categories, to determine averages, and so on, becomes an essential component in the exercise of disciplinary power over whole groups of people – a power that uses the establishment of precise individual differences as a basis for the construction of taxonomic divisions.

Jeremy Bentham's plan for the Panopticon (1791) is, according to Foucault (1979), paradigmatic for the technological scheme by which this linkage of disciplinary power and knowledge is practised. The clever architectural design of the Panopticon makes efficient surveillance of prisoners possible: it consists of a large courtyard with a tower in the centre and a set of buildings, divided into levels and cells, on the periphery. Each cell has a window that faces the tower, from which the supervisor can observe the inmates in the cells without himself being seen. The cells are like 'small theatres in which each actor is alone, perfectly individualized and constantly visible' (ibid.: 200). In such a spatial structure disciplinary control over the behaviour of those confined in the cells becomes possible because they are stuck in the position of objects subjected to the permanent examining gaze of the surveillant: their every move will be observed, noted, and registered. For Foucault, the Panopticon is the metaphor for a technological device whose function is to increase social control. Even if the Panopticon itself, in its pure form, was never actually constructed, the mechanisms exemplified by it serve as the perfect paradigm for disciplinary technology, efficient in its operation, flexible in its applications. As Hubert Dreyfus and Paul Rabinow (1982: 189) have remarked, 'whenever the imperative is to set individuals or populations in a grid where they can be made productive and observable, then Panoptic technology can be used'.

I am reminded of these insights of Foucault in trying to make sense of the developments in audience measurement practices that I have been discussing here. In fact, the principles of panopticism are central to the technological operation of audience measurement: its core mechanism, and ultimate ambition, is control through visibility. Audience measurement too is a form of examination: its aim is to put television viewers under constant scrutiny, to describe their behaviour so as to turn them into suitable objects in and for industry practices, to judge their viewing habits in terms of their productivity for advertisers and broadcasters alike. What audience measurement accomplishes is the production of a discourse which 'formalizes' and reduces the viewer into a calculable audience member, someone whose behaviour can be objectively determined and neatly categorized. As we have seen, this discursive streamlining of 'television audience' is extremely useful for the industry: it effectuates a comforting sense of predictability and controllability in an uncertain environment.

However, it would be misleading to see audience measurement as a regular instance of the disciplinary arrangements Foucault talks about. Television viewers cannot be subjected to officially sanctioned disciplinary control such as is the case with schoolchildren or prisoners. In these institutions disciplinary techniques are aimed at transforming people through punishment, through training and correction. The living room however is emphatically not a classroom or a prison cell, nor is television a 'carceral' institution. After all, watching television takes place in the context of domestic leisure, under the banner of the hedonism of consumer society, in which the idea of audience freedom forms a prominent ideological value.[1] Therefore the commercial television industry cannot have the power to effectuate the conversion of viewers into what Foucault (1979) has termed 'docile bodies', implying total behavioural control over them – that is, the ability to force them to adopt the 'ideal' viewing behaviour (for example, watch all the commercials attentively).[2]

This 'problem' – that is, the problem that viewers are not prisoners but 'free' consumers – accounts for the limits of audience measurement as a practice of control. Indeed, it would even be ideologically impossible to officially present it as a practice of control: instead it is called, as we have seen, a practice of creating 'feedback'. The importance given to methodological accuracy and objectivity in discussions about audience measurement may be understood against this background: emphasizing that audience measurement is a matter of research not control increases its credibility and legitimacy and reduces distrust against it. All this amounts to the fact that audience measurement can only be an indirect means of disciplining the television audience: it is through symbolic, not literal objectification and subjection that ratings discourse, by streamlining 'television audience', performs its controlling function. It does not effect the actual discipline of television viewers, it only conjures it up in its imagination. This leads to a fundamental contradiction in the very motif of audience measurement. Just as the disciplinary technologies described by Foucault, ratings services put viewers under constant examination. But contrary to what happens, for example, in the prison, the visibility of people-watching-television achieved by audience measurement is not linked up with the organization of direct behavioural control: observation and regulation of bodies do not go together here. In other words, audience measurement is an incomplete panoptic arrangement: the power/knowledge linkage is, in a sense, rather precarious. This does not mean that there is no power and control involved in the set-up of audience measurement; it does mean, however, that the production of ever more refined knowledge as such becomes a rather autonomous pursuit: stripped of a direct material effect on its object of scrutiny, audience measurement is carried out in the tacit belief that the production of knowledge as such – that is, the construction of a streamlined map of 'television audience' – must somehow automatically lead to control over actual audiences. To put it in a different way, even if audience measurement cannot be seen as a true panoptic technology, panopticism is inscribed in it insofar as the whole project is inspired by the ideal of such a form of control, and driven by the constant theoretical and practical search for the best mechanisms to do so. We will see, however, that the project has quite contradictory effects, not at all uniformly leading to the desired increased control.

To be sure, the technologies of audience measurement – meter, diary, telephone interview, people meter – do involve actual entry in the living rooms of (a small number of) actual viewers, in order to put them under constant examination. These technologies indicate that audience measurement is basically an ingenious means for the industry to obliquely penetrate people's private spaces, in order to make 'visible', in a roundabout way, what would otherwise take place out of sight (and therefore beyond control). But, unfortunately for the industry, the ratings firms can only incorporate families and households in their samples (and intrude in their homes) when they agree to it. While people's freedom to reject their subjection to surveillance is something to be respected in a free society, it is also unwittingly perceived as an unfortunate cir-cumstance, an inconvenience: think of the concern about 'the non-co-operation problem', the suspense around 'compliance rates'.

The problem has become all the more pronounced with the launch of the people meter technology. The futuristic passive people meter, in particular, comes dangerously close to a literal materialization of panoptic mechanisms: with the (passive) people meter, the process of subjection to the examining apparatus is becoming all too obvious. And indeed, this theme is well reflected in the public controversy around the people meter. With the introduction of the people meter, audience measurement is becoming too explicit and palpable an instance of monitoring viewers. Thus, the people meter has repetitiously been given a bad press as a 'manifestation of Big Brother': observers note 'the new technology's spooky Orwellian overtones' (Waters and Uehling 1985) (is it mere coincidence that public debate on the people meter started in 1984?), while one industry official expressed his personal doubts about the passive people meter as follows: 'My concern is more from the big-brother standpoint. If somehow, somewhere a computer knows this massive weight is a 53-year-old male, that scares me. What else does it know about me?' (in *Broadcasting* 5 January 1987: 63).

But this kind of moral concern about the people meter, cast as it is in the liberal discourse of intrusion of privacy, overlooks the less conspicuously obtrusive, but more structural 'rationality' of the very practice of audience measurement. Not only the people meter, but all audience measurement technologies in principle depend on the propriety of having people submit themselves to permanent monitoring. From this point of view, the people meter is not a qualitative break, but merely represents one more step in the technological sophistication of the enterprise: the old setmeter and the paper-and-pencil diary are simply somewhat more 'primitive' devices ('little big brothers' as it were) whose operation is similarly based upon the principle of control through visibility.[3] Rather than raising the ethical problems surrounding the people meter, then, it may be more insightful to try to unravel the implications of technological progress in audience measurement pro-cedures for the exercise of control over the television audience which is their very purpose. And in this respect, I would suggest that the introduction of ever more intricate measurement methods may not simply lead to ever-increasing control, but on the contrary to less control – or better, a less tight link between power and knowledge.

The relentless search for technological sophistication can easily be explained as being incited by ordinary competition between ratings producers, in their commercial attempts to cater for the proliferating industry demands for more accurate ratings. But at a more theoretical level this very call for more accurate ratings also betrays a sense of desperation over the very possibility of designing a proper map of the streamlined audience in the crowded and chaotic television landscape of the late twentieth century. As I have discussed in Chapter 7, ratings discourse acquires its symbolic effectivity when it succeeds in constructing such a map. But this can only take place when it is utterly unambiguous how audience size should be determined, and this in turn can only be done when there is a consensus within the industry about what the object of measurement is, how 'viewing behaviour' should be operationalized. However, it is precisely this consensus which has now dissolved. Conflicting interests among different branches of the industry have multiplied, leading to intensified competition between networks, cable and satellite channels, independent stations, video rental stores and so on, while advertisers are faced with growing uncertainty about the effectiveness of the different media to reach their potential consumers.

In these delicate circumstances, the very currency upon which negotiations within the industry are conducted – the audience commodity as defined by ratings discourse – has inevitably become a central focus of contestation. Thus, while until the mid-1970s there was no real dissension about the assumption that the Nielsen statistics truly represent the 'viewing behaviour' of the television audience, recent industry debates about audience measurement have been, as we have seen, replete with discontent and distrust about their 'reality value'. Note, for example, the dramatic assessment of the situation as given by Nicholas Schiavone, NBC's Vice President for Radio Research, in whose view electronic media research is 'out of control':

> Now, the thoughtful person will understand that if business is to succeed in the long term, then trust must be established between buyer and seller. In media, this trust is based in part upon the accuracy and reliability of the estimates. . . . But when ignorance prevails and trust is betrayed, when numbers lose their meaning, then the marketplace ceases to function efficiently. Advertisers and media no longer relate in a systematic way. The result is chaos. While plenty of money may be changing hands, without good numbers it's hard to tell just what that money is doing.
>
> (Schiavone 1988: RC13)

As we have seen, the answer to the shattered consensus and trust is sought in putting viewers to more meticulous rituals of examination, under the assumption that knowing more precisely what happens in their living rooms will result in more accurate, more true descriptions of 'viewing behaviour'. Thus, in a review of the state of affairs in advertising research, Leo Bogart (1986: 13) sarcastically described the people meter as 'a laudable though rather belated recognition of the fact that television sets do not watch television; people do'. In other words, greater empirical naturalism in audience measurement practices is somehow expected to forge a new consensus about what constitute true audience 'facts'. In this context, it is not surprising that the passive people meter idea – the panoptic instrument *par excellence* – has been received with so much enthusiasm in industry circles.

However, the people meter (no matter how passive) is only one, and actually a quite limited articulation of the wishful attempt to repair the damaged map of the streamlined audience. More far-reaching aspirations are circulating within the audience measurement community, that go beyond the attainment of more and more detailed data about exactly who is watching what, as is promised by the people meter. In fact, the dissolution of consensus has instigated a concern for incorporating a wider range of viewer variables in the measurement endeavour.[4]

Among advertisers especially, there is a growing interest in knowledge about the relationship between television viewing and the purchase of products being advertised in commercials. After all, this is the bottom line of what advertisers care about: whether the audiences delivered to them are also 'productive' audiences (that is, whether they are 'good' consumers). For example, in more avant-garde commercial research circles the search for ever more precise demographic categories, as the people meter provides, has already been losing its credibility. As one researcher put it:

In many cases, lumping all 18–49 women together is ludicrous. . . .
Narrow the age spread down and it still can be ludicrous. Take a $32\frac{1}{2}$-year-old woman. She could be white or black, single or married, working or unemployed, professional or blue collar. And there's lots more. Is she a frequent flier? Does she use a lot of cosmetics? Cook a lot? Own a car? Then there's the bottom line. Do commercials get to her? These are the items the advertiser really needs to know, and demographic tonnage is not the answer.

(Davis 1986: 51)

The kind of research that attempts to answer these questions, currently only in an experimental stage, is known as 'single source' measurement: the same sample of households is subjected to measurement not only of its television viewing behaviour but also of its product purchasing behaviour (e.g. Gold 1988). Arbitron's ScanAmerica, for example, is such a system. In addition to measuring television viewing (using a push-button people meter device), it supplies sample members with another technological gadget: after a trip to the supermarket, household members (usually the housewife, of course) must remove a pencil-size electronic 'wand' attached to their meter and wave it above the universal product code that is stamped on most packaged goods. When the scanning wand is replaced in the meter, the central computer subsequently matches that information with the family's recent viewing patterns, thus producing data presumably revealing the effectiveness of commercials (Beville 1986b; *Broadcasting* 27 June 1988).[5] Needless to say that this system is technically 'flawed' because it necessitates even more active co-operation than just button-pushing. But the tremendous excitement around the prospect of having such single-source, multi-variable information, which is typically celebrated by researchers as an opportunity of 'recapturing . . . intimacy with the consumer' (Gold 1988: 24) or getting in touch with 'real persons' (Davis 1986: 51), indicates that the purely objective, thing-like variables of size and composition alone are no longer perceived as sufficient markers for categorizing the television audience.

Another, similarly unsettling development in the American ratings scene in the 1980s has been the idea of so-called 'qualitative ratings'. Here, the aim is the measurement, and thus quantification, of the 'quality' of aspects of watching television. For example, an organization called Television Audience Assessment (TAA), based in Cambridge, Massachusetts, has attempted to enter the audience measurement market by developing a system which not only measures audience size and composition, but also viewers' attitudes towards the programmes they watch. A 'Program Appeal Index' is intended to measure the level of enjoyment viewers derive from a programme; while a 'Program Impact Index' rates the intellectual and emotional stimulation a programme gives its viewers. Not surprisingly, test results confirmed our common sense knowledge that programmes vary widely on both variables. TAA marketed its service by stressing the usefulness of these indices for the production of new kinds of knowledge which could be relevant for the industry, because high Impact and Appeal ratings may positively influence viewers' receptivity to commercials. Thus, test results suggested that people were most likely to plan ahead to view programmes with 'high appeal' and to remain loyal over time to such programmes, and that programmes with 'high impact' tended to be watched with more involvement and attention. Another useful kind of 'fact' to know, especially for advertisers, is that for low-impact programmes, 46 per cent of the audience leaves the room during the commercials, compared to only 26 per cent of viewers who rate the programme high in terms of impact. One could guess what impact such 'findings' could have on the negotiations between advertisers and broadcasters (eg Beville 1985; Television Audience Assessment 1984).

What is most important to note here, however, is that such measurements produce new kinds of empirical truth, undermining, or at least relativizing, the existing, cruder, 'facts' constructed by traditional ratings discourse. With the idea of qualitative ratings subjective elements have squarely sneaked into the field of ratings discourse – something that has been so neatly excluded from the basic idea of audience measurement in the United States:[6] head counting based on the binary opposition of watching/non-watching, resulting in hard measures of size of audience and audience segments. And this incursion of the subjective dimension in ratings discourse threatens to put the aura of objectivity surrounding ratings under pressure. Thus, Mal Beville (1985: 131–2) vents his scepticism about qualitative ratings by contending that quantitative ratings (such as produced by the meter, the diary, and the people meter) at least 'report . . . the *actual viewing behavior* of the household or person in the sample' (emphasis in original) and provide, if the measurement is accurate, 'an objective recording of what took place'. Yet isn't Beville overly confident here? We could also put forward an opposing view: the interest in qualitative ratings could just as well be seen as bespeaking a recognition that quantitative ratings do not represent an objective recording of 'what took place'. In fact, what has become increasingly uncertain in the new television landscape is exactly 'what takes place' in the homes of people when they watch television. No longer can it be conveniently assumed – as traditional ratings discourse does – that having the TV set on equals watching, that watching means paying attention to the screen, that watching a programme implies watching the commercials inserted in it, that watching the commercials leads to actually buying the products being advertised. . . . Thus, 'viewing behaviour' loses its convenient one-dimensionality: measuring 'it' can never be the same anymore.

Of course, the industry already 'knew' for a long time that its decisions and negotiations were based on fictive footings. After all, it has been established more than once through research, academic and commercial, that watching television is very often done with less than full attention, accompanied by many other activities, from chatting to reading to love making (Papazian 1986; Collett and Lamb 1986).[7] But this widespread occurrence of inattentive and discontinuous viewing was repressed in the ratings discourse of the old days. Now that the formerly-repressed has returned: too many conflicting interests have made such a manœuvre of 'calculated ignorance' impossible to sustain. As one advertising researcher exclaims: 'To put it bluntly, most of the audience is zapping us. It's nothing new. But what could be new is that we face up to the problem and address it squarely. How do we unzap the viewer. . .?' (in Davis 1986: 52). It is against the background of this problem of control that the feverish search for ever more detailed data about 'real viewers' attains it full significance.

But all this data-gathering, all this preoccupation with better measurement technologies and procedures, may contain its own paradox. It could well be that the more microscopic the panoptic gaze on the viewer becomes, the more elusive 'viewing behaviour' turns out to be, and the more difficult it will become for ratings discourse to draw a streamlined map of 'television audience'.

The problem I refer to here is foreshadowed by a classic study by Robert Bechtel *et al.* (1972), who observed a small sample of families in their homes over a five-day period. Ironically, the method they used is very similar to that of the passive people meter. The families were observed by video cameras whose operation, so the reseachers state, was made as unobtrusive as possible: 'There was no way to tell [for the family members] whether the camera was operating or not. The camera did not click or hum or in any way reveal whether it was functioning' (ibid.: 277). More important however were the insights the researchers gained from these naturalistic observations. Their findings were provocative and even put into question the very possibility of describing and delineating 'watching television' in any simple sense as 'a behavior in its own right': they asserted that their 'data point to an inseparable mixture of watching and nonwatching as a general style of viewing behavior', and that 'television viewing is a complex and various form of behavior intricately interwoven with many other kinds of behavior' (ibid.: 298–9). Logically, this insight should lead to the far-reaching conclusion that having people fill out diaries or, for that matter, push buttons to demarcate the times that they watch television is principally nonsensical because there seems to be no such thing as 'watching television' as a separate activity. If it is almost impossible to differentiate between viewers and non-viewers and if, as a consequence, the boundaries of 'television audience' are so blurred, how could it possibly be measured?

Bechtel *et al.*'s study was certainly ahead of its time, and its radical consequences were left aside within the industry, because they were utterly unbearable in their impracticality.[8] Instead, the passive people meter is stubbornly seen as the best hope to get to know the real 'viewing behaviour' of individual audience members. But as we have seen, recent initiatives in the research field have already resulted in the destabilization of ratings discourse's basic assumption, namely, that watching television is a simple type of behaviour. In the end, the introduction of more and more viewer variables – such as in single-source research and in qualitative ratings – may lead to the inevitable conclusion that the way people relate to television is too capricious and heterogeneous to be reduced to an exhaustive list of measurable units. In fact, Leo Bogart, the prominent market researcher and sociologist and author of the classic overview of 'viewing habits and the impact of television on American life', *The Age of Television* (1956) has repetitively criticized the emphasis on measurement of the audience. 'Improving the quality of our measurements is a meaningless exercise if the measurements themselves

lack meaning', he states (Bogart 1986: 15). Such warnings notwithstanding, however, the call for more, more detailed, and more accurate
measurement is the order of the day.

What appears to take place, then, is a 'revolt of the viewer' against the
powerful disciplinary machinery of American audience measurement. A
revolt, however, that does not have anything to do with conscious
resistance, with active sabotage of the operation of audience measurement practices (although this *is* done by the sizeable group of people that
refuses to co-operate). The revolt we are faced with here is both more
fundamental and more inevitable: it is an epistemological revolt, which
simply has to do with the fact that what actual audiences do with
television is ultimately in excess of uniform, objectifying quantification,
categorization, and representation. The streamlined 'television audience'
only exists in discursive form: it is nothing more than a statistical
construct, which does not reflect a pre-existent, real entity, but evokes it.
And while this has always been the case, for a long time the conditions
were met for the industry to believe in the 'realism' of ratings discourse.
If the streamlined audience were a fiction, then it was a functional fiction
– an usable map all the players in the game agreed to believe in. But now
that convenient illusion has been shattered by the 'revolt of the viewer'.

This whole turn of events, and the crisis in audience measurement it
has generated, coincides, as we have seen, with the proliferation of
options in the television landscape. The 'revolt of the viewer', then, is not
some sort of romantic eruption of viewers' rebellion on the basis of their
'authentic' needs and desires, but is brought to the surface by the very
technological changes introduced by the television business itself. Viewers
have always already 'revolted' by being physically or mentally absent at
any time they choose to, but the VCR, the remote control and the
multiplication of channels have intensified the opportunities to do so
(Sepstrup 1986). These new opportunities have led to a decentralization
of the conditions of watching television, just as, as Simon Frith (1987) has
noted, cassette recorders have decentralized music making and listening.
The television industrial complex is unable to control the uses of its own
technological inventions: as a matter of paradox, the strategy of making
watching television more attractive by offering new technological devices
to do so, only leads to less and less control over audience activity![9]

It is only ironic, then, that the evolution of television bears some striking
resemblances to that of radio, the medium that suffered so much from
television's growth from the early 1950s onwards. The radio audience
became increasingly unmeasurable with the introduction of car radios and
transportable battery radios, as well as the proliferation of stations and
programmes. In the words of one network researcher, the industry faced a
paradox in 'that all the attributes which were assuring radio's survival in a
television world – radio's compactness, its mobility, economy, ubiquity,
and diversity – these were the very factors that were progressively making

the radio medium *a nightmare to measure*' (in Beville 1985: 42, emphasis added). In a similar vein, we can see the increasing sophistication of television audience measurement as a stubbornly persistent attempt to catch up with the increasing unpredicability of 'viewing behaviour' enabled by the new television landscape. The underlying rationale seems to be: if it is not possible to constrain people's freedom to watch television the way they choose to, then one should at least keep track of them – as unrelentingly and painstakingly as possible. Hence, there is now concern over the growing number of portable hand-held TV sets that 'goes unmeasured' (Friedman 1989), as well as all the TV sets in sportsbars, hotel rooms, hospitals, laundrettes, campuses, restaurants, and work spaces (Van der Gaag 1989).

It remains to be seen, however, whether the abundance of new data will ever lead to a renewed streamlined map of 'television audience'. Will it be possible, with a further sophistication of audience measurement technologies, to come to a new consensus over such a map, or will the increasingly microscopic technological gaze on people watching television only lead to an ever greater elusiveness of the 'viewing behaviour' audience measurement is presumed to measure? The 'revolt of the viewer' may have resulted in a permanent disruption of the streamlined audience: perhaps the proliferation of viewer activities will increasingly resist being straitjacketed in a unified discursive construct. The 'revolt of the viewer', then, is an idea that emerges as a result of the (fearful) perception of the increasing 'unmeasurability' of the television audience. In other words, the 'revolt of the viewer' is a symbolic resistance – intended by nobody but the inevitable outcome of real developments and real practices – against the industry's attempts to bring order in the chaos of the social world of actual audiences.

Here the unfulfilled promise of audience measurement as a panoptic arrangement becomes fully clear. Contrary to the panopticist ideal, the subjection of people cannot be guaranteed here, because ultimately no monitoring technology can regulate people's behaviour in a direct, material sense – it can only observe and registrate it. Stronger still, it may well be that the more advanced audience measurement becomes, the less streamlineable the information assembled will be. The more it sees, the less it can get to grips with what it sees, as it were. The calculable audience member tends to dissipate before the ever more sensitive microscope of audience measurement, and increasingly regains his or her status of active subject. Audience measurement, in short, is an example of how the practice of panoptic examination, when severed from the attendant power of disciplining behaviour, turns out to have a contradictory outcome: rather than facilitating control, it makes it more difficult!

Of course we should not diminish ratings discourse's continuing power either. As I have indicated before, the commercial television industry has matched its own map of the streamlined audience with equally streamlined programming and scheduling strategies. As a result, ratings discourse 'controls' actual audiences by limiting the range and surprises of programmes that they get to see on their TV sets: the streamlined audience and streamlined programming tend to reinforce each other in their predictability. It remains to be seen whether the contemporary disruption of the streamlined audience will lead to dramatic changes in American commercial television's programming philosophy, although it should be noted that the transition to the people meter was accompanied by heavy speculation about its possible impact on future programme development (*Broadcasting* 7 September 1987).

For example, the general prospect that certain demographic categories would gain and others lose in the people meter's version of the ratings, inevitably led to considerations about preferred kinds of programmes to be produced. For instance, test results indicated that male audiences would gain in size in people meter ratings (presumably because men are better button-pushers). In response, CBS decided to programme a flourish of new male-oriented shows during prime time in the first season of the people meter. Incidentally, without success: according to the 1987/ 1988 Nielsen people meter ratings, CBS was the least successful of the three networks in that season and the male-oriented shows it introduced (such as *Crime Story*) were no ratings successes at all (Ross 1988). Which brings us to the more general sense of loss within the networks, testified fully by Brandon Tartikoff, NBC's President of Entertainment:

> Lucille Ball said that television changed with the invention of the remote control device. As soon as a guy doesn't have to get up from his chair to switch the channel, television becomes a new ball game. Viewer inertia, which supported many an uninspired show, has given way to viewer impatience.
>
> (In Levinson and Link 1986: 263)

Of course, viewer inertia was only a true fact within the symbolic world of ratings discourse. The 'inert viewer' was the fictional prototype of the streamlined audience member complacently and arrogantly indulged in by the industry. As of viewer impatience, it may be the new fictional construct by which the industry seeks to combat its uncertainty about the television audience – a construct which, if anything, betrays a declining sense of confidence over the power of the medium. Whether the shows will cease to be 'uninspired', however, remains to be seen. Will there be a 'move towards originality', as the buzzword seems to be in some industry circles (*Broadcasting* 12 October 1987)? Only the future can tell whether the new television landscape, with its promise of increased choice, will result in a permanent betterment for actual audiences in terms of programme quality and diversity.[10]

Apart from this practical issue of cultural politics, however, a more fundamental, epistemological issue imposes itself with these developments. It concerns the tricky status of the concept of audience as it functions in audience measurement's discursive work. We have seen an increasing difficulty for the industry in determining beyond any doubt what 'watching television' is. In other words, the very empirical basis on which 'television audience' as object of measurement is founded seems increasingly to escape unambiguous operationalization. Paradoxically, then, audience measurement tends to become a practice in search of its object rather than a practice researching a given object. Contrary to what is suggested by its epithet, it is by no means certain what the object of audience measurement is. The truth constructed by ratings discourse is built on quicksand: it delivers knowledge that is both politically and epistemologically precarious.

In the meantime, the unstreamlined, contradictory, complex and dynamic practices and experiences that shape the social world of actual audiences will remain beyond the institutional considerations of an industry in transition, too busy to recapture control.

Part III

Serving the audience:
European television

11 Normative knowledge: the breakdown of the public service ideal

In the European tradition of public service broadcasting, making money has always been emphatically rejected as the object of television and radio programming. Instead, the aims and purposes of these media were conceived by the overriding consideration that broadcasting is a 'servant of culture', in the words of John Reith, the illustrious and influential first Director General of the BBC. For Reith, the major task in the BBC's cultural mission was the 'systematic and sustained endeavour to re-create, to build up knowledge, experience and character, perhaps even in the face of obstacles' (quoted in Briggs 1985: 54). It is striking – and rather prophetic – that Reith should have made mention of 'obstacles'. He clearly expected difficulties in pursuing the endeavour – difficulties which ultimately resided in resistances on the part of the object of that endeavour: the audience. In fact, a history of European public service broadcasting in general could be written from this perspective: a narrative in which the resistance of the audience against its objectification in the name of highminded, national cultural ideals drives the story forward. Part III is a contribution to the construction of that ongoing story. The recent crisis of European public service broadcasting in the face of increasing transnational commercialization of television is a key episode in the dénouement of the story.

Although Reith's philosophy was especially formative for British public service broadcasting before the Second World War, its influence reached further than Britain alone, if not in its concrete policy impact then at least in its spirit of authoritative idealism. Thus, throughout Western Europe public service broadcasting's classic mission is that it should convey highly imposing cultural ambitions – ambitions extending way beyond the relatively forthright economic ones of commercial profit-making. Public service broadcasting is a prime instance of the rejection of the subordination of cultural politics to economic forces. Public broadcasters therefore often see their work as unremittingly antithetical to that of their commercially-motivated colleagues. They often display a confident disrespect toward the latter. 'Giving the audience what it wants', a principle celebrated within commercial rhetoric as a triumph of cultural democracy, is deeply distrusted in public broadcasting circles, connoted as it is with submission to the easy, unprincipled path of populism. It was Reith himself who wrote that 'few know what they want and very few what they need' (quoted in Briggs 1985: 55). More recently, another European public broadcaster, André Kloos, in the seventies chairman of VARA, the time-honoured Dutch socialist broadcasting organization, characterized the difference as follows:

> Roughly speaking, we can distinguish between two sorts of broadcast-ing organizations. The first sees radio and television solely as a means of satisfying the needs of the mass audience, no matter what needs. Its highest aspiration is to please the largest common denominator of the public, without demanding any effort. . . . The other type of broadcasting organization tries to achieve specific effects with its audience. It is not satisfaction of manifest needs that is the most important, but change of patterns of needs, cultivation of discrimina-tion, orientation towards values that go further than the satisfaction of needs. All this demands effort.
>
> (Quoted in VARA 1983a: 12)

Echoing Reith's 'obstacles', 'effort' here is seen as required from both sides: not only from the public broadcasters themselves who must pursue higher aspirations than easy success, but also, more emphatically so, from the audience, who is gently solicited to rise above its prevailing ways. This normative discourse shows how, philosophically speaking, public service broadcasters require more from the audience than commercial broadcasters. It is not enough for audiences to just pay attention to the programmes offered them: they must get something out of those programmes that is presumably 'good' for them. Watching television as an activity is not considered meaningful or worthwhile as an end in itself, but is seen as a means towards a larger process of cultural change.

This stated ideal to regulate audiences so that they become integrated in a preferred design of the nation's cultural life, is clearly associated with an attempt to pursue control over people from above. As Stuart Hall has remarked,

> 'Cultural change' is a polite euphemism for the process by which some cultural forms and practices are driven out of the centre of popular life, actively marginalised. Rather than simply 'falling into disuse' through the Long March of modernisation, things are actively pushed aside, so that something else can take their place.
>
> (Hall 1981: 227–8)

In short, public service broadcasting is explicitly conceived as an interventionist institutional practice: it should presumably contribute to the construction of 'quality' citizens rather than merely catering to, and therefore reinforcing and reproducing, the already existing needs and wants of consumers. Succinctly, in classic public service philosophy the project of broadcasting is an 'art of effects' (Foucault 1979: 93) aimed at reforming the audience.

From this perspective, nothing could be more spurious and inadequate than knowing the audience within the vocabulary of ratings discourse. As we have seen in Part II, ratings discourse says nothing about effects, nor does it give any clue about communicative accomplishment. It only provides *post-hoc*, quantitative information about size and composition of the given audience. Ratings discourse is the logical outcome of a system geared at 'audience maximization' – a principle that is fundamentally at odds with the classic public service ideal. While in commercial television all institutional activities are attuned to the larger design of keeping a sufficient number of people tuned in, public service television needs to keep a sufficient number of people tuned in to adequately perform its 'service' task. Success, in other words, cannot be gauged by purely quantitative measures of popularity; it must encompass more qualitative and substantial achievements, ideally amounting to the persuasive transmission of ideas, values and tastes. Thus, Asa Briggs, in his voluminous history of broadcasting in Britain, specifies how Reith's theory of public service engenders a conception of the broadcasting audience which is entirely antithetical to the one foregrounded by the logic of commercialism:

> The 'publics' are treated with respect not as nameless aggregates with statistically measurable preferences, 'targets' for a programme sponsor, but as living audiences capable of growth and development.
>
> (Briggs 1961: 239)

In this context, the practice of audience measurement does not have a 'natural' place, as it has in commercial television institutions. However, many public service institutions in Europe now make extensive use of audience measurement information to develop and manage their policies and practices. Nowadays, talk about the audience in terms of numbers has pervaded public service institutional discourse, so much so that, paradoxically enough, the people meter, the measurement technology that caused so much unrest in American television industry circles, was already introduced in several European countries years before it was in the United States (McCain 1985).[1]

The growing prominence of audience measurement within European public service broadcasting is often associated with an increasing 'commercialization' of the public service institutions, at least in spirit if not in structure and finance. The adoption of commercial marketing strategies, including that of audience measurement, is seen to have been propelled by the introduction of commercial competition in the European broadcasting field (e.g. Garnham 1983; 1989; Richeri 1985; Blumler *et al.*

1986; Verstraeten 1988). And by 1990, Britain, Italy, France, West Germany, Belgium, Spain, Denmark, Ireland and the Netherlands have seen the gradual demise of the national monopoly or oligarchy that public service broadcasting institutions had mostly enjoyed. Furthermore, the advent of cable and satellite television has spurred the launch of several transnational, commercially-run channels. In short, there is no doubt that by the late 1980s, principles and methods derived from the commercial system had gained the power to subvert the terms in which broadcast television had been practised for decades in Western Europe (Connell and Curti 1985). From this perspective, the rising significance of ratings discourse can be explained as a natural and logical outgrowth of a more general tendency in European broadcasting to move 'from service to business'. Or, to put it in terms of the principal theme of Part III of this book, the ascendance of audience measurement as a prevalent way of knowing the television audience represents a shift away from reliance on the a priori, normative knowledge about how the audience should be addressed, which is part and parcel of classic public service philosophy, towards dependence on empirical information about the audience.

Indeed, after more than sixty years of operation, public service broadcasting institutions in Europe are undeniably in crisis. The very basis of their legitimacy is being eroded in societies that are more and more caught by an entrepreneurial, commercial spirit. Furthermore, the 'general public', in whose name broadcasting as a 'public service' has been envisioned in the first place, seems to be less and less taken by the blessings of the public service tradition in radio and television now that it has the opportunity of expanded 'consumer choice'. As some commentators proclaim, 'there seems to be little evidence to suggest that some kind of "save our public service" campaign would secure the necessary popular support to maintain public service operations' (Connell and Curti 1985: 90).[2] In the light of this crisis, the future of public service broadcasting is very insecure indeed.

However, it is insufficient to locate the grounds for this crisis solely in the competitive environment in which public service institutions now have to operate. It is important also to look at the internal contradictions of public service philosophy itself to understand why neither public service broadcasters themselves, nor politicians and other policy-making groups have managed to find creative responses to overcome the crisis. As Nicholas Garnham has pointed out,

> behind the concrete economic and political problems facing public service broadcasting lies a crisis of the imagination – an inability to conceive of an alternative to broadcasting controlled by profit-seeking private capital other than as centralised, bureaucratic, inefficient,

arrogantly insensitive to the people's needs, politically subservient to the holders of state power and so on.

(Garnham 1983: 21)

It is important then to examine the discursive context of this crisis of imagination: how is it that public service broadcasting could not hold its own when it was confronted with the assault of commercial competition?

An examination of public service broadcasting's complex and uneasy relationship to its audience may clarify the problem. As I have pointed out in Part I, public service broadcasting's ideal-typical concept of audience does not constitute a market, but a public. This audience-as-public consists of citizens, in whose interest it presumably is to be reformed. In most neutral terms, this reform is said to be established by serving the audience a comprehensive and responsible diet of information, education and entertainment – as stated in the official mandates of most European public service broadcasting institutions. In this context, the importance of radio and television programmes lies in their potential to transfer meaningful messages rather than in their capacity as vehicles to deliver audiences to advertisers: programmes and programming matter for their symbolic content rather than as agent for economic exchange value. As a result, programming policy is an issue both more central and more complicated for public service television than for commercial television. After all, 'information', 'education' and 'entertainment' are not unambiguous categories: neither their meanings nor their functions are clear and evident. As Tom Burns has noted, the duty to inform, educate and entertain is really no more than a discretionary formula:

The prescription of itself poses a number of questions about the nature of the information, education and entertainment to be provided, about the quantity and the quality of each element, and about the proportion of the total broadcasting output which should be allocated to each, as well as about what will promote and what will prevent their successful presentation.'

(Burns 1977: 40)

It is therefore not surprising that public service broadcasters put a great deal of energy into translating the abstract principles of public service philosophy into concrete guidelines, schemes and criteria to be used in decisions about programming policy. The formulation of programming policy, in other words, is a normative issue for public service broadcasting – an issue about which divergent conceptualizations are possible and about which, therefore, consensus is not pregiven but needs to be constructed.[3] This need to construct institutional consensus in normative terms is one of the reasons why public service organizations have exhibited such bureaucratic tendencies.[4] Indeed, the work of public service institutions is in many respects much more difficult and onerous than that of commercially-motivated ones. In fact, one American network executive, interviewed by Jay Blumler (1986), could astutely reason why the profit motive is so convenient from an organizational management perspective:

> Profit is not a bad thing. When profit is around, it provides a focus for everyone's thinking. There tends to be less political activity, less back-biting, looking around, memo writing, when you're in a profit-making organisation. But when it's a non-profit organisation, when the focus is unclear, when you're not sure about what you're doing today versus tomorrow, politics can be rampant. . . . Little children can get killed in those organisations. With the goal of profit . . . it can be very clear exactly who's doing what, and it's relatively simple to measure performance.
>
> (In Blumler 1986: 2)

And indeed, part of the tragedy of public service broadcasting institutions is that their immaterial goals often do not afford them sufficient clarity of purpose to come to unambiguous, ready-made priorities. The histories of the BBC and of VARA, to which I will turn in Chapters 12 and 13 respectively, are perfect testimony to this. Both histories are characterized by fierce internal struggles about the direction their programming policies should take. These controversies are articulated in an endless production of procedural discourse: policy plans and documents, memos, working notes, evaluation reports, as well as discussion meetings, seminars, and so on, all intended to clarify and determine the normative criteria for the setting up of programming. Central in this ongoing discursive search for criteria is the question, implicit or explicit, of how the audience-as-public should be defined and addressed. In other words, it is in these discourses that normative knowledge about the audience emerges from the public service institution's point of view.

I will describe how over the years, the truth value of this normative knowledge has been eroded as the solid conviction that public service broadcasting should reform the audience gradually gave way for a recognition of the ultimate impossibility to achieve this goal: actual audiences turn out to be too intransigent or recalcitrant to submit unproblematically to such reform attempts. As will be clarified in Chapter 14, this erosion of conviction was compensated by embracing the same forms of empirical knowledge, particularly audience measurement information, that was already routinely used within the American commercial television industry. In this sense, the crisis of the imagination Garnham (1983) talks about can be seen as a lack of imagining new ways of knowing the audience that are qualitatively different from the commercial way of knowing. I will trace the ramifications of this crisis through two case studies: the British BBC and the Dutch VARA. In both cases, the crisis implies the loss of a particular normative construct of 'television audience': the 'disciplined audience' in the case of the BBC, and the 'natural audience' in the case of VARA.

12 Britain: the BBC and the loss of the disciplined audience

John Reith, who started his career as the BBC's Managing Director in 1922, had a clear view of the task of broadcasting, which he could develop under the rather felicitous circumstances of deliberate disregard of the real world of actual audiences. He saw the BBC as a ship of which he was the chief pilot – a nautical metaphor which suggested a mission of leading and directing the audience in the modern world (Kumar 1977). Echoing the legacy of cultural theorist Matthew Arnold (1963[1867]), he developed a highly commanding philosophy about the BBC's responsibility towards the audience: 'As we conceive it, our responsibility is to carry into the greatest possible number of homes everything that is best in every department of human knowledge, endeavour, or achievement' (quoted in Briggs 1985: 55).

Reith's discourse securely articulated the values, standards and beliefs of the British upper middle-class, especially that part educated at Oxford and Cambridge. Emanating from it was a preference for radio programmes featuring classical music, plays, poetry, talks and discussions. More popular programmes such as comedy, popular music, and variety were also included, but in a manner, context, and style that revealed an upper middle-class approach and orientation. For example, the BBC had an active musical policy in the hope to 'raise' the musical taste of its listeners because Britain was considered a backward musical nation. Entertainment, then, was not so much rejected as it was defined educationally.[1] In an attempt to oppose the 'Americanization' of popular culture which already started to concern British cultural critics in the 1920s, the BBC aimed to develop a sense of discrimination in the audience by giving it the opportunity to listen to 'better, healthier music' than pop music. It was assumed that once people heard classical music, they would realise its superiority to popular tunes (Frith 1983). One Labour Party MP referred to the inherent class bias of BBC culture when he suggested in Parliament in the 1930s that the BBC was 'run very largely by people who do not know the working class, do not understand the working class point of view, but are seeking evidently to mould the working class' (Briggs 1985: 151). But such criticism did not prevail, nor did it affect BBC policy in most of its inter-war years. On the contrary, in Reith's interpretation public service broadcasting was meant to be a form of enlightened cultural dictatorship, in which a single set of standards and tastes was imposed upon the entire national audience (Scannell and Cardiff 1982). Any idea of a stratified audience was rejected, as was any division of the programme output into 'highbrow' and 'lowbrow'. What Reith strived for was the creation of a common national culture: the BBC's self-conception was that of a 'national church' (Reith's own words) to whose authority all citizens must be subjected.[2]

Such rightminded authoritarianism should not be too easily dismissed as manipulative or elitist. Rather, these ideas were linked to a well-intentioned stance on broadcasting as a means for the democratization of culture and society, in the sincere belief that democracy was directly related to principled and conscientious cultural leadership and guidance, to giving people access to established cultural forms from which they were previously excluded. As Reith stated in his memoirs:

> We have tried to found a tradition of public service, and to dedicate the service of broadcasting to the service of humanity in its fullest sense. We believe that a new national asset has been created . . . the asset referred to is of the moral and not the material order – that which, down the years, brings the compound interest of happier homes, broader culture and truer citizenship.
>
> (Quoted in Frith 1983: 108)

These ideas were translated into explicit norms for the preferred way in which the audience should listen to radio. Habitual non-stop listening or using the radio as background noise were discouraged. Instead, the audience was summoned to listen seriously and constructively, as the 1930 BBC Yearbook states: 'the listener must recognise that a definite obligation rests on him to choose intelligently from the programmes offered to him' (quoted in Scannell and Cardiff 1982: 185). The BBC attempted to encourage this dutiful style of radio listening through very specific programming devices. Generally, standardisation, continuity and regularity, already common in those days in American broadcasting, were rejected. For example, contrary to present-day programming strategies, the principle of fixed scheduling (i.e. placing programmes at the same time on the same day from week to week) was avoided. Furthermore, four to five minutes of silence were inserted in-between programmes so as to allow listeners to switch off. In short, BBC programming policy at that time was based upon highly idealist and utopian expectations about the audience: an image of the ideal listener was constructed to which actual listeners were presumed to comply. They were not supposed to engage in 'easy listening', to use the wireless as a service which is 'on tap' all day long. Indeed, radio listening was defined as a very serious, well-controlled activity.

Thus, in this early period BBC discourse about the audience was both normative and speculative: knowledge about how to address the audience was determined theoretically, not empirically. The discourse was prescriptive not descriptive: it was preoccupied with what the audience required, not what it wanted. It was not the BBC's concern to be popular. Instead, it wanted the audience to be a disciplined audience.

But soon some doubts were raised within the BBC as to the real effectivity of its programming endeavours. Thus, programme consultant Filson Young raised the question whether the audience was really made up of the 'serious listeners' envisioned by Reith:

> What is the attitude of the ordinary listener towards broadcasting? Is he going to regard it as a means of filling the vacuum of idle hours, carping at everything which does not make immediate and facile appeal for him and being amazed when the programmes are not continually filled with the kinds of items that do so appeal?
>
> (Quoted in Briggs 1965: 74)

There was no way to answer this question in any systematic way, but it was a hauntingly disquieting one and it stimulated calls among programme makers to search for empirical knowledge about listening habits. Here then we have the origins of interest in audience research within the BBC: it was led by a concern about the effectivity of its attempts to fulfil its self-imposed cultural task. Thus, as early as 1930 Val Gielgud, then Head of the Drama Department and active proponent for the setting up of some form of 'listener research', stated in a memorandum:

> I cannot help feeling more and more strongly that we are fundamentally ignorant as to how our various programmes are received, and what is their relative popularity. It must be a source of considerable disquiet to many people besides myself that it is quite possible that a very great deal of our money and time and effort may be expended on broadcasting into a void.
>
> (Quoted in Briggs 1965: 259)

He went on to complain that 'nothing handicaps me more than the non-possession of anything in the nature of a thermometer which would correspond in the theatre to the acid-test of box office returns' (quoted in Chaney 1986: 269). Despite the commercially-sounding overtones of this last remark, however, early debates within the BBC about the uses of empirical surveys among the audience were not predicated upon the wish to singlemindedly determine the size of the audience. Rather, what many felt was needed was finding out more about 'types and tastes among the various classes of society and in the various parts of England', as stated in a 1930 memorandum by Director of Talks Charles Siepman (quoted in Briggs 1965: 260). The interest, in short, was substantially sociological rather than merely statistical. Furthermore, Siepman stated very clearly that empirical information should not dictate programming policy: 'However complete and effective any survey we launch might be, I should still be convinced that our policy and programme building should be based first and last upon our own conviction as to what should and should not be broadcast'(ibid.).

Underlying these early concerns was an increasing awareness within the BBC that the listening public was not an abstract entity, an ideal-typical national community characterized by 'unity in diversity', as Reith's philosophy assumed, but a fundamentally stratified category, both socially and culturally, with sectional interests and differentiated preferences and habits. In particular, the predominance of 'serious listeners' was gradually being called into question and more and more attention was being paid to attracting 'the man in the street'. As a result, programming policy began to be based upon the acceptance of a separation between the 'serious' and the 'popular', for instance in style of presentation of talks programmes. 'Serious' talks were presented in a dispassionate and 'neutral' manner, whereas in 'popular' talks programmes attempts were made to represent the opinions and experiences of 'ordinary people' and to use lighter styles of presentation such as the round-table discussion, interviews and the magazine format. Undergirding this differentiation was the assumption that the audience could be divided into the 'intelligent and the well-informed', the 'intelligent and not so well-informed', and the 'not-so-intelligent and mostly uninformed'. The second group, not the third (which was considered too 'vulgar' to be reachable) was seen to be the most important target for the popular talks programmes (Cardiff 1980).

All in all, BBC programming in the last few years before the Second World War exhibited an unmistakable drift towards popularization. This development did not so much represent the abandon of a commitment to reform the audience (although Reith, who departed in 1938, was very embittered by the tendency), but can be seen as a first recognition of the difficulty of realizing that goal as a result of an awareness about 'resistances' among actual audiences to take up the role of the disciplined audience that was so well-intentionedly assigned to them. Letters from listeners and all sorts of 'opinion polls' – early versions of ratings research – carried out by newspapers in the 1930s showed a clear 'preference for entertainment' among the people (Briggs 1965; 1985). Furthermore, there was evidence that large sections of the audience were attracted to the transmissions of commercial radio stations based on the European continent, such as Radio Normandie and Radio Luxembourg. In other words, the BBC needed to begin to deal with competition. As a result, programming policy discourse became preoccupied with a fundamental contradiction between the wish to edify the audience on the one hand, and the need to *attract* the audience on the other.

The process of popularization was greatly accelerated by the war, when the BBC was assigned the task of maintaining the morale of both the workforce at home and the troops in France. Here, especially, the accumulation of empirical knowledge became a crucial factor in the development of new patterns of programming. Thus, the BBC's Listener Research Department, set up in 1936, acquired unprecedented importance during the war as it provided systematic information about the population in a period of great uncertainty. And the troops in France were treated to the visit of a high BBC official, A. P. Ryan, who was appointed to investigate their listening habits. In his influential report he came to some extremely sobering conclusions:

> It is idle to hope for serious listening, if that be defined as putting on programmes which will only appeal to people that broadcasting may give them something of the satisfaction as is to be got from, say, reading Shakespeare or listening to Bach. . . . This obvious fact cannot be too emphatically stated. The troops won't mind if a proportion of good serious stuff is included in their programme out of deference to policy views as to what constitutes good balance. They won't mind – and *they won't listen*. They will simply accept good serious stuff as one of the facts of life, like blackouts, and absence of hot water and being away from home. If they were ordered to listen they would do so with resignation, and even perhaps with growing interest, but they will not be ordered to listen, and so they will switch off or turn to Haw Haw or some other obviously entertaining alternative.
>
> (Ryan 1940, quoted in Cardiff and Scannell 1981: 62; italics in original)

This piece of evidence led the BBC to grudgingly accept the need to increase the amount of light entertainment. As a result the Forces Programme – which was set up as a service for the troops but was soon to be widely listened to at home as well – became filled with a flurry of cheerful music, variety, and popular talks programmes. In this, the BBC recognized the success of the programming strategies of the commercial radio stations. American formulae, styles and formats were gradually adopted, such as continuity, regularity and slickness of presentation, as well as audience participation devices such as musical request programmes, quizzes and amateur performances. This process of 'Americanization' was intensified by the arrival of US troops in Britain. The BBC tried to cater for them by including more American material, such as baseball commentaries and American popular music (Cardiff and Scannell 1981). By the end of the war then the BBC found itself heavily involved in emulating the very style of programming which was so detested before the war. As Cardiff and Scannell (ibid.: 76) conclude, 'in a very general sense the war showed the BBC that serving the public could no longer mean leading and guiding the audience but must involve a more pragmatic effort to cater for its differing needs and requirements'.

This process was fundamentally mediated through the availability of empirical information supplied by the Listener Research Department. After the war, the importance and legitimacy of in-house empirical research into the audience was no longer contested, and the Audience Reseach Department rapidly grew in size and centrality. It was during the war that Robert Silvey, the first head of the department, initiated the setting up of the Continuous Survey of Listening, aimed at measuring the number of listeners for each programme, and it was this research machinery which later became the BBC's ratings service for both radio and television (Silvey 1974). As a matter of fact, from the very beginning the BBC's television planners were more readily prepared to use research in their search for policy criteria then their radio colleagues, such as an investigation into the usefulness of programme scheduling and sequencing for viewers (Chaney 1986).

However, these developments should not be interpreted as a wholesale capitulation to the principles of commercialism, nor as a complete waning of normative discourse within the BBC. If Reith's philosophy was put under severe pressure after the war, it certainly did not completely lose its hold on the BBC's way of knowing how it should relate to the audience. According to Scannell and Cardiff (1982: 187) after the war 'the BBC no longer sought to lead and reform public taste; it now tried to match or to anticipate it'. But this could misleadingly suggest that the BBC had unreservedly succumbed to the commercial dictum of 'giving the audience what it wants'. This was not the case, either at the level of policy discourse or at the level of programming practice. The set of values and attitudes established during the Reithean era remained influential as a figure of conscience, as a general reminder of the normative role the BBC had to play as a public service institution. In other words, these values and attitudes remained a constitutive element in the BBC's sense of corporate identity, if only as a faint echo of a glorious past or, to put it more positively, as a key marker of the corporation's unique tradition, of what Burns (1977: 43) has called the 'platonic idea of the BBC'.

Still, enormous changes were brought about during the postwar period. The popularization of wartime radio programming implied a recognition that the British public could no longer be addressed as a unified and homogeneous whole, but, in the words of William Haley, Reith's successor after the war, as 'a cultural pyramid slowly aspiring upwards' (quoted in Kumar 1977: 246). This recognition was formalized with the introduction of a tripartite service system of sound broadcasting: the Light, Home, and Third Programmes. According to Haley, the pre-war single service system 'plunged [the listener] straight from popular to unpopular material, from highbrow to lowbrow and vice versa', which resulted in the BBC's reputation for being didactic, 'something of a governess'. On the other hand, the new system would 'lead the listener on to more serious things' by 'curiosity, liking and growth of understanding'. He or she would be encouraged to switch from one programme to another and gradually 'move up the cultural scale' (in Briggs 1985: 244). There is no doubt then that the paternal, educational attitude was still alive and well in these years: the audience was still considered to be a disciplined audience, at least in potential. Haley firmly believed that, 'while satisfying the legitimate demand for recreation and entertainment, the BBC must never lose sight of its cultural mission' (ibid.: 245).

It must come as no surprise, however, that the Light Programme soon proved to attract the vast majority of the listeners, most of them of working class background (as the Audience Research Department found), while the audience for the Third Programme, the service for high culture, did not widen, thereby disaffirming Haley's idealist philosophy. The limitations of the paternalistic, normative model of public service broadcasting became ever starker, although still cherished.

But the most important changes were triggered by the emergence of television. BBC Television was initiated as early as 1936; it was discontinued during the war and reopened in 1946. In the beginning, many reservations against the new medium were expressed, especially at the top of the BBC hierarchy, typically born out of the concern that it would dominate the home, encourage passivity and lead to an excess of entertainment. An often-quoted remark were Orson Welles' words: 'If the home is to become a non-stop movie-house, God help the home.' (ibid., 276) In other words, television, due to the assuaging experiences with radio, was no longer surrounded with too high hopes about its reforming potential. The difficulty of disciplining the audience had implicitly become an accepted fact, although sounds of caution continued to be heard. In 1952, Haley told his staff: 'Fight against too many hours. Fight against lowering of standards. . . . Television must not become a film industry. Television must remain civilized and adult. You are fighting great issues.' (ibid.)

The installation of a second, commercial television channel in 1955 destabilized even further the situation in which the BBC operated.[3] Commercial television, not incidentally named Independent Television (ITV), actively and shrewdly exploited the BBC's patronizing reputation in its claim of presenting an alternative, 'people's television' (Sendall 1982). In practice, this meant the introduction on British television of many obviously popular genres such as spectacular quiz shows and imported American drama series. But the most important result of these events is not the so-called 'trivialization' of television programming as a whole. More fundamental is the fact that the BBC was now confronted with the need, not only to attract the audience (which could be seen as the main drive behind the earlier popularization of radio), but to fight for it in a competitive environment. And so, the ratings game – and ratings discourse – was introduced in British television. Thus, the *BBC Handbook* of 1957 stated that it was 'of obvious importance to the BBC to know how those of the television public who have a choice of programmes divide their viewing time' (Briggs 1985: 300). The apparent 'obviousness' of 'the battle of the figures' was reflected, for instance, in the development of more competitively-organized television schedules and the setting of minimum average shares of audience which the BBC should seek to establish,[4] although in terms of overall programming policy the BBC first refused to compete with ITV on the same terms. It continued to insist on maintaining the standards of 'responsibility' and 'quality'. In the first years of competition, then, the BBC's output of 'serious' programmes went up rather than down (ibid.). It was only in the late 1950s and early 1960s that the range of entertainment programmes was expanded and more 'popular' styles of news and current affairs programmes were introduced. According to Burns (1977: 54), 'by 1960, most people within the BBC had been made aware that, whatever else it did, it had to deliver programmes which were entertaining'.

And this leads us to the changed cultural relationship between the BBC and its audience. Commercial television's most significant impact was the breaking of the BBC's cultural monopoly in defining what broadcasting should be about. Commercial television challenged the BBC's status as a unifying national force, it led to 'the intrusion of other renderings of Britishness and of rightmindedness, and the consequent shrinking of BBC values to something sectional and questionable' (ibid.: 43). Its hegemony undermined, it was no longer possible for the BBC to revel in its mission of cultural enlightment as the 'natural', taken-for-granted purpose of public service broadcasting. It became too clear that what the BBC represented and promoted was a very partisan version of British citizenship, which excluded the social realities of large sections of the general public. The BBC therefore needed a different self-concept to keep up its legitimacy as the national public service broadcasting institution *par excellence*. This shift in self-conception was accomplished during the 1960s when the hierarchical idea of society as a cultural pyramid gave way to a more liberal vision of cultural pluralism. Hugh Greene, the BBC's Director General from 1960 to 1969, introduced a new metaphor to conceive of the BBC's altered social role: not that of a ship, as Reith would have it, but that of a mirror. The BBC must, in his view, mirror a changing society and culture: 'I don't care whether what is reflected in the mirror is bigotry, injustice and intolerance or accomplishment and inspiring achievement. I only want the mirror to be honest, without any curves, and held with as steady a hand as may be' (in Briggs 1985: 331).

This change of metaphor implies a dramatic shift of the place assigned to the audience *vis-á-vis* broadcasting in public service philosophy. Abandoned was the explicit desire to take the audience on board, as it were, and lead it in a previously determined direction – as implied in Reith's model of public service. Instead a far more neutral task was formulated: that of representing and 'registering' society's many different voices and faces. The BBC came to embrace a new conception of 'serving the public' by taking up, in the words of Krishan Kumar (1977), the role of 'honest broker', of manager and impressario, of middleman of all possible sectional positions and interests in an increasingly pluralist and conflict-ridden society.

It is this version of public service philosophy that has come to predominate to this day. Thus, a recent summary of the guiding principles of public service broadcasting formulates its importance in terms of its provision of 'a forum in which all citizens can find an expression of national concerns and communal interests. In its universality of appeal and geographic and social reach broadcasting can help create a shared sense of national identity' (Broadcasting Research Unit 1986). In this context, diversity has become the most prominent substantive principle in programming policy: diversity of interests represented and of tastes catered for, even if it concerns minority interests and tastes. In practice, this leads to a will to provide something for everyone, by appealing to every conceivable minority or majority group. As Janet Morgan, a consultant for the BBC, has observed:

> Just as a speaker who wants to keep the attention of his audience will have a remark for each sector or opinion, will quote each view, so the BBC balances the requirements of each constituent part of its whole audience. There is a bit of intellectualism, a bit of pseudo-intellectualism, and . . . a good deal of anti-intellectualism. There is extreme vulgarity . . . and there is a more lofty side.
>
> (Morgan 1986: 27)

If this modern emphasis on diversity (as a reflection in the mirror of society which the BBC strives to be) seems to be an adequate response to the heterogeneous profile of late-twentieth-century social and cultural life, it also makes the public service institution's relationship to the audience more problematic. In Reith's normative model, the place assigned to the audience was at least clear: on the ship (or, to use Reith's other metaphor, in the church). But what is the audience supposed to do with the multiperspectival mirror? Look into it and pass it by? In other words, what happens to the assumption of a disciplined audience in this new philosophy?

For one thing, the metaphor of the mirror – as well as that of related metaphors such as 'forum' – is premised upon the deceptive idea of value-neutrality: the ideological aspect of representation (i.e. the fact that a completely true-to-life mirror is impossible due to the inevitably selective and constructive nature of programming practice) is suppressed in favour of a primarily technical conception of the task of the public service broadcaster: his or her job is confined to that of holding the mirror in front of the already existing diversity of voices, visions and tastes in society.

This ideologically-unspecific conception of public service broadcasting has marked consequences for the values the BBC as an institution has come to live by. If it is no longer supposed to defend and promote specific cultural values, as Reith had envisioned, then it needs other guidelines to give direction to its activities. These guidelines were provided by the adoption of 'professionalism' as a value in its own right within broadcasting practice.[5] As Briggs (1985: 324) has noted, 'by 1960 there was as much talk [within the BBC] of professional standards of the producer and of the teams of people who worked with him as there was of the "social purposes" of broadcasting'. And it was professionalism which was seen as the means to prevent television from becoming a 'distorting mirror'. Writing in 1977, Kumar noted that

> more than ever before the BBC cannot afford to be identified with any sectional interest in the society – even something as indefinite as 'high culture'. It must, to some extent, go as the wind blows it. But a rudderless ship soon ends on the rocks. What keeps it on an even keel, increasingly, is the 'management' function performed by the professional broadcasters.

(Kumar 1977: 247)

According to Kumar, the professional attitude is most visibly articulated in the style of presentation adopted by the BBC's newscasters, announcers and other presenters – a style which is 'compounded equally of aggressiveness, scepticism, irony and detachment' (ibid.: 248), in other words, a style which stresses non-partisan, trustworthy expertise rather than well-bred aloofness, as in the earlier days. It is, indeed, the style of the middleman. It seems right to state that this style has not only gradually become naturalized as *the* preferred mode of presentation, but also that being 'professional' in general (as opposed to 'amateurish') has become accepted as the taken-for-granted goal each contemporary broadcaster strives to achieve.

But the problem with the discourse of professionalism is that it implies an inward-looking, production-oriented attitude which, logically, insists upon the autonomy of the professionals in making judgements about the 'quality' of the product, without compliance to 'outside' demands. In other words, it is a discourse which tends to protect and cut the professionals off from those who do not belong to the profession – including the audience-out-there for whom the work is, logically, ultimately done. For example, Philip Schlesinger (1987), who has undertaken a close ethnographic analysis of BBC news production, has noted that 'the audience' remains an abstraction in the day-to-day routines of broadcast journalism. He concludes that '"the problem" of the audience it not an urgent one for the communicator' (Schlesinger 1987: 107). Furthermore, the obsessive reliance on peer group competition and recognition as points of reference for the broadasters tends to bring with it an implicit distancing from, and even a devaluation of, concrete feedback from actual audiences, articulated in what Schlesinger (ibid.: 107–8) has observed as 'the apparently general conviction that "the bulk of audience reaction is from cranks, the unstable, the hysterical and sick"'. Professionalism then is an essentially self-indulgent discourse, in which the audience is ultimately relegated to the domain of the irrelevant.

On a more general institutional level, what this amounts to is a radical loosening of the ties with the audience as inscribed in the BBC's philosophy of broadcasting. Burns has struck the point extremely well in remarking that

> the transition of broadcasting from an occupation dominated by the ethos of public service, in which the central concern is with quality in terms of the public good, and of public betterment, to one dominated by the ethos of professionalism, in which the central concern is with quality of performance in terms of standards of appraisal by fellow professionals [marks] a shift from treating broadcasting as a means to treating broadcasting as an end.
>
> (Burns 1977: 25)

To put it differently, the reformulation of public service commitment in terms of the obligation to provide a mirror of society has led to emphasizing the professionally-accountable production of the mirror – operationalized in terms of a broad and diverse 'range' of programming of good 'quality' (cf. Blumler *et al.* 1986) – at the expense of a preoccupation with the potential meaning or impact of that mirror on the audience.

While the classic ideal of cultural enlightenment presumed the construction of a disciplined audience, today a much more noncommittal attitude towards television is expected from the audience. It would now be absurd, for instance, to even wish to draw up guidelines for the right way of watching television; nowadays it is accepted as given that audiences are free what to watch and how to watch. As Richard Rose has remarked in his book, *Ordinary People and Public Policy* (1989: 178), 'a defining characteristic of a free society is that there are limits to the obligations of citizenship', and it is this fundamental principle that an institution like the BBC had to come to terms with. The modern citizen – the quintessential audience member of contemporary public service broadcasting – has come of age; she can no longer be addressed in a paternalistic manner, but is assumed to make her own choice out of the diversity of programmes laid out before her. However, this vision makes the contact between public service television and its audience a rather diffuse, indistinct one. The classic model was based upon the enunciation of a clear moral and aesthetic order, anchoring the sense of responsibility towards the audience which is at the heart of any official public service broadcasting philosophy. In the contemporary model, however, that responsibility is freefloating and directionless: what the public service institution purports to do is give the audience the opportunity to look into all parts of the mirror, but it acquiesces in its essential powerlessness in summoning audiences to actually take up that opportunity. The audience member/citizen is now a sovereign individual. The Reithean aspiration to create a disciplined audience has disappeared: at best, public service broadcasting in Britain is now praised for its 'catering for popular tastes with high-quality production standards and offering diversity to stretch interests and horizons without creating an impression that uplift was being imposed' (Blumler *et al.* 1986: 354).

In summary, the history of the BBC indicates how normative discourse on the television audience has slowly eroded. In classic public service philosophy, the stakes were high: the audience-as-public was positioned as citizens who must be reformed. But the obstacles that were foreseen by Reith turned out to be too great. The objectification of 'television audience' as a set of citizens ready to be unified and disciplined under the central cultural leadership of the BBC was impossible to sustain in the face of what the institution came to know about actual audiences in empirical terms. There is a sense of capitulation here. The contemporary ideals of diversity and quality are in fact nothing more than an attempt to reflect, as comprehensively and professionally as possible, the given cultural profiles of a plurality of potential audience groups. Thus the audience-as-public is no longer objectified so as to be reformed, but is to be reproduced in its existing identities and divisions. In this respect, public service broadcasting has indeed retreated from its mission as an interventionist cultural practice; it has come to content itself with a far more modest conception of what it means to 'serve the public'. A 'take it or leave it' attitude is thus unwittingly built into public service broadcasting's normative relationship with the audience: actual audiences are now granted the freedom to choose to do whatever they want with the diverse range of programmes supplied them.

But it is precisely this premise of free choice that threatens to unsettle the foundations for public service broadcasting's legitimacy and authority. After all, in the paradigm of free choice legitimacy and authority can logically only be derived from the actual choices made by audiences. Against this background, the relevance of empirical knowledge about the audience, not only pragmatically but principally, is clear. Empirical information fills the gap that has grown between the BBC and the audience as a result of the loss of a normatively defined disciplined audience. Empirical audience research is often justified in public service contexts not for marketing reasons but, more idealistically, in order to be 'in touch with public opinion'.[6] But there is only a thin line between the two: when it comes to 'free choice', there is not so much difference between the free consumer and the free citizen.

This is reflected in the British government's most recent official policy document, the Home Office's White Paper *Broadcasting in the '90s: Competition, Choice and Quality* (1988). Even the document's title suggests a convergence of market discourse and public service discourse. In this White Paper, audiences are squarely conceived as consumers whose freedom of choice must be extended by opening up the British broadcasting market to new channels. The document explicitly constitutes 'diversity' and 'quality' as the central values for broadcasting in the 1990s, but it also adds a third: 'popularity', a norm that, contrary to the first two, is directly related to the audience. The value of 'popularity' principally foregrounds audience-derived judgements about what counts as satisfying 'diversity' and 'quality', thereby subverting the independent authority of professional judgement. This tends to upset the public service institution's proud self-presentation as the exclusive guarantors of 'diversity' and 'quality' (Collins 1989a). The White Paper even suggests replacing the licence fee as basis for funding BBC Television with subscription finance, reasoning that this would improve consumer freedom because individual viewers could then decide for themselves whether the BBC offers them 'value for money'. This would of course mean the end of the BBC's time-honoured status as a universal and comprehensive public service for all citizens. Shocking as such a development may be – and it is highly uncertain whether it will ever be implemented (e.g. Miller 1989) – it does indicate how the BBC's public service discourse has lost so much of its normative distinctiveness that it could easily be incorporated in a discourse in which 'quality' and 'diversity' are seen as a matter of 'competition' rather than as pregiven institutional guarantees.

This discursive convergence in public service and commercial philosophy, I suggest, explains why audience measurement despite the continuing scepticism with which it is regarded by BBC executives and programme makers (see Madge 1989: 93–95), could become such an entrenched part of the institutional process of broadcasting as a whole, not only within the BBC, but in many other European public service institutions as well. This happened only gradually, however, and it was paralleled by the erosion of an institutional point of view that could no longer depend upon the authority of normative knowledge alone to gain control over the audience, and became less and less at odds with the empiricism of market thinking. The case of VARA, to be addressed in the following chapter, illustrates the subtleties of this process of transformation even more dramatically.

13 Netherlands: VARA and the loss of the natural audience

The Dutch broadcasting system, like the British, is essentially based upon the assumption that broadcasting should be a question of public service. However, its philosophical and organizational foundations differ considerably from the British emphasis on national broadcasting, as embodied by the BBC. The nationalist principle has never succeeded in becoming the prevailing organizational force in Dutch broadcasting. Since its inception, it has been based upon a very different set of loyalties and commitments. To be sure, attempts to found a national, monopolistic, BBC-like broadcasting organization were undertaken, both in the very beginning of radio (early 1920s) and after the Second World War, but several social, cultural and political forces, which need not be explicated here, have led to the emergence and institutional consolidation of a broadcasting system in the Netherlands which is unique in the world, and which has come to be known as a system of 'pillarization' (Van den Heuvel 1976). In an early article which aimed to explain the Dutch system to foreigners, for example, it was characterized by the authors as a 'third way' of regulating broadcasting, alongside the American commercial system and the British national monopoly system (De Boer and Cameron 1955).

As a regulatory principle, pillarization was not restricted to broadcasting, but extended to the structuring of almost all facets of organized activity within Dutch society, including party politics, schooling, trade unionism and the press.[1] At the heart of the principle of pillarization was the idea that Dutch society was divided into so-called pillars, that is, social groups separated from each other not along class lines, but along the lines of religious or ideological convictions. Emanating from this idea was a corporatist social system with a high degree of vertical oneness and solidarity, thus unifying leaders and followers, elite and mass, middle class and working class, within each pillar. While the catholics and the protestants formed the most well-organized pillars (and were the most active proponents of a pillarized society), they were complemented by the liberals and the socialists, leading to four main pillars formally recognized as such. There were, then, catholic, protestant and socialist political parties, trade unions, youth clubs, schools, universities, women's organizations, housing corporations, hospitals, welfare organizations, newspapers, sporting clubs, and so on.[2] All believers were officially summoned to cluster themselves within these pillarized organizations. The system was functional insofar as it promoted peaceful co-existence and cooperation between the diverse pillars, and effectively neutralized the disruptive effects of class conflict and class struggle, because it divided the population up along the lines of value systems rather than economic interests. The system operated under the condition of obedience, real and perceived, of the rank and file.[3]

Historians usually designate the period between the end of the First World War and the mid-1960s as the high tide of pillarization in Dutch politics and culture; in the Netherlands, as in the rest of the Western world, the late 1960s marked the end of postwar consensus and stability and the beginning of a rapid process of 'depillarization'. Today, the Dutch people no longer predominantly define themselves in terms of exclusive membership of one of the pillars; social identifications have become much more fluid and multiple. However, powerful remnants of the pillarized tradition still live on, certainly at the institutional level. This is also the case for the institutional structure of broadcasting.

When radio started to outgrow the stage of amateurism and became a mass medium in the mid-1920s, each pillar began to set up its own broadcasting organization. There was no legal framework for broadcasting yet at that time, and when the legal framework came in 1930, the principle of pillarization within broadcasting triumphed over that of national unity, and granted formal, institutional status to the then already existing, flourishing broadcasting associations.[4] Each organization derived its legitimacy and identity from the pillar to which it 'belonged'. Each organization was given independent responsibility to fill a fixed amount of air time with its own particular programming, although the government determined the general rules to which all programming had to comply. Each organization selected its personnel from inside the ranks of the pillar. Each organization depended for its income on the number of members it attracted, and these members were generally recruited from those considering themselves as belonging to the religious or ideological grouping represented by the organization. Each organization directed its programming to its own following rather than to the general public. Thus, not only radio transmission, but also radio listening became defined in principle as a matter of ideological commitment. And so the principle of formalized diversity, bordering on a kind of apartheid, conceptualized in terms of a fixed set of representative currents of thought or world views within society, was built into the very premises of the Dutch public service broadcasting system.[5]

One of these organizations is VARA, the socialist broadcasting association, founded by a group of socialist radio enthusiasts in 1925, and inspired by the example of German workers' radio clubs that already existed in the Weimar Republic (Swierstra 1975). VARA had managed to acquire a full and equal position in the system, which was an extraordinary feat in light of the then existing mood of anti-socialism and fear of the 'red danger' in society at large. There was then a fundamental difference between VARA and its catholic and orthodox-protestant counterparts, KRO and NCRV. These confessional organizations saw broadcasting primarily as a means of strengthening their own members' sense of religious identity. VARA, however, defined itself as an instrument of the social-democratic labour movement, and as such aimed at contributing to the struggle for progressive social reform rather than merely representing and reinforcing a philosophy of life. Against this background, VARA sought to speak for and reach all workers, not only those of socialist conviction but also catholic or protestant ones, as its potential members and listeners – which, of course, met with resistance from the confessional organizations (Van den Heuvel 1976).

VARA's rebellious and disruptive stance can be gathered from a number of prohibitions imposed on it during the interwar years: for example, it was not allowed to transmit the singing of the 'International', while anti-religious programmes were banned as well as explicit references to class struggle and expressions of other 'deviant' views on politics and morality, such as a lecture about birth control (Bardoel *et al.* 1975; Bank 1986). However, VARA's position was moderate enough for it to become integrated in the system as a whole, and VARA officials themselves considered being part of the system so important that they accepted the prevailing rules and norms of the permittable through forms of internal censorship (Bardoel *et al.* 1975). Even so, the organization was fondly cherished by social democratic activists as a true achievement of their own – 'a cathedral built in togetherness by hundreds of thousands of little men' (Sluyser 1965: 7). This populist sentiment remained a major thread in VARA history, although by the 1980s it has taken on, as we will see, a rather different form.

In the 1930s, then, VARA's relationship to its audience was direct and reciprocal: as part of the 'Red Family', it presented itself as the broadcasting organization of and for ordinary working class people, the 'little men and women'. Almost all listeners were also members of the association of VARA (or at least this was the assumption, for no systematic survey data about radio audiences were available at that time); members, gathering together in regional districts and local chapters all over the country, participated actively by collecting funds, organizing listening evenings and setting up yearly, massively attended open-air festivities;[6] VARA's programmes, consisting not only of typically propagandistic material such as addresses of leaders of the Social

Democratic Workers' Party and celebrations of the First of May, but also popular entertainment (drawing upon and incorporating elements of existing folk culture, e.g. through the use of well-known working class popular artists: 'our own' artists), were immensely popular among the members/listeners (Weijers 1988). Contrary to Reith's BBC, then, which in the interwar years operated in splendid isolation from the social world of actual audiences, VARA, as an association rather than a corporation, functioned in that period as a powerful cement within a tightly-knit and strong-willed social community, determined to establish the political and cultural emancipation of the working masses. In other words, VARA could luxuriate in a position of secure knowledge about who its audience was because it identified itself with its audience, as becomes clear in continuous, self-evident references within the organization to its 'natural constituency': no fundamental gap between 'us' and 'them' was perceived, because both were imagined to be part of the same community.

This sense of unity between institution and audience was not, of course, VARA's idiosyncratic privilege, but was inscribed within the structure of the Dutch broadcasting system itself. Every broadcasting organization, certainly the religious ones, relished the certainty of having a distinct part of the nation's population as its natural audience. The population/audience was neatly divided in ideologically-based segments, as it were, and each broadcasting organization presumed to cater for the cultural needs of one of those segments. In other words, just as the system was pillarized, the audience was presumed to be pillarized as well.[7] This is a reason why the need for knowledge about the audience, quantitative empirical style, took a long time to be felt.[8] As De Boer and Cameron (1955: 67) noted, 'there is a decided lack of enthusiasm in Hilversum [where Holland's broadcasting industry is located] for listener research. The Netherlands is a small country . . . and most Dutch broadcasters feel they know their audiences well.'

However, this cosy atmosphere of oneness between broadcasting institution and audience has never been as harmonious as it seems. This becomes clear when we take into consideration the concrete policies VARA needed, and continues to need, to develop the practice of broadcasting. Within VARA too, then, as within the BBC, the question of programming policy has always been a thorny issue and here again, the question of how to define and establish a normative relationship with the audience through programming is the central problem to be solved. And in this respect, VARA's dilemmas prove to run parallel to those of the BBC: how to adapt an essentially interventionist philosophy of public service to the stubbornness of actual audiences.

Of course, VARA's ideological problematic is quite different from the BBC's. The BBC's national status prevents it from explicitly aligning itself with any sectional interest. For VARA, however, the opposite is the case: its partisan identity is its very *raison d'étre*; were it to become 'neutral' or, to use a term often employed in Dutch discourse on broadcasting, 'identity-less', then it would have lost its legitimacy.[9] Within VARA, then, the issue of programming policy is always, in one way or another, related to the issue of institutional identity.

Two key terms form the general discursive framework within which VARA has attempted to construct its identity throughout its contentious history: the twin terms 'popular' and 'progressive'. It is over the meaning of these two terms, as well as the complicated relationship between them, that VARA discourse about programming philosophy has evolved. In general terms, VARA's ambition has always been to be both popular and progressive: it is through this combination that the socialist broadcasting organization has attempted to forge its special, reformist relationship to the audience. But how to achieve this?

VARA never wanted to restrict itself to transmitting political propaganda for the social democratic movement. It was the idea of cultural emancipation – a cornerstone of the general political agenda of social democracy – that formed a central lead for VARA to develop its definition of 'progressiveness'. Furthermore, VARA definitely wanted more than just entertainment. As Meyer Sluyser (1965: 63), one of VARA's most passionate early activists and champion of the interests of the 'little man', once noted, 'if VARA never wanted to be more than a pleasure machine, then it would not have been worth setting it up. There are enough merry-makers in Holland.' Thus, although entertainment was even mentioned as the first obligation VARA had to meet in its first statutes in 1925 – the 'little man' has a right to be entertained – in its cultural politics VARA opted for the reformist idea, as in Sluyser's words, 'the advancement of the average standard of general knowledge and cultural education in the country' (ibid.). In this sense, VARA's philosophy was remarkably in line with the way in which the purpose of public service broadcasting was originally defined within the BBC. The difference was that Reith's BBC wanted to impose audience reform 'from above', from an upper middle-class perspective, while VARA's project of reforming the audience was in a sense a voluntarist initiative 'from below', from the perspective of the socialist labour movement.

The unique features of broadcasting, with its capacity to penetrate from a central point of transmission into hitherto unreachable corners of society, propelled VARA to conceive cultural education in terms of distribution and access: VARA's task was to enhance the accessibility of cultural forms to the people by distributing it to them. But distribution and access are merely formal, not substantial goals: they remain silent about what should be passed on to the audience. So, the ideal of cultural emancipation quickly became translated in terms of access of working class people to more 'serious', established forms of culture, because these were considered self-evidently worthwhile.[10] Most of all, however, the ideal implied a first, inevitable seperation between 'us' and 'them'. VARA chairman De Vries, a school teacher, in the 1930s evoked this affectionate image of what VARA can do:

> If you look outside, then you see everywhere in the polder little houses and people live in them who know nothing about music and poetry and of theatre. But now there is radio, and everything beautiful in the world will now penetrate those little houses as well. We do a piece of educational work, men. In a few years' time those people will not be content with the music and the recitations of today, then they will want better music and more difficult radio plays. *That* is education.
>
> (Quoted in Weijers 1988: 116, emphasis in original)

If the reformist perspective articulated here reminds us of Reithean discourse, its origins were, unlike BBC ideology, certainly not fed by elitist distance towards the common people, but on the contrary by an almost sentimental love for them. This ideologically-motivated blend of populism and paternalism – a populist paternalism, a paternalist populism – was one way in which VARA attempted to articulate the 'popular' and the 'progressive', and it has remained a prevalent discursive motif within the organization until well into the 1980s. Thus, a typical phrasing of this particular option for defining VARA's identity, made by an authoritative VARA figure, Milo Anstadt, many years later, sounds like this:

> The VARA can help to disseminate the socialist message . . . [But it must] as a mass medium be prepared to accept as starting point the world of ideas inhabited by the broad masses. To speak with Roosevelt: one has to be one step ahead of the people; those who distance themselves more than one step, will no longer be followed.
>
> (Anstadt 1976: 78)

That this populist/paternalist stance was not the inevitable trajectory which VARA could have taken in defining its relationship to the audience, becomes apparent from the way it was constantly contested inside VARA and within the larger social democratic movement. Thus, in the 1950s, novel strands within this movement (assembled, for example, in a renewed Labour Party), wished to modernize Dutch society by breaking the rigid dividing lines between the traditional pillars, and by developing a unified, national cultural politics. Proponents of this 'breakthrough' were generally high-minded intellectuals who did not exhibit any affection for the culture of ordinary folks. Instead, they emphasized the need for cultural leadership in more truly Reithean fashion, aimed at correcting the masses from a position of aloof distance. 'Vulgar fun' must be replaced by 'civilized enjoyment', according to Professor G. van der Leeuw, who was the Dutch Minister of Education,

Arts and Sciences in 1947: 'In the Netherlands of the new spirit, it should no longer be possible that a child on the street has nothing decent to sing, or that the boys and the girls who want to dance know nothing else but the newest negro products' (quoted in Weijers 1988: 120).

Clearly, this implied a very unpopular, even antipopular idea of reform and VARA administrators, keen on defending its acquired institutional position, responded by rejecting this vision of cultural politics as 'autocratic', leading to a deep cleavage between the masses and the cultural leaders. They opted for a 'democratic' form of cultural reform, one that preserved the organic relationship between VARA and the people who make up its popular constituency (Rengelink 1954).

However, the pre-war VARA tradition, with its self-evident attachment to and identification with the social democratic subcultural community, increasingly became an anachronism in the postwar period. VARA too needed to modernize in order to keep up with the larger social context in which it operated. This modernization process has been a very painful one, and in a sense it still goes on today. It is a process which can be described as one of VARA in feverish search for a new concept of audience. By the late 1980s, VARA had come a long way from being an association fostered by rank-and-file socialists as 'our' mouthpiece, to a modern broadcasting organization which, as we shall see, aggressively attempted to enlarge its share of the audience market. This transformation was only possible through a rethinking of the articulation of the popular and the progressive – a process which instigated intense, often heated debate tormenting VARA managers and programme makers for years.

The 1960s are still generally remembered and celebrated by Dutch sociologists and journalists alike as the 'Golden Age' of Dutch television (Bank 1986). Because television has the potential to familiarize the entire population with ideas and worlds they had not known before, the medium as such was perceived to have a progressive impact on Dutch society by breaking open the closed parochialism of pillarized culture (Ellemers 1979; Wigbold 1979; Manschot 1987). VARA has been credited with playing a major part in this by operating at the cutting edge of the then emerging 'current affairs' programming, in which journalists took a much less submissive stance towards authorities than had until then been usual, and by transmitting irreverent satirical programmes.

It is worth noting, in passing, that these programming strategies were heavily influenced by developments within the BBC at that time, under the leadership of Hugh Greene. For example, VARA adapted the BBC's well-known satirical programme *That Was The Week That Was* to a Dutch version, called *Zo is het (That's the way it is)*, which became a *cause célèbre* in the history of Dutch television for its heavily controversial impact, both inside and outside VARA.[11] One instalment in which the act of television viewing was depicted as a ritual of religious devotion, transmitted in January 1964, provoked such widespread official and popular indignation that VARA management decided to cancel the programme – much to the dismay of the programme makers concerned (Daudt and Sijes 1966; Pennings 1985a). In more general terms, this incident marked a new direction in public service programming: a programming that included iconoclastic items that could provoke, even shock and disturb the audience. 'Serving the public' here even implies antagonizing substantial proportions of the audience, as Greene would have it (Briggs 1985: 331).[12]

All in all, these programmes were cancelled because they were based upon a philosophy that was neither 'progressive' nor 'popular' in the traditional sense. But they indicated that at least some VARA programme makers had become increasingly self-conscious about the relative autonomy of their job. Like their BBC colleagues, they too, especially the younger ones who got their jobs in the early 1960s, had begun to embrace the professional attitude (Bardoel *et al.* 1975). In defining what was progressive, they departed from a formal alliance with the ideas of democratic socialism and exhibited a more detached, anti-establishment attitude better suited to the ambition of editorial autonomy that went along with the values of professionalism.[13] And by aiming at shocking the audience their programmes were decidedly antipopular. In a fundamental sense, then, these provocative programmes represented a profound break with VARA's dominant, populist/paternalist relationship to its audience. They never became a major programming strand, however, precisely because they disrupted VARA philosophy too much (Pennings 1985a).

In the early 1970s, another group of programme makers, gathered within the Documentaries Division, put forward an even more radical programming philosophy, which aimed at restoring the tight and close affiliation with the audience. They opted for a reinvigoration of VARA's socialist credentials, and demanded an explicit, sectional, Marxist-inspired commitment to the plight of the working class within capitalist society. Between 1972 and 1974, this group produced a series of documentaries, titled *Van Onderen (From Down-under)*, which typically featured the exploitation and oppression of workers in large capitalist corporations. This programme strategy was interventionist with a vengeance. Its presumed effect on its audience was far-reaching: it was hoped that the programmes would induce not only the raising of (class) consciousness, but also a sense of solidarity and, eventually, active struggle for social change. It must be clear then that these programmes were not directed to a general public, but to a very specific, politically defined target group: the oppressed (Bardoel *et al.* 1975; Pennings 1985b).

The programmatic experiments of the 1960s and 1970s were carried out and defended by their proponents, inside and outside VARA, with zealous passion. These were the times of intense commitment to radical visions of 'progressiveness' (Ang 1987). Especially in the 1970s, the interventionist ambitions built into VARA's particular version of the public service idea were pushed to an extreme by the experimentalists: a truly socialist VARA, so it was proposed, should use television as an instrument of political mobilization. The audience's role should not be limited to that of (responsive) viewers; they should also be active participants in the production of the programmes, for example by organizing discussion groups about the programmes and by using their comments as starting point for the next programme – a procedure, therefore, that went radically beyond the conventional arrangement of broadcasting as a one-way process of central transmission and privatised reception. This heavily politicized concept of what it means to serve the public, which echoes Hans Magnus Enzensberger's (1979 [1969]) influential theory of the 'emancipatory' (as opposed to 'repressive') use of the media, was, according to Tom Pauka (1974), leader of this group of radical programme makers, populist but not popular: it did not aim to attract large audiences (which indeed it never did), but resolutely took the side of the victims of an unjust society.[14]

I have described these programming experiments here to illustrate some of the daring efforts that were made within VARA to modernize its normative relationship to the audience. In one sense, these experiments were possible because there was little consensus within the organization in the 1960s and 1970s about what that relationship should look like now that the organic social-democratic community, which VARA considered the basis of its institutional identity, has fallen apart. In other words, VARA did not know how to modernize itself. But the experimental mood never caught on in VARA as a whole: in fact, it only existed at the margins of mainstream VARA policy, and the reason for this can ultimately be found in the impossibility for VARA to move too far beyond the structural limits within which a broadcasting institution, no matter how socialist, has to take care of its own conditions of reproduction. The popular/progressive couplet served as the preliminary guarantee in this respect.

Lack of popularity was the main criticism issued against the programming strategies of the experimenters: while the 1960s' satirists were accused of elitism, the 1970s' radical socialists were accused of 'proletarian romanticism' (Pennings 1985b). However, it is important to note that the requirement for VARA to be popular was never meant to be at odds with its identity as a progressive broadcasting organization. Again and again, the management continued to formulate idealistic visions of VARA's normative purpose. In 1969, it was stated that VARA should be a broadcasting organization 'for all those in the Netherlands who demand a progressive and radical policy on the cultural, social, and political terrains' (VARA Gids 1969: 10).[15] In 1978, chairman André Kloos reiterated that VARA is 'a political and cultural instrument for progressive Netherlands' (Kloos 1978). In 1983, under the leadership of chairman André van den Heuvel, a shift in choice of words: VARA needs to be a 'left-wing people's broadcasting organization' (VARA 1983b). And in 1987, chairman Marcel van Dam states that VARA wants to be a 'progresssive humanist organization' (in Ang and Tee 1987). All these discursive formulas, abstract as they are, are intended to sustain, again and again, the assumption that VARA does not have to choose between being popular and being progressive, but can be both. How to be popular *and* progressive, that's the question.

The desire to articulate popularity and progressiveness then is both a normative and a strategic issue for VARA, having everything to do with the widening gap between broadcasting institution and audience from the early 1970s onwards. In a sense, all the debates in the experimental phase were conducted in the comfortable assumption, right or wrong, that in principle there was a natural audience out there for VARA programming: these were generally debates which revolved around VARA's philosophically-constructed relationship to some ideal-typical audience (the audience that needed to be reformed, shocked, or mobilized), not about VARA's practical relationship to actual audiences. Gradually, however, VARA was confronted with a new situation: it became aware that having an audience, a very basic question, could not be taken for granted; that the audience should be conquered.

In the Netherlands too, it was the emergence of competition that propelled this situation. In 1967, a new Broadcasting Act was implemented that opened up the Dutch system for newcomers. A new organization, TROS, came into being and contrary to the established, pillarized broadcasting organizations, VARA included, TROS did not seek legitimacy by referring to an ideological or religious identity, but by – the phrase sounds familiar – 'giving the audience what it wants'. TROS derived its programming strategies from American commercial examples: it transmitted showy programmes with a style of presentation full of pizazz, with which Dutch audiences were largely unfamiliar until then. While not a commercial organization in the economic sense of the term, TROS's methods were. Popularity in its strictly quantitative meaning was its chief aim. Not surprisingly, it did attract large audiences, at the cost of the other, established organizations. The latter panicked, and began to search for ways for the counter-attack. They mostly did this by adopting the very same programming methods TROS used: providing more light entertainment, American drama series and snappy current affairs

programmes – a development that came to be known as the 'trossifica-
tion' of Dutch television (Ang 1985b). And so, concern with the necessity
of *fighting* for the audience entered VARA discourse.

In fact, it had been clear for a long time that many viewers and
listeners did not behave in the loyal and obedient manner that the
pillarized system expected them to do. For example, as early as 1954, the
very first representative survey among Dutch radio listeners provided
data that audiences were rather independent in their programme choice:
the socialists, catholics and protestants certainly did not listen only to the
programmes of their 'own' broadcasting organization, but also to the
others (Centraal Bureau voor de Statistiek 1954). Almost a decade later,
similar conclusions were drawn about the television audience (Centraal
Bureau voor de Statistiek 1962). Thus, the audience was never so neatly
segmented along the pillarized lines as the system presumed: the
pillarized audience was more a convenient fiction than a social fact. In
fact, awareness of this can be illustrated by a prohibition the episcopate
imposed upon its Roman Catholic following, in 1954, to become members
of the 'red' VARA or even listen to or watch its programmes – a
disciplinary rule that was bound to be subverted!

The broadcasting organizations were aware that the fiction of the
pillarized audience was based on shaky ground, and this was one of the
reasons why they took the initiative to set up an audience research
service, which began to operate in 1965. But as long as the established
broadcasting organizations formed a closed oligopoly, competition was
not really an issue. There was a kind of implicit 'gentlemen's agreement'
built into the system to live and let live: a situation of peaceful
coexistence. This comfortable situation was cruelly disturbed by the
advent of TROS, and later even more by yet another 'Americanized'
organization, Veronica, a former pirate pop music station, which entered
the system in 1976. These new organizations aggressively drained many
viewers off from the ideologically-based organizations, and effectively
blew up the idea of the loyal, pillarized audience.

VARA was fully aware of the problems these developments raised.
Typically enough, then, VARA management commissioned market
research firms to explore its position in the audience 'market'. These
surveys provided VARA with disturbing empirical knowledge: for
example, that many people who voted for the Labour Party preferred to
be members of TROS not VARA, and that young people were much less
attracted to VARA than the older generation – something which, so the
report concluded, did not predict a rosy future for VARA (De Hond
1977a; 1977b).

But the idea of the 'natural constituency' was so deeply inscribed in
VARA's assumptive world that it was difficult for VARA to adapt to the
new situation. Instead, it preferred to cherish the thought that there
was still a part of the audience, defined in the 1970s and early 1980s

either in political terms ('left-voting Netherlands'), or in politico-demographical terms ('the people with less power, knowledge and income'), that should rightfully and automatically 'belong' to VARA's natural audience. The observation that VARA did not occupy a spontaneous 'warm spot in the heart' (De Hond 1977b) of these groups was implicitly interpreted as their 'false consciousness'!

How much resistance there was within the organization to give up the idea of the 'natural constituency', becomes clear in the following diagnosis, made by a business consultant in the early 1980s:

'The VARA finds itself in a peculiar position. You claim to be the broadcasting organization of and for the progressive movement, but a part of that claimed constituency prefers the competition . . . What amazes us is that, even though you recognize the situation, you react to it with a kind of 'reverse market behaviour'. You scold at your competitors and, especially, at those people who do not show a preference for you, but you don't seem to look at home for the cause. If the clients no longer come, you do not blame your own store, but the clients and the other stores.'
(Quoted in a letter from chairman Albert van den Heuvel to the Kerngroep TV [Heads of the Television Divisions], 1 October 1982)

What is most significant about this assessment, however, is the language in which it is put. Terms like 'market behaviour' and 'clients' imply the acceptance of a marketing perspective towards the audience which was never part of VARA discourse. The management, however, took great pains to transform the programme makers' way of thinking along these lines, and this meant the introduction of a new perspective on the institution's relationship with the audience. This was sometimes done by carefully adding new words into VARA discourse, as by secretary Herman van Wijk in 1978. 'If we care about the social effect of our work, we must take more account of the realities of society', he stated, by which he meant that the target audience must first of all be reached. And he patiently explained:

'To reach' means, in this context, to enhance VARA's appeal, to instil affection for it. Only when that has been provided for, that is when at least some uninhibited viewing or listening contact has been made, can we think about transmitting a 'message' and contributing to social development.

(Van Wijk 1978).

What Van Wijk called for, in fact, was a more consumer-oriented approach, and in this he set the tone for VARA policy in the years to come, although as late as 1982, chairman Van den Heuvel still felt the need to explain the importance of 'getting to know our "market"' through research to his programme makers: 'It concerns the desires and appreciation of the potential target group, that is, the opinion of those for whom we claim to work and about whom we regretfully have to observe, that only one third of them is willing to belong to us' (Van den Heuvel 1982). In his view, VARA programmes did not sufficiently take account of the preferences and competences of the audience they were intended for:

> Workers are hardly able to recognize themselves in our programmes. Our information is too difficult, too inbreeding-like, too jargony, too presumptuous, too quickly criticizing, and offering too little real insight. Furthermore, often too elitist in the sense of more interested in the particular than in the normal, aiming too high, and too trendy.
>
> (ibid.)

In these words, the perceived need to direct programmes more to the mass audience was still cast in idealistic, reformist terms. But when the situation became more critical – at least when considered in marketing terms: VARA's position in relation to the competition was lamentable – the tone became more impatient, more threatening, as in a policy plan from 1984, where it was bluntly stated that 'it is not our identity that is our first problem, but our popularity' (VARA 1984: 23).

In this development the meaning of the term 'popularity' tended to shrink to its most trivial, quantitative dimension, devoid of the political and cultural meanings of 'the popular' which informed VARA discourse in earlier years. 'Popularity' has become little more than 'reaching a large audience': something which, of course, can be measured by ratings! But on the other hand, it was impossible for VARA to completely forsake the ideological dimensions of its 'identity', if only to differentiate itself from shamelessly 'commercial' organizations such as TROS and Veronica. Thus the task was to forge a synthesis of a commercial definition of popularity and a populist sense of progressiveness (Ang 1987). This led to quite supercilious rhetorical constructions in official VARA discourse:

> It is VARA's mission to make programmes – in every category – that are best viewed, listened to, and appreciated. . . . Not because high viewing and listening figures are an end in itself, but because VARA in its totality has something to say and to show, that it deliberately wants to bring to the public's attention. VARA is a broadcasting organization with an ideal and that is the reason why she consequently strives to get the biggest reach. VARA programmes must win from all others.
>
> (VARA 1984: 14)

Here, popularity (in terms of ratings success) was now squarely seen as instrumental to, and relatively independent of, achieving progressiveness.

The popular and the progressive were now conceived as two entities external, sometimes even in opposition, to each other: the first embraced the idea of audience-as-market (consisting of consumers to be reached), the second retained the idea of audience-as-public (consisting of citizens to be educated and reformed). In a particularly strident 1983 policy statement, a magical solution to this contradictory construction of VARA's audience was forged in the the evocation of the 'ordinary people' as its 'natural constituency' (VARA 1983b). However, now this 'natural constituency' is defined not by referring to a pre-existent political and cultural community, but by applying the commercial instrument of market segmentation: it consists of those 'between 25 and 55 with such a low income that they are covered by the National Health Service, and whose schooling ranges from elementary education to lower vocational training'. This market segment makes up, as the writers of the plan would have it, at least 40 per cent of the Dutch population.[16] But the plan did not leave it at this juggling with demographics. It also constructed the 'ordinary people' as those who are most vulnerable to the dangers of 'reproletarization' (as a result of watching too much commercial television), which VARA wishes to combat:

> VARA has nothing against the audience watching violent scuffles and relationships in the lives of oil magnates [this was the time that *Dallas* and *Dynasty* were at the top of their popularity], but wants to serve as counterpoise by putting other gripping, exciting and surprising elements of Dutch culture on the screen. For ordinary people. No artistic expressions that only few can understand. By reproletarization we thus mean the effecting of a lower and narrower level of interest by a one-sided supply of programming.
>
> (VARA 1983b)

Discursively speaking, then, the 'ordinary people' are a *deus ex machina*, a handy rhetorical device that enables VARA to renew its waning bond with a 'natural constituency' by reconciling the normative and the pragmatic, the reformist and the entertaining, public mission and market exigencies, paternalist populism and audience maximization. The category of 'ordinary people' is not just a market segment, it is also an imaginary construct of 'television audience' with political bearings, reminiscent of, although certainly not derived from, Gramsci's concept of 'the people' as those who are excluded from the realm of political and ideological power.[17]

On the basis of this formulation of VARA's ideal-typical audience, the managers developed a totalitarian scheme of qualitative criteria for VARA programming policy which looked like this

Popular – ordinary $\left\{\begin{array}{l}\text{accessible}\\\text{understandable}\\\text{'close to the people'}\end{array}\right.$

– quality: love for the ordinary man: NOT $\left\{\begin{array}{l}\text{pedantic}\\\text{cynical}\\\text{tiresome}\end{array}\right.$

Left – identity: $\left\{\begin{array}{l}\text{militant making}\\\text{elevating}\\\text{emancipatory}\end{array}\right.$

(unsigned internal report, 7 May 1984)

Such a scheme betrays a desire to totally control the way VARA programmes should address and influence the audience; and indeed, the management announced the intention to quantify this set of criteria, in order to be able to submit all VARA products and all VARA personnel to rigorous evaluative measurement of performance. Panels consisting of representatives of the target group (the 'ordinary people') were suggested, information about audience needs and interests in general were now considered indespensible (VARA 1983b). Articulated here is a bold managerial attempt to rationalize, formalize and objectify *ad absurdum* the relationship between VARA and the 'ordinary people'. And although the plan eventually failed to be implemented, it did pave the way for a change of direction in VARA discourse which more forthrightly than before legitimated the prominence of empirical information about the audience, as collected by research, as both starting point and ultimate yardstick for programming decisions.

In this respect, the strategic, central position of the term 'quality' in the scheme of performance criteria above is significant. 'Quality' forms the formal bridge, at the level of programming philosophy, between 'popularity' and 'progressiveness'. And indeed, while totalitarian plans such as those explicated above were dropped a few years later, 'quality for a large audience' has now become the pivotal benchmark, the key signifier for VARA's institutional identity.

Thus, VARA's current chairman, Marcel van Dam, emphatically rejects the 'ordinary people' as VARA's target audience: 'In the past, people did indeed say sometimes: "We are just ordinary people". But in our contemporary culture nobody wants to be ordinary any more, does he?' (in Ang and Tee 1987: 18). Van Dam, a former Labour MP and an eloquent rhetorician, is also the first leader who has proposed a radical break with VARA's pillarized past by renouncing any residual reference to a 'natural constituency': 'No organization in the Netherlands still has a natural constituency, certainly not when we speak about the younger generations' (in ibid.: 19). At last, then, any essentialist, a priori notion of the necessary belongingness of a section of the audience to VARA was dropped.[18] He justifies this through a kind of postmodernist discourse, in which contemporary culture is regarded as individualized, privatized, de-ideologized (Mollema and Voskuil 1989).

> In the past our aura was: when you are on the left, you ought to be a member of VARA. That is definitely over. The people must now appreciate you for the products you offer them . . ., and only then political colour plays a role. First they want to get their money's worth.
>
> (in Ang and Tee 1987: 19)

In this situation, Van Dam opts for VARA to be a 'modern, independent, progressive–humanist broadcasting organization' who must conquer the audience by providing 'VARA quality'. And so VARA's institutional identity – its difference from the competitors – has become a much more conditional question, something that must be based upon the proven 'quality' of the programmes it actually transmits, rather than on a set of pregiven ideological principles and assumptions. Thus, in a 'product formula' written by Van Dam to create a new, coherent philosophy for VARA's 'corporate identity' he defines the audience as:

> Clients who demand quality and who want to be treated kindly and with respect. They do not have obligations to us, but we do to them. Of course there is in the Netherlands space for a progressive broadcasting organization, just as there is space for progressive newspapers. But that space must be fought for.
>
> (Van Dam 1987: 2)

While Van Dam again and again emphasizes 'quality', however, he at the same time states that 'quality is hard to define' (in Ang and Tee 1987). Therefore, he says, it must be operationalized in such a way that all VARA workers can agree to it: 'Quality is that which is measured as such according to a certain measurement system' (Van Dam 1987: 16). And if ratings success alone cannot justify VARA's existence nor define 'VARA quality', it is the values of professionalism which provide the main points of anchorage. This is reflected in some of the variables that Van Dam (ibid.: 17–19) proposes to operationalize 'quality': 'attention value' (i.e. is the programme varied and exciting enough?); 'accessibility' (i.e. is the information offered clear and understandable?); 'presentation' (i.e. is the programme sympathetic, inviting, smooth, to the point?); 'standing' (i.e. does the programme reflect good taste?); 'technical production value'.

In stressing 'quality improvement' as internal policy spearhead, then, VARA discourse under the leadership of Van Dam has acquired striking similarities with BBC discourse, where the professional quest for 'quality' has reigned since the 1960s and still prevails in the self-conception of BBC programme makers today (Burns 1977; Blumler *et al.* 1986). As we have seen in Chapter 12, 'quality' tends to be part of a specialist, insider's discourse of judgement, reserved to professional experts not laymen. By embracing 'quality' broadcasters symbolically declare themselves independent of the exigencies of the outside world: it gives them the alibi for a withdrawal into what Burns (1977: 141) dramatically describes as 'the autistic world within which they could sustain the complex system of commitment and belief their work [calls] for'. A world, in other words, in which the audience must remain at a proper distance, because too much closeness would disturb the relative security that world, as an occupational milieu, affords (ibid.: 132–4).

However, VARA's case makes clear that emphasizing 'quality' is not only an institutional strategy to enable professional complacency. It is also propelled by a desire to preserve a distinctive identity as a public service institution: in an increasingly competitive world 'quality' has become the preferred marker by which institutions such as VARA and the BBC now wish to keep themselves from sliding completely into a commercial working logic. In this sense, 'quality' is not just a facilitating discourse for the broadcasters' sense of autonomy; at a larger institutional level, it is also perceived as a pure necessity for public service institutions to stress their 'surplus value' *vis à vis* commercial institutions. As Blumler *et al.* have observed,

> whereas in American network television, audience maximization is the test that almost all programmes must pass sooner or later (and more often sooner), British broadcasters [and VARA broadcasters too] tend to see it more as a matter of building an audience and retaining its allegiance for a varied provision. . . . British programme-makers felt it was possible to have good-quality programmes in all genres. . . . 'Good' in such cases implies an attempt to add something to sheer audience-holding ingredients, an important distinction in support of programme quality that seems much fainter in the United States.
> (Blumler *et al.* 1986: 352–3)

It seems fair to conclude, then, that this vague notion of 'quality' serves first of all as a rhetorical device to boost public service broadcasting's truncated sense of 'public service'. 'Quality', as institutionally operationalized and used, is not sought after to reform the audience in any direct sense; rather, the professional discourse of quality functions primarily as a defence mechanism in that it theoretically constructs a favourable image of what the public institution has to offer to the consuming audience, even though it is difficult to determine 'quality' in practice.[19]

All this does not mean, of course, that VARA's social democratic legacy does not continue to have an important impact on the 'structure of feeling' in which VARA operates. But that impact is no longer object of extensive ideological debate within the organization: rather, it is a matter of mentality, of attitude, of tradition, of inherited institutional common sense. It manifests itself in the continuing adherence of most VARA workers to accepted progressive humanist notions about politics and culture, society and morality, concretized in the self-evident importance given to a list of social issues such as justice, world peace, the problems of the Third World, the environment, or social equality, which according to Van Dam (1987) are of particular interest to progressive people; in caustic assertions as to why *Hill Street Blues* ('critical approach of police work') would fit in VARA's television schedule, and *Miami Vice* ('unrealistic') would not (Van Dam, in Ang and Tee 1987); in the propensity to intersperse quiz shows, comedy series and other popular entertainment programmes with items which give the audience 'something to learn' (Ang 1988) and so on. Thus, contrary to the BBC, VARA still does not consider it its role to provide an objective mirror of national life in its full diversity; it still cherishes a partisan, progressive – or rather progressivist – 'message' that it wants to get across.

But that 'message' is no longer translated into a clearcut missionary role of VARA toward the audience: as Van Dam (1987: 6) puts it, VARA should no longer seek to 'tell people *what* they should think, but *that* they should think'. It should no longer seek to reform the audience according to some complete, preformulated ideology, but only offer a series of 'progressive' views and opinions considered worthwhile to whom it may concern. And so, what is left of the interventionist idea of 'public service' has dissolved into a generalized, but detached, 'journalistic attitude' (ibid.), in the assumption that it is more important to raise the right questions rather than imposing the right answers. If VARA still wants to reform the audience, it is by arousing people's curiosity, in the conviction that, as Van Dam (ibid.) so nicely puts it, 'an open mind is a joy forever'.

All in all, VARA's history indicates, just as the BBC's does, how the a priori normative knowledge about the institution/audience relationship has gradually disappeared from public service philosophy. That relationship has become much more conditional, provisional, indefinite. As a result, as Burns (1977: 143–4) has noted, 'communication with audiences is reduced to the common *Gestalt* of a programme "stream" . . .; public issues are translated into methods of programme construction, moral problems into professional judgements'. For better or worse, in this pragmatic atmosphere empirical information about the audience as provided by research forms about the only connection with the audience that the institutions can officially rely on. In this light, it is telling to cite the rhetorical deftness with which VARA management cast the logic of gaining more information about the audience in the early 1980s:

Precisely because VARA, as broadcasting organization for the left movement, has hefty pretensions and thus makes an appeal to its target audience, is continuous research into questions, expectations and wishes in the group it wants to reach of the utmost importance.

(VARA 1984: 28–9)

Similarly, VARA's current policy of 'quality improvement' explicitly foregrounds the role of research in gauging the success of the policy (Van Dam 1987). The tendency to rely on empirical information (rather than on normative knowledge stemming from a preconceived ideology) to develop policy manifests itself more generally in repeated reliance on a whole range of market research-type investigations: from repeated research into VARA's corporate image to smaller-scale pretesting of programme concepts and pilots, which has become common practice within VARA in the late 1980s (VARA 1987). And so, when VARA fully realized that it had lost its 'natural audience', market thinking finally became integrated within VARA practice.

14 Repairing the loss: the desire for audience information

The hard, economic need for ratings data is missing in television systems that are not dependent on competition for advertiser investments. Still, audience measurement has become a large-scale enterprise in many public broadcasting institutions, including the BBC and VARA. How did this happen? And to what effect?

Anthony Smith, former director of the British Film Institute and a leading proponent of public service broadcasting, gave vent to the ambivalence typical in European views on audience measurement:

> The measurements have the same kind of precision as pre-election polling. Better methods are constantly being devised and tried out and complex though interesting technical arguments take place concerning the comparative reliability of methods. Happily, we have never chosen to use these systems to replace elections in the political sphere. It is one thing to sample an electorate and enquire about preferences in politics in a given week. It is quite another to sample television receivers, which may be switched on without anyone being in the room, or with people in the room who are not actually watching, who may be asleep or playing cards or listening to music on headphones. It is fortunate that in Britain the measuring of audiences has been carried out not to decide the levels of revenue for any system, but merely *to satisfy curiosity* and to feed institutional rivalries. In a truly competitive commercial system the measurement of audiences through crude methods of sampling is paramount; programmes, channels, whole companies even, can be swept away through the presence of unknown statistical bugs. In America vast quantities of investment in pilot programmes are regularly junked on the basis of ratings divergences well within the margins of statistical error. It is the extension of roulette into culture.
>
> (Smith 1986: 7; emphasis added)

Smith's observations are interesting, particularly in their omissions. Can the existence of such an expensive endeavour as audience measurement really be explained as mere curiosity? And if so, why should this curiosity be satisfied precisely by measuring audiences?

While European and American measurement practices have become more and more similar in their epistemological and methodological assumptions, the motives for embarking upon the research enterprise as such were rather different. As we have seen in Chapter 12, it is the perceived structural isolation of the broadcaster from the invisible audience which made the BBC decide in 1936 to hire Robert Silvey to set up a listener research division. The felt need for pure information gave research its justification. To what use that information was going to be put, however, was unclear. Reith, for example, had mixed feelings about research. He feared it might inhibit programme makers, and warned against the dangers of building programmes on the basis of empirical information about listeners' preferences (Briggs 1985: 149). Another BBC official put his rejection of any kind of survey research even more militantly:

> As I hold very strongly that the ordinary listener does not know what he likes, and is tolerably well satisfied, as shown by correspondence and licence figures, with the mixed fare now offered, I cannot escape the feeling that any money, time or trouble spent upon elaborate enquiries into his tastes and preferences would be wasted.
>
> (In Briggs 1965: 261)

This stance is quite understandable given the BBC's authoritarian paternalist ambitions in the Reithean period, which aimed to change, not anticipate, audience taste. Others within the BBC, however, were more excited. As Silvey (1974: 32) recalled, while some 'simply refused to believe that any systematic study of the public was possible at all', others had a 'greatly exaggerated' view of the potentiality of research. Silvey himself held that audience research is a matter of duty: the duty for a public service broadcasting organization like the BBC 'to take proper account of the opinions and needs of all its many different publics' (ibid., 12). In other words, information seeking is presented here as a means of communication, as an act of responsibility and accountability towards the public.

In the Netherlands, too, the setting up of audience research did not originate in commercial motives and interests. In the early 1960s, the five pillarized broadcasting organizations, including VARA, began to realize their lack of knowledge about the audience, their assumed closeness to their respective 'natural constituencies' notwithstanding. Because separate research efforts by each broadcasting organization would be too expensive, a joint initiative was taken to set up a continuous audience measurement system, which started to operate in 1965. Its justification was entirely cast in the expectation that research could serve as a compensation for the institutional invisibility of the broadcast audience:

The programme makers are interested in 'hard' audience figures for individual radio and television programmes, and in how they are rated by the audience. Programme makers need to know to whom a particular programme appeals so that they can reach their intended audience. They would like to have their finger continually on the audience's pulse in order to see whether the aims of their programme policy are being realized.

(Werkgroep Luister- en Kijkonderzoek 1963)

Silvey's Audience Research Department had already acquired a fine reputation and one Dutch researcher was sent to London to learn from Silvey and his co-workers (Bakker 1964).

But why research – and particularly, why did the expensive, large-scale, continuous, quantitative, survey-style research eventually become so all-important? Why give priority to *measuring* the audience? There seem to have been no clearcut reasons for this, at least not in the consciousness of the institutions themselves, although there was enormous confusion and discussion within the BBC in the 1930s about the kinds of things (listening habits, listener preferences, efficiency of different broadcasting techniques, the role of the wireless in family life) research could investigate (Briggs 1965). As Silvey recalled:

Curiously, perhaps, this role [of audience research within the BBC] was never specifically defined by my superiors. I had to work it out for myself and, whenever necessary, make it explicit. I can only assume that my conception of audience research's role coincide with the Corporation's for I was never called upon to amend my formulation of it.

(Silvey 1974: 33)

There were no natural reasons why BBC audience research should have been modelled, conceptually speaking, after commercial market research; why, in short, public service research has become so similar to commercial audience measurement.[1] But from the very start Silvey's ideas went in the direction of measuring the size of audiences, thus providing broadcasting with a substitute for the 'box office' (ibid.: 61), and in an early talk he clarified the aims of audience research by utilizing an analogy between the BBC and a department store with the audience members being seen as equivalent to customers: the purpose of research then would be to effectively anticipate consumer demand (Briggs 1965: 278; Chaney 1986). While the market metaphor was first considered 'indecent' by some, Silvey's work has gained increasing endorsement at all levels of the corporation, particularly since the war. In 1939, Silvey set up a continuous service of audience measurement which would later become known as the Survey of Listening and Viewing. For this service, a representative sample of 4000 people were individually interviewed each day about the broadcasts of the preceding day, a huge operation for which no less than 300 trained interviewers a day were needed (BBC 1961). It is interesting to note at this point that the BBC did not make use of the meter technology to measure audience size, at least not until 1981, when the hand-held people meter device entered the British audience measurement scene.[2]

In 1964, the Dutch researcher who visited London, Lo Bakker, was impressed by the quantity of research material produced by Silvey's department, but he was less impressed by its quality: 'There is too little scientifically based reflection upon exactly what is being done'. And he concluded: 'Although the BBC will always be our big brother, also in the field of research, it must be possible to at least equal the quality of continuous registration in the Netherlands.' (Bakker 1964: 5) He specifically referred to the danger of routinization: 'The whole thing makes the impression that the work . . . has fallen into a daily rut' (ibid., 3). This should have been a warning. Twenty-five years later, however, audience measurement in the Netherlands has become as much a routine as its British example. In 1965, the Dutch carefully started with measuring the audience through the diary method; two years later, the set meter was introduced as measurement technology.[3]

The large-scale, institutionalized, day-to-day repetition of data production tends to suppress a questioning of the purposes of research; instead, continuous audience measurement is now a fully integrated practice in the broadcasting machinery. As the Annan Committee for the future of broadcasting in Britain observed in 1977, 'the [BBC Audience Research] department often seems to have to function like an overworked market research firm, hurriedly assembling studies with no time to bring to bear a broader perspective' (Home Office 1977: 451). And while the logic behind the audience measurement routine cannot be explained by the need to have 'hard facts' to bring back to the advertiser, the very availability of viewing figures for every programme, every day, has created for public broadcasters an opportunity to satisfy their curiosity in a way which, as we shall see, is neither innocent nor inconsequential. The integration of continuous audience measurement data in the operation of broadcasting organizations such as the BBC and VARA signifies a general shift in the prevailing discursive modality of knowledge about the audience within public service broadcasting: more philosophical, normative knowledge about how the audience should be conceived tends to be replaced by a reliance upon aggregated empirical information about existing audience formations.

Of course, there are differences between commercial and public service audience research, not only in function but also in form. The most significant difference is the importance granted in European audience measurement to the variable of 'audience appreciation'. Silvey started to think about this during the Second World War, because in his view 'knowing the size of a programme's audience told one nothing about the nature of that audience's listening experience, what it was about the programme that they had liked or not liked or why they felt about it as they did' (Silvey 1974: 113).

In a sense, this kind of consideration does echo the normative aims of public service broadcasting, where subjective reactions of viewers to programmes are by definition more important than for commercial broadcasting. Not surprisingly, measuring audience appreciation was, from the very beginning, justified against this background. Silvey (ibid.) felt that what marks 'a properly balanced audience research service' is the combination of a continuous measurement of audience size with a continuous assessment of audience reaction. In the Dutch case too measuring appreciation was advocated because it was presumed to provide qualitative information about viewers' judgements of programmes (e.g. Bekkers 1988).

In both the BBC and the Dutch systems 'appreciation' has been operationalized in a linear scale (a five point scale in the BBC's case and a ten point scale in the Dutch case), resulting in a very rough index indeed. But it is not without its pragmatic merits, because it allows for the construction of facts not possible with purely quantitative ratings. For example, the acquired data can be used to detect programmes with low ratings but high appreciation scores, to compare different programmes within one genre in terms of their appreciation scores, and to compare the reaction of different segments of the audience to the same programme – all forms of factual information which could in principle be applied in decision-making processes about programming and scheduling in ways that escape the gross verdict of audience maximization, although it remains unclear to what extent and how such use is actually made in practice (Silvey 1974: 113–9; Bekkers 1988).

Registration of audience appreciation has been considered so important that a unique, ultra-sophisticated version of the people meter was introduced in the Netherlands in the summer of 1987,[4] containing the possibility of electronic measurement, within the same sample, of both audience size and audience appreciation. Thus, every time a viewer 'signs off' or switches channels, when the set is turned off, and at the end of each programme on the three Dutch channels, a request is made of panel members to rate their appreciation by pushing certain buttons on their people meter key pads (Saarloos 1989; NOS 1989). As a result, Dutch audience measurement now proudly delivers a meticulously streamlined map of 'television audience' consisting of minute-by-minute ratings and appreciation scores for all domestic programmes, divided up into up to eighty demographic categories (Bekkers 1988).[5]

The appreciation index is a kind of fetish for public service audience measurement: it is seen as the key difference between public service and commercial research. But the privileging of 'appreciation' as the pre-eminent variable to capture viewers' subjective responses to television also presents problems, signifying an unprompted, contradictory capitulation to the logic of the market after all. First of all, it has already been said that what is exactly measured here is not particularly clear: many varieties of 'appreciation' are lumped together into a one-dimensional scale of something like 'general satisfaction'. The researchers themselves are quite aware of this shortcoming. For example, the Dutch did attempt to develop a multidimensional measurement instrument, breaking down 'appreciation' into 'informational value', 'entertainment value', and 'effort required by the viewer'. However, this experiment did not lead to changes in the regular measurement practice because of high costs and stated difficulties in interpreting the findings (De Bock 1974; Bekkers 1988). As a result, 'work on audience appreciation is too broad in sweep', as the Annan committee put it with regard to the British situation (Home Office 1977: 455).

More fundamental than the problem of methodological validity, however, are the implicit assumptions about the value of the information imparted by the appreciation indices. Of course it is true that more dimensions of audience activity than merely watching/non-watching should be relevant to the project of public service broadcasting. After all, it is nothing less than communication effectiveness, i.e. the effect of programmes on viewers' tastes, preferences, interests, knowledge, and so on, which underlies the classic mission of public service broadcasting. Inscribed in public service philosophy then is a critical, self-reflective perspective on its own performance, and in theory research could play an important role in giving a clue about the extent to which its normative goals are achieved. However, measurement of appreciation does nothing other than register the volume of applause, and as a form of information applause generally tends to be particularly meaningful from the narcissistic perspective of the institutions themselves: in a sense, the subjective feelings of viewers about programmes are mobilized and quantified in the service of institutional self-confidence. Seen in this way, addition of the appreciation index to that of plain measures of audience size does not in itself represent a fundamental departure from the objectivist epistemology of ratings discourse: it is merely a more sophisticated version of it, providing the institution with a measure of its own performance without having to consider the truly qualitative, specific and probably complex and contradictory responses of actual audiences. The audience remains an abstracted, objectified other.

The knowledge provided by audience measurement then does little justice to the official ambitions of public service broadcasting. This is not to be blamed on the individual researchers working within the audience research departments, but on the structural constraints imposed on the uses and applications of research. It is significant, for example, that little interest is displayed by the broadcasting institutions for research into the larger social impact of their programmes. To be sure, apart from measuring audience size and appreciation, the public service audience research departments in Britain and the Netherlands do regularly carry out what are called *ad hoc* investigations, intended to gather more specific information about audience responses to concrete programmes or types of programme. But not only do these special studies take up a relatively small amount of the total budget and energy available for the research endeavour (Home Office 1977); they also generally address questions that do not go beyond the direct, institutionally defined interests formulated by the management or the producers of the programmes: the reduction of uncertainty.

In the 1950s, for example, the BBC Audience Research Department in response to the then widespread public concern about the social impact of television, occasionally embarked upon forms of research into the effects or effectiveness of programmes, but it is telling that Silvey (1974: 173) himself was 'thankful' that research in what he called 'the field of the social – as distinct from the broadcasting-centred – effects of viewing' was eventually left on the side.[6] Similarly, most *ad hoc* studies commissioned to the Dutch Audience Research department are surveys examining issues that are extensions of regular ratings research (e.g. the response of specific target categories to specific programmes), and do not concern larger issues of social effects or impact, much to the regret of the current head of the department, Wim Bekkers.[7] In general, then, the Annan Committee's complaint that 'the research efforts of the broadcasting organizations have been too piecemeal, too narrow and too superficial' still has not lost its pertinence (Home Office 1977: 452). But how realistic would a restructuring of research in more satisfactory directions be?

From the institutional point of view, it is of course not surprising that public service audience research is almost completely instrumental to the institutional interests of the broadcasters themselves – 'broadcasting-centred' in Silvey's words. Audience measurement information tends to be used as a form of public relations, as a sustainer of legitimacy, as a means of probing market conditions, in short, it provides the broadcasters with a discourse of symbolic reassurance. As Burns (1977: 134) has noted, with ratings the relationship between broadcaster and audience is 'taken care of' through a procedure which 'reduces awareness of the public to the safe dimensions of percentages'. In this sense, Burns holds that audience measurement is a barrier, rather than the bridge it was intended to be, between public service broadcaster and audience. Indeed, it is hard to see how ratings, including the appreciation indices, can articulate the fundamentally qualitative, living relationship with the audience which public service broadcasting has striven to achieve.

Evidence for the institutional complacency reinforced by ratings discourse can be derived from observations of the way in which programme makers deal with the numbers their programmes get. Thus, Burns saw how 'the figure' tends to take on a life of its own on the BBC studio floor:

> The shock of a reported A.R. figure of 63 for a programme in a 1963 comedy series which had touched 75 was enough to disrupt the first hour or two of rehearsal of a subsequent production. Very little work was done. The atmosphere of dejection deepened with every new arrival. Clusters formed around the leading actors, the floor manager, and the assistant floor manager, with the producer circulating between them and the telephone. 'This', it was explained to me, 'is what it's like on a morning you've got a low audience figure.' For cast and production team, it was 'the figure'. Even after rehearsal began, the figure returned to the centre of the stage during waits: '63 – and I thought it was such a bloody good show.' The whole gathering was, in fact, engaged in a more preoccupying task than rehearsal for the next show: the search for a reassuring explanation. It was found eventually in the concurrence of a sports film on the commercial network.
>
> (Burns 1977: 141)

Within VARA, too, a whole organizational culture around ratings has developed. For example, VARA's *TV Magazine* now unrestrainedly publishes a weekly Top Ten of programmes with the highest gross ratings, creating an image of success to which Silvey (1974: 185) strenuously objected because such hit lists 'encouraged an entirely fallacious impression of the real significance of audience size' and 'would make it even more difficult to dissuade people from the heretical belief that Bigger always meant Better'. Furthermore, there are cases in which bottles of champagne are opened when a programme gets a high figure; daily pools are organized to predict the figures of tomorrow; and VARA's in-house researcher often finds himself requested to offer ready-made explanations for unexpected fluctuations in the figures (even if the differences are not statistically significant). In this respect, it is telling that the researcher's help is called for only when the figures are disquieting or disappointing.[8] In short, the figures have come to play an autonomous role in indicating success or failure, supplanting any more specific interest in what actual audiences have made of the services they were provided.

Audience measurement data then inevitably channel the institutional view of the audience in the direction of taxonomic abstractions which create distance, not proximity to the ways in which actual audiences respond to the programmes and to television in general. But it should be emphasized that ratings discourse has never gone completely uncontested among self-respecting public service broadcasters. As much as managers, producers and programme makers are inclined to take account of the figures made available to them, there is also a widespread sense that actually there are more important, more respectable things to achieve than satisfying ratings results and beating the competition. The cult of fact induced by the very existence of ratings and related information is countered by the continuing articulation of more normative forms of discourse which serve to sustain a commitment, at least in words and in sentiment, to other ideals, such as diversity, quality and, in VARA's case, progressiveness. These discourses are more oriented towards what should be than what is, they are more prescriptive than descriptive, more philosophical than empirical. Even Silvey was aware of the limitations which the empiricism of his work brought about:

> We were sometimes chided for attaching so much importance to knowing what people *had* listened to. What about the programmes they *would have* listened to, if only they had been broadcast? A good question, but an extremely difficult one to investigate. . . . It takes a lively imagination to conjure up the taste of a new dish from reading the recipe.
>
> (Silvey 1974: 110, emphasis in the original)

This slip into empiricism, embodied by audience research, articulates the basic dilemma of the project of public service broadcasting. It is undeniable that empirical knowledge does have a liberating potential in that it can supply broadcasters with a clearer map of the audience out there, but in privileging fact over value it tends to marginalize the normative aspects involved in the very idea of public service broadcasting. It encourages the treatment of existing, empirically observable audience behaviour as given not as something to be changed. It is for this reason that research as such has a fundamentally ambiguous place in public service broadcasting. As the Annan Committee has so eloquently put it:

> Audience research can be an aid for the producer and a guide to the scheduler; but it cannot take the place of the judgement of either. As David Hume long ago showed, the social sciences cannot usurp the role of moral judgement. Inferences from the one are no substitute for the excercise of the other.
>
> (Home Office 1977: 459)

In this respect, it is interesting to note that in some other European countries audience measurement has long been much less important than in Britain or the Netherlands. The Scandinavian countries, where commitment to reformist public service ideals has remained very strong so far, are a case in point. In Norway, any form of research has been met with widespread opposition until well into the 1980s, in the belief that programming should not be influenced by empirical audience information (Rolland 1989). The Danish Broadcasting Corporation only started to develop in-house audience research in 1973 (Svendsen 1989). In both countries, however, the felt need for audience information has grown as a result of the waning of public service monopoly, resulting in a considerable increase of research activity, to the point even that ideas for implementing continuous audience measurement using people meter technology are taking root. Swedish broadcasting does have a long and extensive research tradition, but all explicitly carried out 'in the spirit of public service', one of its central motifs being the consideration that 'educational content must continue to be able to reach its audiences effectively' (Cronholm 1989: 26). Significantly, the Swedish Broadcasting Corporation is one of the very few European public broadcasting institutions that has decided not to convert to a metred audience measurement system for the time being.[9]

In general, however, the seemingly unstoppable European trend, just as in the United States, is an ever more singleminded emphasis on, and preoccupation with sophistication of audience measurement technologies and procedures, warnings as expressed by the Annan Committee notwithstanding. Ever more expensive and more comprehensive systems are being proposed by several competing research firms such as AGB and Nielsen, not only nationally, but also at an international, pan-European level – a development instigated by the coming integration of Europe as a single market in 1992 (De Bock 1984; Durand 1988). As one British commentator cynically notes, 'We are all stuck with the meter as a means of measuring TV audiences and no-one believes we can survive without it' (Billet 1989: 20).

It is significant to see then that there is little active resistance against this trend in public service broadcasting circles. If criticism is expressed at all, it is mostly cast in subjective not structural terms. In 1983, for example, an internal inquiry within the BBC revealed widespread dissatisfaction about the people meter figures delivered by BARB (the Broadcaster's Audience Research Board), but at the same time the broadcasters proved to be thoroughly dependent on the confirmations the figures provide (Madge 1989: 93–5).

This situation, I suggest, decisively marks the crisis of imagination in which public service broadcasting finds itself today. The current prominence of ratings can be read as a way of solving public broadcasting's crisis, which is fundamentally a *cultural* crisis, by turning it into a crisis of information. In the words of Lawrence Grossberg, in such a perspective

the crisis is not located in the social changes that have taken place but rather, in our failure to respond properly to these changes. To know what would constitute a proper response, one must have accurate, descriptive information about the world. Thus, the crisis is located in our inadequate knowledge and in those attitudes which interfere with the acquisition of this information.

(Grossberg 1979: 57)

Hence, the solution is sought in the accumulation of even more information.

But what do public service broadcasting institutions really gain from all the information now available to them on their on-line computer terminals? Already in 1977, even before the introduction of the people meter which churns out vastly more data, the Annan Committee observed that the BBC researchers are 'swamped by their collection of so many facts and figures about the ratings' and unable 'to find time to stand back from the information they collect, critically to evaluate it and to detect trends' (Home Office 1977: 452–3). In the Netherlands too a sense of information overload is clearly felt. Thus, recently NOS (the Netherlands Broadcasting Foundation, of which the Audience Research Department is a division) has sought the advice of two external communication research experts to find new ways to apply the information:

> NOS wishes a theoretical deepening of viewing and listening research. By accompanying the collection of data with theorizing we hope to enlarge the meaning of these data. A better understanding of viewing and listening behaviour will enable a better explanation and prediction of audience responses to radio and TV programmes. In some cases this will also render unnecessary the collection of new data, in other cases it will influence the way in which data are collected.
> (Letter NOS, 24 Dec 1987; quoted in Van Cuilenburg and McQuail 1988: 2)

In response the outside consultants, professors Jan van Cuilenburg and Denis McQuail of the Netherlands Press Foundation, have suggested the development of a TV programme databank, essentially based upon statistical, multivariate correlations between programme variables and viewer variables, in such way that in the long run it will be possible to predict audience response (a set of dependent variables) for certain programmes with specified characteristics (a set of independent variables).[10] Imagined here is the prospect of a computerized information processing instrument for programming policy which no longer has to depend upon past ratings as information, but has the power of forecasting future ratings!

The Audience Research Department took this suggestion seriously and has attempted to implement it (Bekkers 1988). However, this has run into problems, not least because those within the broadcasting organizations who are directly responsible for the making of programmes seem to be unable and reluctant to transform the ingredients of their programmes into formalized, measurable variables.[11] The discourse of the professional programme maker – creativity, intuition, talent, *Fingerspitzengefühl,* professionalism! – rebels against the rigorous hypothetico-deductive discourse implied in computerized prediction. Whether or not it will ever be realized, then, the idea of the programme databank represents a desire to rationalize programming policy so that it becomes a manageable process whose outcome is, ideally, known in advance, or at least controllable to a considerable extent. Disappeared from this utopian dream (or megalomanic fantasy), however, is any consideration for the living, qualitative, meaningful, truly cultural relationship with the audience – which, it should be remembered, was the very *raison d'être* of public service broadcasting.

This example indicates how far audience research has been removed from the purpose originally claimed for it, namely to enhance communication with the audience, to alleviate the lack of insight broadcasters felt into the social and cultural impact of their work. Empirical knowledge could in principle contribute to develop that insight. However, the evolution of audience research in the direction of large-scale measurement has tended to emphasize technical rationality rather than understanding, aimed at producing statisticized, taxonomized and objectified audience information rather than attempting to gain insight into the complex world of actual, flesh-and-blood audiences.

According to John Durham Peters (1988: 15), 'information is a form of knowledge that rearranges the significance of everyday realities, sapping them from substance'. He refers in this respect to population statistics, whose production dates back to the rise of bureaucracy, enabling the modern state to know a population's behaviours – birth, marriage, death, crime and so on – in a single, cross-sectional glimpse, a disembodied form of knowledge that provides a panoramic vision of the entire nation but is beyond the range of experience: 'One can quite accurately predict, statistically, that about 150 people will die on American roads this day. But the meaning of death as a structuring principle of those lives as the people experienced them falls through the cracks of the statistical model' (ibid.). The same can be said about audience measurement statistics: it makes us know the audience in terms of patterns of a limited number of behavioural displays, but it remains silent about the ways in which television becomes meaningful and has an impact in people's everyday lives and the larger culture.

That empirical knowledge can potentially serve as a tool of communication as well as a tool of control, however, is suggested by reactions of programme makers to focus group sessions in pretesting research. VARA researcher Dick Wensink observed at first hand how they are often appalled or surprised by what actual viewers have to say about and do with 'their' programmes. Often, this is the first time a programme maker is confronted head-on with views from 'the other side'. A sense of disbelief predominates: how could people miscomprehend, dislike, or overlook things put into the programmes with so much dedicated professionalism? All sorts of defence mechanisms are mobilized to find a reassuring explanation for viewers' 'misconceptions'.[12] In another instance, a British programme maker, watching a video of viewers watching his programme, was reportedly so shocked by what the viewers 'did' to his programme that he couldn't bear it any longer and decided to stop watching.[13] Research begins to take on disturbing qualities here: the actual audiences come too close, become too 'real'.

'Audience research is valuable because its results can be disconcerting', states the Annan Committee in its assessment of the potential uses of research. 'The results may upset long cherished myths held by broadcasters and make them rethink the way to achieve their objectives' (Home Office 1977: 458). Quite so, but in practice it is precisely when results are disconcerting that the truth value of research tends to be questioned, because it undermines the programme maker's professional self confidence. It is in such situations that sentiment grows that 'TV researchers risk becoming dictators', as *The Independent* reports (Douglas 1989).

In their overview of work on professional mass communicators, Ettema, Whitney and Wackman (1987: 759) have noted that 'individual creators need not have a clear idea of whom their audience is or what the audience wants. They need not even grasp the full meaning of their work; it is the industry system as a whole through box office receipts and track records that attunes content to audience and to critic.' This institutional state of affairs is shared by all broadcasters alike, whether they work in commercial or public service settings. Public service broadcasters too, then, work in a structural context which bolsters a love/hate relationship with actual audiences. Their institutional point of view makes it almost impossible for them to avoid seeing the audience – in whose benefit they are assumed to work – as a nuisance, as a recalcitrant other whose visibility needs to be held in check. Perhaps this is the fundamental reason why in the end, despite all criticism and warnings against its dangers, it is the conveniently objectifying information provided by ratings discourse, useful as a management tool of control but principally inadequate as a form of cultural and philosophical self-reflection, that has become the dominant way of knowing the audience in public service broadcasting institutions as well.

Conclusions
Understanding television audiencehood

We must make allowance for the complex and unstable process whereby discourse can be both an instrument and an effect of power, but also a hindrance, a stumbling-block, a point of resistance and a starting point for an opposing strategy.

Michel Foucault (1980a: 101)

BEYOND THE INSTITUTIONAL POINT OF VIEW

First, a short recapitulation of what this book has argued so far. Television audiencehood is a pervasive social and cultural reality in the late twentieth century. In a multitude of ways, sometimes routine sometimes exceptional, television plays an intimate role in shaping our day-to-day practices and experiences – at home but also outside it, at work, at school, in our conversations with friends, family and colleagues, in our engagements with society, politics and culture. However, our understanding of what all these practices and experiences mean, what they imply and implicate, has remained scant. We do not have a sophisticated vocabulary with which we can usefully speak about the nuanced predicaments of our television-saturated world, either in a general sense or in particular instances. The 'we' I am incorporating here refers to the rather loose community of scholars, critics and other intellectuals, whose general task in a free and democratic society it is to interpret and comment upon important developments and events that affect our common conditions of existence. Given television's conspicuousness in contemporary culture and society, this poverty of discourse, this lack of understanding is rather embarrassing indeed, if not downright scandalous.[1]

In this book, I have tried to relate this lack of understanding with the preponderance of the institutional point of view in existing knowledge about the television audience. This point of view is primarily advanced and materialized in the knowledge produced within the television institutions – knowledge that is explicitly aimed at facilitating the institutions' ambition to 'get' the audience. Institutional knowledge is not interested in the social world of actual audiences; it is in 'television audience', which it constructs as an objectified category of others to be controlled. This construction has both political and epistemological underpinnings. Politically, it enables television institutions to develop strategies to conquer the audience so as to reproduce their own mechanisms of survival; epistemologically, it manages to perform this function through its conceptualization of 'television audience' as a distinct taxonomic collective, consisting of audience members with neatly describable and categorizable attributes.

What I hope to have shown in Parts II and III, however, is that even in its own terms institutional knowledge is lacking. Institutional knowledge does not only offer us limited insight into the concrete practices and experiences of television audiencehood; it is also ultimately unable to supply the institutions with the definitive guarantee of control they so eagerly seek.

In Part III, I have traced the tendency toward increasing rationalization of institutional knowledge about the audience within European public service broadcasting organizations. It is a tendency characterized by a change in emphasis from ideological, normative and philosophical knowledge, in which 'television audience' is defined in terms of 'what it needs', to empiricist, factual and informational modalities of knowledge, pre-eminently demonstrated by the mounting prominence of audience research, and audience measurement in particular. This change signifies an eclipse of the classic idea of 'serving the public' in favour of a more market-oriented approach, in which 'television audience' is defined in terms of 'what it wants'. Public service institutions no longer address the television audience as 'citizens', but as 'consumers' – at least at a general, organizational level.

In Part II, however, we have seen that the taxonomic construction of 'television audience' (or segments of it) along the purely objective axis of size in order to come to a streamlined empirical map of it is less unproblematic than it seems: as the pre-eminent form of institutional knowledge in commercial television institutions, ratings discourse is too replete with ambiguities and contradictions to function as the perfect mechanism to regulate the unstable institution–audience relationship. Epistemologically, the whole controversy around the people meter suggests one thing: namely, that in the end the boundaries of 'television audience', even in the most simple, one dimensional terms, are impossible to determine. Those boundaries are blurred rather than sharply demarcated, precarious rather than absolute.

This dissolution of 'television audience' as a solid entity became historically urgent when 'anarchic' viewer practices such as zapping and zipping became visible, when viewing contexts and preferences began to multiply, in short when the industry, because of the diversification of its economic interests, had to come to terms with the irrevocably changeable and capricious nature of 'watching television' as an activity. However, from the institutional point of view this proliferation and dispersal of forms of television audiencehood can only be seen as a problem, because it only makes it more difficult for the television institutions to bring their relationship to the audience under control. Therefore, television institutions can only be reluctant to give up their calculated ignorance of the dynamic complexity of the social world of actual audiences. Instead, they are likely to continue to quest for encompassing, objectified constructions of 'television audience' – as the continued search for the perfect audience measurement technology suggests.

If we abandon the institutional point of view, however, the current disruption brought about by the changing television landscape becomes the historical backdrop that provides us with an excellent opportunity finally to take seriously the challenge of developing understandings that can do justice to the differentiated subtleties of television audiencehood. In order to do this, we must resist the temptation to speak about the television audience as if it were an ontologically stable universe that can be known as such; instead, our starting point must be the acknowledgement that the social world of actual audiences consists of an infinite and ever expanding myriad of dispersed practices and experiences that can never be, and should not be, contained in any one total system of knowledge. To round off this book, then, I shall explore the epistemological and political consequences of such an acknowledgement.

THE ACADEMIC CONNECTION

Academic mass communication researchers, I noted in the Introduction, have often all too easily complied to the institutional point of view in their attempts to know the television audience, not necessarily in a political sense, but all the more in an epistemological sense. This is a bold statement that needs to be substantiated. Perhaps I can best do this by pointing at the cognitive authority inhabited by ratings discourse, not only within television institutions, but also within the academic communication research community.

If ratings discourse derives its effectivity from its assumption that 'television audience' is a taxonomic collective consisting of the sum of audience members defined exclusively in terms of their measurable 'viewing behaviour', this very assumption has also predominated in the search for knowledge about the television audience in academic discourse. For instance, in their prestigious overview of social scientific television research, *Television and Human Behavior*, Comstock *et al.*, to come to a 'depiction of the audience', have decided to draw heavily on data from the A.C. Nielsen company 'because of their freshness and comprehensiveness' (1978: 86). The chapter concerned goes on to extrapolate 'trends and patterns' from the data, which are taken to 'reflect the social phenomena of time use and taste'. Through an array of impressive-looking charts, figures, tables, and graphics, representing things like average hours of viewing per week or by time of day, for different demographic groups, for different types of programmes, and so on, a sense of total overview of 'television audience' is created – a comprehensive map on which all important 'facts' are systematically identified and classified.

In a book simply and revealingly entitled *The Television Audience: Patterns of Viewing*, Goodhart *et al.* have carried out an even more sophisticated discursive streamlining of 'television audience'. It is based upon (mainly British) audience measurement data and is, again, presented as a systematic study of 'how the viewer actually *behaves*' (1975: vii, italics in original). Applying advanced statistical techniques, the authors have managed to construct a dazzling range of curious forms of aggregated audience behaviour, such as 'audience flow' (the extent to which the same audience watches subsequent television programmes), 'repeat-viewing' (the extent to which the same people view different episodes of the same programme), and 'channel loyalty' (the extent to which viewers show a consistent preference for one channel over another). Their mathematical *tour de force* leads the authors to conclude that 'instead of being complex . . . viewing behaviour and audience appreciation appear to follow a few general and simple patterns operating right across the board' (Goodhardt *et al.* 1975: 127). As a result, Goodhardt *et al.* claim to be capable of mapping audience behaviour with all but law-like precision. For example, what they call the 'duplication of viewing law' signifies that for any two programmes the level of 'duplication' or overlap in their audiences can be predicted on the basis of the ratings of the programmes, and not on their content: 'people who watch one particular western are no more likely to watch other westerns than are other viewers' (ibid.: 129).[2] A statistically constructed, objective 'fact' about viewing behaviour is thus established without any reference to the subjectivity of viewers. In this instance the streamlining process has become all but complete: 'television audience' is reduced almost entirely to a set of objective regularities, and seems to be more or less completely purged from any subjective peculiarities in people's engagements with television.[3]

The point here is not necessarily to refute the scientific quality of these conscientiously conducted research projects or to reject their value out of hand, but more positively to examine exactly what is known through such totalizing inquiries into the television audience, to query the discursive horizon they construct, as well as what vanishes beyond that horizon.

Thus, Goodhardt *et al.*'s duplication of viewing law has led them to conclude that watching television does not have much to do with people's preferences and is a quite aselective practice: 'there are discrepancies between what viewers say or feel they would like to watch and what they watch in practice' (ibid.: 127). But to infer from here that what people say or feel they would like to watch is of little interest or significance – because it is not reflected in manifest, measurable 'viewing behaviour' – would be a truncated kind of knowledge, which all too easily reveals its complicity with the institutional point of view. Several authors (e.g. Gunter and Svennevig 1987) have pointed to the 'mediating influence of others' as an explanation for why what people watch does not correlate with what people say they would like to watch: especially when people watch in groups, they often end up watching programmes not of their own choosing, because the choice has been imposed upon them by the dominant individual in the group – usually the father when the group is the family (Lull 1982; Morley 1986). Such discovery of 'intervening variables' between 'viewing behaviour' and 'programme choice' already begins to subvert the decontextualized, one-dimensional definition of 'watching television' that is implied in knowledge that takes for granted the institutional point of view. As David Morley (1986: 19) has remarked, 'to expect that we could treat the individual viewer making programme choices as if he or she were the rational consumer in a free and perfect market is surely the height of absurdity when we are talking of people who live in families'. More generally, what begins to become visible here is the uneven and variable everyday context in which the practices and experiences of television audiencehood are shaped and take on meaning for actual audiences.

Ironically George Comstock, one of the leading figures in mainstream communication research and principal author of *Television and Human Behavior*, has himself inadvertently recognized the limited vision of the knowledge produced by academic researchers. In an article revealingly titled, 'Television and Its Viewers: What Social Science Sees', he notes:

> It is sometimes said that very little is known about television and people beyond the popularity of the former and the fickleness of taste of the latter. This is not really true, if one is willing to accept a scientific definition of 'knowing'. That is, there is a great deal 'known' if one is willing to define the concept of knowing as a state in which there is verifiable evidence that disposes an observer toward one or another set of possible facts or explanations without establishing that such is the case with absolute certainty.

(Comstock 1981: 491)

He then goes on to review the findings which fit in his definition of scientific knowledge, only to come to the conclusion that 'There is no general statement that summarizes the scientific literature on television and human behavior, but if it is necessary to make one, perhaps it should be that television's effects are many, typically minimal in magnitude, but sometimes major in social importance' (ibid.: 504). Even the most fervent supporter of positivist social science must admit that such a conclusion, with its abstracting emphasis on quantified generalizations ('many', 'minimal', 'major'), can at best be called disappointingly trivial. Is this really all that can be said about 'television and its viewers'?

One might object that I have given a rather unfair picture of the accomplishments of communication research here. Indeed, I do not want to risk the danger of slighting all the more focused research efforts that have been made by generations of communication scholars into the television audience, for example, in the contexts of the uses and gratifications approach (which roughly tries to explain 'viewing behaviour' in terms of people's needs or motives) (e.g. Blumler and Katz 1974; Rosengren *et al.* 1985), and of the cultivation analysis perspective (which roughly tries to examine the effects of 'viewing behaviour' on people's conceptions of social reality) (e.g. Gerbner 1969; Gerbner *et al.* 1986). However, even though these research traditions originated in a genuine interest in what watching television implies for the audience not the institutions, I would argue that they unwittingly tend to deepen, rather than challenge the institutional point of view, because they overwhelmingly hold on to the conceptual assumption that 'television audience' is a given taxonomic grouping of serialized individuals who can be described and categorized in terms of measurable variables: not only the conventional variables of ratings discourse but also a host of other ones (depending on the research project concerned): socio-demographic variables, personality variables, television use variables, function variables, gratification variables, effect variables, and so on.[4] The kind of knowledge about the television audience generated from such research strategies, mostly using techniques of multivariate analysis, is generally directed toward condensing measured repertoires of individual responses into aggregated types of audience activity or experience, ultimately resulting in the isolation of distinct viewer types.

One of the most famous viewer types constructed by communication researchers is the 'heavy viewer', on whom all sorts of concerns are projected. Thus, Comstock *et al.* (1978: 309) take some pains in singling out four demographic categories who 'typically are heavier viewers of television': these categories are 'females, blacks, those of lower socioeconomic status, and the elderly', about whom the authors speculate that 'because of psychological and social isolation [they are] particularly susceptible to influence by television'. Indeed, in a substantive review of the international research conducted on 'heavy viewing' from 1945 to the present, Frissen (1988) has shown that communication scholars have been relentlessly preoccupied with describing and explaining 'heavy viewing' as a problematic behavioural phenomenon, related to invariably negative and disturbing psychosocial characteristics such as depression, anxiety, lack of ambition, fatalism, alienation and so on, resulting in a so-called 'heavy viewer syndrome' (Gerbner and Gross 1976). Combined with repeated attempts to set viewers who presumably suffer from this syndrome apart from other groups, 'heavy viewers' tend to be objectified as a category of stereotyped others. In one recent representative article, which sets out to construct a typology of European television viewers using a combination of the uses and gratifications approach and cultivation analysis, the researchers permit themselves to typify the category as follows:

> For those viewers who are interested in all types of programme [i.e. 'non-selective' viewers], watching television is probably a habit, a ritualized way of occupying free time; little time would then be left over for other activities and for the use of other media. An ideal type in this category would be an older manual worker with a low level of education and low income. The image that emerges is of an unresourceful, uncritical, passive person who apparently prefers the world of television to his own world.
>
> (Espe and Seiwert 1986: 320)

Such a characterization, which is by no means untypical (see Frissen 1988), can only be made from a distant, exterior perspective on this trumped-up audience category.[5] So, what started as a genuine interest in viewers apparently unrelated to the institutional concern for audience control, ends up foregrounding a discourse that is just as objectifying and othering as institutional knowledge! By concentrating so heavily on differentiating between groups of viewers, academic communication researchers are driven toward drawing 'fictions' of rigid, reified audience categories, a kind of knowledge that forecloses understanding of the concrete practices and experiences of people because those 'fictions' are regarded as reflecting essential viewer identities that are taken to sufficiently explain certain patterns of 'viewing behaviour'. Consequently, in a paradoxical leap of argument it is (some categories of) the viewers that are implicitly put on trial, not the institutions that provide the programming – as the case of the 'heavy viewer' suggests.[6]

The epistemological limitations of the pull toward generalized categorization implied in the search for viewer types can be illustrated, in an anecdotal but telling fashion, by returning to the couch potatoes, whom we encountered at the very beginning of this book. They are self-proclaimed heavy viewers, who cannot be understood by referring to the academically constructed fiction of this type of viewer. Faced with the idiosyncratic, self-reflective, witty, utterly recalcitrant 'behaviour' of the couch potatoes – and there is no reason to dismiss them as 'atypical' in advance – communication researchers are ultimately left with empty hands, or better, want of words. This suggests that the pull toward categorization should at least be complemented by the opposite one of

particularization (Billig 1987): rather than reducing a certain manifestation of 'viewing behaviour' to an instance of a general category, we might
consider it in its particularity, treat it in its concrete specificity,
differentiate it from the other instances of the general category. Only
then can we begin to understand the multiple practices and experiences of
actual audiences, rather than get stuck with abstracted, simplified fictions
of categories of 'television audience'. Only then can we go beyond
(statistical) 'significance without much signification', as James Anderson
(1987: 371) has put it.

More fundamentally, the very notion of 'viewing behaviour' which
undergirds any taxonomic demarcation of 'television audience' and its
partitioning into fixed categories needs to be questioned. In her review,
Frissen (1988: 149) has concluded that after decades of researching heavy
viewing, 'communication researchers apparently have not yet reached the
point where they describe and explain heavy viewing from an explicit
theoretical standpoint'.[7] What's more, she found that even the very
operationalization of 'heavy viewing' itself has been done rather sloppily,
in purely arbitrary and pragmatic ways, in some cases in terms of number
of hours watching (e.g., two hours, three hours, four hours, ten quarters
of an hour per day, sixteen and a half hours per week), in other cases just
by slicing a certain percentage of the total population that spends the
most time watching television (e.g., 25 per cent, 30 per cent) (ibid.: 142).
This raises the question whether 'heavy viewing', as a type of 'viewing
behaviour', is not an artefact designed to simplify the researcher's task
rather than an actually existing 'syndrome' of a definite category of
people. As a generalized concept, it is devoid of meaning.

To avoid the unwarranted construction of such artefacts which is one of
the liabilities of taxonomic thinking, we should seriously recognize that
'watching television' is always in excess of the sum of the isolatable,
measurable 'viewing behaviour' variables in which it is operationalized. It
should be seen as a complex and dynamic cultural process, fully
integrated in the messiness of everyday life, and always specific in its
meanings and impacts.

FROM THE POINT OF VIEW OF ACTUAL AUDIENCES

My critique of mainstream communication research, then, is directed at 'the
overly condensed character of the variables' (Fielding 1989: 9) used in too
many research projects which claim to try to examine the television audience,
resulting in quite simplistic, empiricist assumptions about what 'watching
television' implies as an activity. As Pierre Bourdieu has remarked,

> the absence of . . . preliminary analysis of the social significance of the
> indicators can make the most rigorous-seeming surveys quite unsuitable
> for a sociological reading. Because they forget that the apparent

constancy of the products conceal the diversity of the social uses they are put to, many surveys on consumption impose on them taxonomies which are sprung straight from the statisticians' social unconscious.

(Bourdieu 1984: 21)

The solution is not simple:

the only way of completely escaping from the intuitionism which inevitably accompanies positivistic faith in the nominal identity of the indicators would be to carry out a – strictly interminable – analysis of the social value of each of the properties or practices considered – a Louis XV commode or a Brahms symphony, reading *Historia* or *Le Figaro*, playing rugby or the accordion and so on.

(ibid.: 20–1)

What Bourdieu calls for, in other words, is the evocation of the irreducible dynamic complexity of cultural practices and experiences, and 'watching television' is no exception.[8]

Consider, for example, a woman's account of the TV viewing habits of her family, mentioned by Hermann Bausinger in his article, 'Media, Technology and Daily Life' (1984: 344): 'Early in the evening we watch very little TV. Only when my husband is in a real rage. He comes home, hardly says anything and switches on the TV.' Here, comments Bausinger, 'watching television' has a very particular meaning, profoundly immersed in 'the specific semantic of the everyday': 'pushing the button doesn't signify, "I would like to watch this", but rather, "I would like to hear and see nothing".'

This example suggests clearly that 'viewing behaviour' can only be adequately accounted for when it is grounded in the concrete situation in which it takes place. 'Watching television' is always behaviour-in-context, a generic term for heterogeneous kinds of activities whose multifarious and shifting meanings can only be understood in conjunction with their contexts. Of course, 'context' itself cannot be reduced to a fixed number of 'background' variables, because contexts are indefinite, and indefinitely extending in time and space.

The practical consequences of this fundamental undecidability of 'watching television' and its 'contexts', can already be traced in the increasing difficulties encountered by the ratings services to measure 'television audience', as we have seen in Part II. Developments within the television industry and the changing television landscape have forced the ratings services to expand the scope of their operationalization of 'viewing behaviour' so as to include an ever increasing number of individual and situational variables. To date, it is unclear when and where, if ever, this stubborn search for more encompassing objectification of 'television audience' will stop. Theoretically, however, it is clear that the loss of control in the audience measurement endeavour signifies a fundamental epistemological crisis. Karin Knorr-Cetina has given a fine characterization of this crisis:

> As the fineness of the grid and the number of relevant attributes increases, we are less likely to guess what the outcome of each arrangement of attributes that marks a social situation will be. This is one way in which we can make sense of the definitive role and the unpredictable dynamics of the situation.
>
> (Knorr-Cetina 1989: 28)

For all practical purposes, the consequences of this crisis cannot be acknowledged as such within the television institutions because their very existence depends upon clearcut measures of 'television audience'. But they can be taken up by academic scholars as a starting point for charting new avenues for understanding television audiencehood. Rather than despair over the insolubility of the crisis, I suggest, we should gladly embrace it, and develop another kind of knowledge on its ruins. Such alternative knowledge – knowledge that is constructed 'from the point of view of actual audiences' – would differ from established knowledge, not only in substance, but also in its political uses. It goes without saying that I can only sketch the outlines of this alternative, for it is only in the process of developing it and articulating it that we will be able to refine and sharpen its focus.

So far as epistemology is concerned, we can follow Knorr-Cetina's (1989) proposal to adopt the principle of 'methodological situationalism' in developing new research strategies, in replacement of the methodological individualism that underlies most research on the television audience (see also Lindlof and Meyer 1987). Giving analytic primacy to concrete situations of television audiencehood rather than to decontextualized forms of 'viewing behaviour' implies a recognition that the social world of actual audiences only takes shape through the thoroughly situated, context-bound ways in which people encounter, use, interpret, enjoy, think and talk about television.

The analysis of micro-situations of television audiencehood should take precedence over either individual 'viewing behaviour' or totalized taxonomic collectives such as 'television audience' because micro-situations cannot be reduced to the individual attributes of those participating in the situation. Thus, the viewer as such does not exist as the stable and unproblematic source of 'viewing behaviour'. As John Fiske (1989: 57) has put it, 'any one viewer . . . may at different times be a different viewing subject, as constituted by his or her social determinants, as different social alliances may be mobilized for different moments of viewing'. In other words, rather than conceiving viewers as having a unified individuality that is consistent across circumstances, they should be seen as inhabiting multiple and mobile identities that fluctuate from situation to situation.[9] Furthermore, situations not psychological dispositions (needs, preferences, attitudes and so on) tend to determine the kind of 'viewing behaviour' that people actualize. For example, Bausinger (1984: 349) refers to the apparently contradictory situation of 'the same man who swears because the sports programme has been delayed by ten minutes because of the Pope's visit, then spends the sports programme working on the flower stand he is making, and hardly notices the programme'. This suggests that in everyday contexts the distinction between viewing and non-viewing is radically blurred. In day-to-day reality audience membership is a fundamentally vague subject position;[10] people constantly move in and out of 'television audience' as they integrate 'viewing behaviour' proper with a multitude of other concerns and activities in radically contingent ways.

Pushed to the extreme, the principle of methodological situationalism holds that 'we cannot ever leave [the] micro-situations' (Knorr-Cetina 1989: 32) in which 'watching television' is practised and experienced in an indefinite number of spaces, at indefinite times. However, this does not mean that micro-situations are completely self-contained, merely following their own, unique principles of organization. On the contrary, micro-situations as interrelated in many different ways and things happening in such situations often transcend the immediate situation. Occurrences in a situation always have references to, and implications for, other situations (ibid.: 36).

One obvious situation-transcending factor is presented by the institutionally-defined constraints placed upon the structural conditions in which watching television can be practised in the first place.[11] The very framework of broadcast television implies the imposition of when and what people can watch. Prevalent scheduling and programming practices impose a temporal arrangement based upon predictability, regularity and repetition (Scannell 1988); the very composition of the menu of programmes being served is determined by the institutions. People cannot, in whatever situation they watch television, outdo these constraints; they can only negotiate with their terms and develop fragmentary tactics to subvert those constraints without ever escaping them (Silverstone 1990). As a result, all micro-situations of watching television are virtually connected to one another in so far as they have to realize themselves in relation to given institutional constraints. This, of course, is the ultimate power of the television institutions, the ultimate basis of their control over the audience.

However, the fact that instances of watching television are 'controlled' in this way 'does not catapult them out of micro-situations', as Knorr-Cetina (1989: 36) has put it. Thus, recognition of the situational dependency of actual audience practices and experiences can shed a new light on the fundamental unpredictability of 'viewing behaviour' – that irritating 'fickleness' of the audience that television industry managers often complain about. It is only in concrete situations that people do or do not comply to the rules for 'watching television' that the institutions implicitly lay down through their scheduling and programming strategies in their attempts to conquer the audience as effectively as possible. Statistically constructed differentiations between categories of viewers notwithstanding, concrete viewers sometimes zap or zip, sometimes don't. This time they watch the commercials, another time they don't. Sometimes, when the situation is right, they decide to watch an educational programme attentively in order to learn from it, at other times they wouldn't bother.

Seen from this perspective, then, variability rather than consistency of 'viewing behaviour' is the order of the day. From this perspective, what are called 'viewing habits' do not represent a more or less static set of characteristics moored in an individual or a group; they are no more than the temporary and superficial snapshots of a never-ending, dynamic and complex process in which 'the fine-grained interrelationships between meaning, pleasure, use and choice' (Hall, in Morley 1986: 10) are shaped in millions of situations.[12] From this perspective, 'television audience' is a nonsensical category, for there is only the dispersed, indefinitely proliferating chain of situations in which television audiencehood is practised and experienced – together making up the diffuse and fragmentary social world of actual audiences.

This brings me to the broader implications for the kind of knowledge emerging from the thoroughly ethnographic thrust of this perspective.[13] Obviously, emphasis on the situational embeddedness of audience practices and experiences inevitably undercuts the search for generalizations that is often seen as the ultimate goal of scientific knowledge. In a sense, generalizations are necessarily violations to the concrete specificity of all unique micro-situations; therefore, it is knowledge about particulars not the general that this perspective tends to highlight. As Stephen Tyler (1986: 131–2) has put forward in a suggestive metaphor, 'It is not just that we cannot see the forest for the trees, but that we have come to feel that there are no forests where the trees are too far apart, just as patches make quilts only if the spaces between them are small enough.' This is not to imply that as researchers we can say something only about one singular micro-situation – one tree or patch – at a time. We can, through some procedure of comparative analysis, look for what situations have in common and in what ways they differ (cf. Marcus and Fischer 1986). But it is unwarranted to add up the results into an ever more generalized, comprehensive system of knowledge that comprises the forest or quilt, i.e. the whole social world of actual audiences, because the very fluid nature of that world resists full representation. The epistemology this implies cannot be reconciled with received notions of cumulative scientific progress, and the partiality at stake is stronger than the normal scientific dictates that we study problems piecemeal, that we must not over-generalize, that the best picture is built up by an accretion of rigorous evidence (Clifford 1986). There is no whole picture that we can strive to gradually 'fill in', because actual audiences are temporally and spatially dispersed and continuously changing formations that can never be pinned down as such.

In other words, if the alternative knowledge we have in mind here can be said to ensue from the standpoint of actual audiences, it should be stressed that by taking it up we cannot presume to be speaking with the authentic voice of the 'real' audience, because there is no such thing. Rather, 'the standpoint of actual audiences' is a discursively constructed, virtual position from which we can elaborate always partial and provisional understandings that evoke the dynamic complexity of television audiencehood rather than imprisoning it in static grids of information. Which brings me to a last point: what relevance can such understandings have, not only within the academic world of communication scholarship but, crucially, outside it?

THE POLITICS OF TELEVISION AUDIENCEHOOD

What I have tried to uncover here is the profundity of the gap between the institutional point of view on the one hand, and the virtual standpoint of actual audiences on the other. From the institutional point of view, watching television is the decontextualized, measurable viewing behaviour that is taken to be the indicator for the existence of a clear-cut 'television audience' out there; from the virtual standpoint of actual audiences watching television is the ill-defined shorthand term for the multiplicity of situated practices and experiences in which television audiencehood is embedded. It is a gap that can be understood in terms of what has been referred to, in a variety of theoretical contexts, as the opposition between macro and micro, the formal and the informal, control and creativity, structure and agency, strategy and tactics, communication as transmission and communication as ritual, the view from the top and the view from the bottom. It is also a gap that gives rise to opposing types of knowledge: one that strives toward prediction and control, and another that aims at reaching what could be called ethnographic understanding, a form of interpretive knowing that purports to increase our sensitivity to the particular details of the ways in which actual people deal with television in their everyday lives.

Meanwhile, television institutions and actual audiences remain locked into one another in so far as the former still to a large degree determine and constrain what the latter can see on their TV sets. These institutional constraints are being thoroughly reshuffled by recent changes in the television landscape. The European public service institutions, especially, are facing a severe crisis, not only in practical (economic, organizational) terms, but also in terms of their normative founding philosophies. The institutions themselves, as we have seen, have responded to this crisis by adopting the discourse of the marketplace in their approach of the audience: defining 'television audience' as a collection of consumers rather than citizens, thinking in terms of 'what the audience wants' rather than 'what it needs'. The residual markers of difference are formulated within, not beyond the boundaries of this overall consumerist framework: 'diversity' and 'quality'. Whither public service broadcasting? This is a complicated and multifaceted political issue which cannot be fully addressed in this context. But I would like to end this book with a few notes that shed light on this issue from the perspective I have tried to develop in the previous pages.

What contribution can ethnographic understandings of the social world of actual audiences make to assess the dilemma? To put it bluntly: little, in a direct sense at least. It cannot – and should not – give rise to prescriptive and legislative solutions to established policy problems, precisely because the ironic thrust of ethnography fundamentally goes against the fixities of the institutional point of view. What it can do, however, is encourage public debate over the problems concerned, by informing critical discourses on television – as a cultural form, as a medium ever more firmly implanted in the everyday texture of modern society – that are independent from established institutional interests. Seriously taking up the virtual standpoint of actual audiences is likely to highlight the limitations of any particular institutional arrangement of television, and can thus serve as a vital intellectual resource for the democratization of television culture.

Let us assume that there is something truly worthwhile to be lost if the seemingly unstoppable process of commercialization would wipe out all institutional undertakings of television provision that are not based upon the overall motive of profit making. Let us assume that some sense of 'public service' should indeed be upheld against the risk for all cultural and social values to be subsumed to purely economic ones. But such political judgements, which presumably must eventually lead to decision making at the level of macro-institutional policy, need not necessarily concur with a defence of the existing institutional embodiments of the public service idea. Nicholas Garnham has usefully remarked that a much more profound cultural politics is at stake here:

> In the battle for the hearts and minds of the public over the future of public service broadcasting it is important to stress that the historical practices of supposedly public service institutions, such as the BBC, do not necessarily correspond to the full potential of public service and may indeed . . . be actively in opposition to the development of those potentials.
>
> (Garnham 1983: 24).

What we should discuss, then, is what that 'full potential of public service' could be in a time so engrossed with 'free enterprise' that the very idea of public service broadcasting seems hopelessly oldfashioned, at least when we persist to conceive it in its conventional, historically-rooted institutional form. As Graham Murdock (1990: 81) has asked, 'can we arrive at an alternative definition of public broadcasting which is capable of defending and extending the cultural resources required for citizenship?'

It is in this respect that ethnographic understanding of the social world of actual audiences may feed the imagination needed to come to such alternatives. We have seen how public service institutions have generally originated in some idealized, mostly rather patronizing concept of what 'serving the public' means, but that it proved to be impossible to uphold such utopian, philosophical definitions of the 'full potential of public service' in the dirty reality of broadcasting practice. I would suggest that we should take this dirty reality seriously if we want to come to new visions of public service television, that do not prematurely comply with the limitations imposed by existing institutional arrangements. This dirty reality, of course, is ultimately nothing other than the intransigence of the social world of actual audiences.

Take the issue of 'quality', one of the spearheads of modern-day public service institutions such as the BBC and VARA. 'Quality' as formally defined and operationalized by the institutions in their programming decisions may well not at all correspond with what in practical terms counts as 'quality' in the social world of actual audiences. We should realize, as Charlotte Brunsdon (1990) has remarked, that people constantly make their own judgements of quality when they watch television, judgements which can vary from situation to situation, depending on the type of satisfaction they look for at any particular time. From this perspective, 'quality' is not a fixed standard of value on which the professional broadcaster holds a patent, but is a radically contingent criterion of judgement to be made by actual audiences in actual situations, 'something that we all do whenever we channel hop in search of an image or sound which we can identify as likely, or most likely, to satisfy' (ibid.: 76).

This is to point out that there is much more to 'quality' than the assurance from the broadcasters that they will try to provide us with what they define as quality programmes: apart from professional quality, presumably a formal characteristic of programmes, there is 'lived' quality as it were, related to the concrete ways in which television is inserted in people's everyday lives. To put it differently, rather than being seen as a predetermined yardstick, 'quality' should be posed as a problem, a problem of value whose terms should be explicated and debated, contested and agreed upon in an ongoing public and democratic conversation about what we, as publics, expect from our television institutions. Ethnographic understanding of the social world of actual audiences can help enrich that conversation because it foregrounds a discourse on quality that takes into account the situational practices and experiences of those who must make do with the television provision served them by the institutions – an open-ended discourse that conceives quality as something relative rather than absolute, plural rather than singular, context-specific rather than universal, a repertoire of aesthetic, moral and cultural values that arises in the social process of watching television rather than through criteria imposed upon from above.

A similar case can be made about 'diversity', the second ideal which contemporary public service broadcasting claims to represent. Several problems pertain to how this concept is generally treated. First of all, defending diversity is often conflated with the expansion of consumer choice, that is, with quantitative rather than with qualitative diversity. It is in this respect that public service discourse becomes almost interchangeable with commercial discourse. Of course, 'diversity' is often defined in more formal terms, that is, in terms of the broad range of programme genres that public service institutions are obliged to transmit, corresponding to the multiplicity of functions that broadcasting is supposed to fulfil, i.e. 'information', 'entertainment' 'drama', 'education' and so on. However, such formal diversity easily overlooks the fact that from the standpoint of actual audiences, these functions often overlap: a popular drama series for example can in some situations, for some people, be more 'informative' or 'educative' than a news or current affairs programme. A formal conceptualization of diversity, in other words, can easily be out of touch with the concrete experiences of those who watch the programmes. Such formalism can be softened by a second, more sociological definition of the ideal of diversity, namely in terms of the responsibility of providing programmes aimed at a variety of 'target groups', including those minority groups that are not of interest for advertisers and are thus not well served in a commercial system. This is a laudable idea, but precisely by equating the concept of diversity with a more or less fixed range of sociologically observable categories within the population (e.g. ethnic minorities, women, the elderly and so on) one risks objectifying those categories and their presumed needs and preferences, and seeing 'diversity' as a static prescript rather than a dynamic and flexible cultural principle which, as Murdock (1990: 81–2) has put forward, aspires to 'engage with the greatest possible range of contemporary experience' and 'offer the broadest possible range of viewpoints on these experiences and the greatest possible array of arguments and contexts within which they can be interpreted and evaluated'. In short, in a programming policy that takes seriously the dynamic complexity of television audiencehood the principle of 'diversity', like that of 'quality', cannot be institutionally predetermined, but should imply a constant and ongoing responsiveness towards and engagement with what is going on at all levels of the larger culture.

From such a perspective, we can only suspend judgement about the most desirable institutional arrangement of television provision in the

1990s and beyond: there is no guarantee that more commercial offerings would necessarily lead to lower quality and less diversity, and that a defence of public service broadcasting based upon established footings would necessarily be the best way to promote these values. Such relativist pragmatism may sound unsatisfactory to those who want unambiguous, once-and-for-all pros and cons. Against this I would argue that ethnographic understanding can be useful precisely because it can be potentially disturbing for the existing institutions, by keeping them from being too arrogant and self-assured about themselves, too self-contained in their cultural policies. More positively, I would suggest that the stance of relativist pragmatism endorsed by ethnography is the only way to create a democratic element in the organization of our television culture, in the sense of enlarging people's opportunity to deliberate and choose, in endlessly varied ways, for what they consider the 'best' television.[14] Against this background, institutional solutions for the regulation of the changing television landscape, especially in Europe, should be sought not in establishing fixed, formalist definitions of quality and diversity, but in securing more flexible conditions in which a plurality of qualities can find their expression.[15] The further political task would then be the construction of institutional arrangements that can meet these conditions.

But this is not the end of the story. What ethnographic understanding of the social world of actual audiences also enables is a critique of facile nominalist notions of 'the consumer', 'the market' and 'what the audience wants' that seem to have been so pervasively embraced by television institutions of all kinds. The ascendancy of these notions in public service institutional settings has been accompanied by a waning of normative discourse on what 'serving the public' should be about, and the adoption of purely empiricist forms of 'feedback'. However, the streamlined information delivering this 'feedback' ignores and obscures the fact that actual audiences are never merely a collection of consumers who happily choose to watch 'what they want'. Indeed, ethnographic knowledge can provide us with much more profound 'feedback' because it can uncover the plural and potentially contradictory meanings hidden behind the catch-all measure of 'what the audience wants'. It can help us to resist succumbing to all too triumphant allegations that commercial success means the victory of the sovereign consumer, for what is discursively equated with 'what the audience wants' through ratings discourse is nothing more than an indication of what actual audiences have come to accept in the various, everyday situations in which they watch television. It says nothing about the heterogeneous and contradictory inter-minglings of pleasures *and frustrations* that television audiencehood brings with it.

The importance of ethnographic discourse, in short, lies in its capacity to go beyond the impression of 'false necessity' (Unger 1987) as prompted by the abstracted empiricism of taxonomized audience information.

It promises to offer us vocabularies that can rob television audiencehood of its static muteness, as it were.

We are living in turbulent times: the television industries and the governments that support them are taking aggressive worldwide initiatives to turn people into ever more comprehensive members of 'television audience'. At the same time, television audiencehood is becoming an ever more multifaceted, fragmented and diversified repertoire of practices and experiences. In short, within the global structural frameworks of television provisions that the institutions are in the business to impose upon us, actual audiences are constantly negotiating to appropriate those provisions in ways amenable to their concrete social worlds and historical situations. It is both the dynamic complexity and the complex dynamics in the interface of this dialectic that ethnographic understanding can put into discourse – a never-ending discourse that can enhance a truly public and democratic conversation about the predicaments of our television culture.

Notes

Introduction

1 The Couch Potato World Headquarters can be reached at PO Box 249, Dixon, CA 95620, USA.
2 See, for the most elaborate theoretical exploration of the clashes between the institutional and the everyday, De Certeau (1984); also Silverstone (1989).
3 Foucault's work is wide-ranging and complex, and interpretations and critiques of his work abound. Personally, I have been particularly convinced by the perspective developed in Dreyfus and Rabinow (1982). In this book, the authors argue that Foucault's distinctive contribution has been the elaboration of a precise theoretical and methodological approach for the study for contemporary forms of social power, called 'interpretive analytics'. Herein, a pragmatically oriented, historical interpretation of the coherence of the concrete practices within society is proposed which avoids both objectivist, totalizing analysis (as in structuralism) and the subjectivist search for deep, intrinsic meaning (as in hermeneutics).
4 In general, a discourse refers to a regulated and systematic set of statements. Foucault more specifically analyses discourse in the context of the institutionalized social practices within which statements are made. Discourse obeys specific rules of operation that provide the space – the concepts, metaphors, analogies, rhetorical figures and so on – for making concrete statements within the boundaries of the sayable. For a further theoretical exploration of the poststructuralist concept of 'discourse' underlying Foucault's theorizing, see MacDonell (1986). For other overviews of the broad field of discourse analysis, see Van Dijk (1985); Potter and Wetherell (1987).
5 Lazarsfeld meaningfully called himself a 'managerial scholar'. His success was forcefully propelled by the emergence of positivist social science on the academic scene. For a painstaking historical study of the gradual institutional legitimization of positivist communication research, see Rowland (1983).
6 These characteristics are typically conceptualized in social psychological terms, i.e. in terms of both independent and dependent 'person' and 'activity' variables (cf. 'attitudes' and 'behaviour', 'persuasion', 'selectivity', 'choice', and so on). See Katz (1987), who defends the Lazarsfeld legacy by stating that its critics pay too little attention to what Lazarsfeld said rather to what he actually did, but never grapples with the fundamental psychologism that pervades and limits the scope of the legacy, no matter how sophisticated its spin-offs.
7 As a matter of pure coincidence, another edited book using the very same title as Barwise and Ehrenberg's (1988) was published in the very same year, namely Drummond and Paterson (1988). This book however does not treat

the television audience as a unified object of research. The perspectives offered are more multivocal, critical, and open-ended. The coincidence does indicate that questions of audience remain continuingly central in studies of television communication.

8 Feyes suggests that some more recent, more sociologically-based mainstream models of media effects – i.e. those of agenda setting, spiral of silence, the knowledge gap and media dependency – provide some relevant notions that can 'bring the audience back into critical communications research' (1984: 230).

9 I will have more to say about this in the Conclusions.

10 I have commented on some aspects of this trend in Ang (1989).

11 Allor (1988) discusses several branches of critical approaches to mass communication (e.g. political economy, feminist theory, cultural studies and postmodern theory) and finds them all epistemologically wanting in their – in his view – monolithic conception of audience. In other words, according to Allor's severe judgement, not only positivist audience research but also theoretical traditions that pretend to be anti-positivist tend to fail in this respect.

12 In the philosophy of knowledge, there has been continuing debate about the nature of the relationship between knowledge and reality. The debate has often centred around the rival assumptions of empiricist and conventionalist philosophies of knowledge. In poststructuralism (which is the most sophisticated branch of conventionalism, and under which Foucault's work has often been put), the foregrounding of the effectivity and power of discourse as the terrain in which meanings, concepts, and categories are constructed, has often led to a nullification of the material existence of 'the real world out there': since we can only speak about the real in and through discourse, it is superfluous to assume and address a pre-existent real at all. Such discursive determinism however is problematic because it collapses the question of ontology into one of epistemology. To shortcut the debate I would like to quote Ernesto Laclau and Chantal Mouffe (1985: 108), who have given the following dissection of the problem: 'The fact that every object is constituted as an object of discourse has nothing to do with whether there is a world external to thought, or with the realism/idealism opposition. An earthquake or the falling of a brick is an event that certainly exists, in the sense that it occurs here and now, independently of my will. But whether their specificity as objects is constructed in terms of "natural phenomena" or "expressions of the wrath of God", depends upon the structuring of a discursive field. What is denied is not that such objects exist externally of thought, but the rather different assertion that they constitute themselves as objects outside any discursive conditions.' See also Lovell (1980); Sayer (1984); Outhwaite (1987).

13 See also Fiske (1987: 16–17).

14 Although I cannot think of any other, more suitable term, naming this whole range of practices and experiences by the single phrase 'social world of actual audiences' is in fact a rather clumsy and inadequate thing to do, because the phrase still runs the risk of retaining the presumption of some self-evident unity of those practices and experiences, while it is exactly this unity that I find problematic.

PART I

1 Institutional knowledge: the need to control

1 Docherty *et al.* (1987) criticize the technological determinism implied in the

popular explanation of the decline of the cinema audience as being directly caused by the rise of television as the most important mass visual medium. The authors claim that both developments can be explained, in Britain at least, by the same sociological factors, most importantly the expansion of home-based consumer culture after the Second World War. Gomery (1985) discusses the American context of the same phenomenon.

2 It is worth noting here that television was not naturally destined to be a medium for private, domestic consumption. Early experiments with television technology were set up with several alternative uses in mind. Television's initial entertainment setting was that of public showings on large-screen television in theatres, while it was also envisioned as a monitoring device for factory production and as a surveillance device in military settings. Furthermore, the possibilities of two-way television as a replacement for the two-way telephone were explored by AT&T in the 1920s, while radio amateurs were also enthusiastic about the interactive potential of television communication. However, these alternative uses were finally marginalized in favour of a development of television analogous to that of radio broadcasting. See Allen (1983). For a historical study of the social construction of television's place in the (American) home, see Spigel (1988).

3 Audience as taxonomic collective

1 Williams' (1974) concept of 'flow' emphasizes that television output is a continuous stream of images and sounds rather than a succession of distinct programmes. Ellis (1982) foregrounds the segmented nature of television's flow of narratives and mini-narratives. According to Ellis, this structure of television discourse already reflects the unconcentrated nature of much home television viewing: it is characterized by the glance rather than the gaze.

2 For some critical assessments of Channel Four, see e.g. Blanchard and Morley (1982); S. Harvey (1989).

PART II

5 Commercial knowledge: measuring the audience

1 There are dozens of ratings firms operating in the United States, all of them attempting to compete for a share in the ratings market, not only for television, but also for radio. In the field of national television ratings, Nielsen has been occupying a hegemonic position since the early 1950s. However, this is not the case in local television ratings, where Nielsen's biggest competitor is the Arbitron Ratings Company. In 1983, a British firm, AGB (Audit of Great Britain), entered the American television measurement field. AGB played a significant role in the controversial introduction of so-called 'people meters', which (temporarily) caused a crisis in Nielsen's hegemony. The European audience measurement scene is dominated by AGB and the Swiss firm Telecontrol.

2 For example, in January 1984, it was estimated that there were 83,800,000 television households in the United States. A programme with a rating of 20, then, can be said to have reached about 16,700,000 households (Beville 1985: 295).

3 Other methods are, among others, the telephone coincidental, the telephone recall, and the personal interview. These methods are generally seen as less

accurate or too expensive and therefore are not much used for the production of television ratings in the United States.

4 It goes without saying that part of the sample will somehow fail to do this. The response rate for the diary method is consequently rather low: 40 to 50 per cent.

5 A distinction is made, then, between 'household data' and 'people data'. In the first, not individual people, but households are taken as the basic unit of measurement, as in Nielsen's National Television Index (NTI). The electronic setmeter can only supply such household data, as it only registers whether the set is on and not who is watching. 'People data', or so-called 'demographics', have traditionally been collected through the diary method. Demographics have been offered, among others, in Nielsen's National Audience Composition (NAC) service. In 1987, Nielsen introduced the 'people meter' (NPM), which offers an integrated measurement service.

6 Other often cited criticisms of ratings from a more or less high culture point of view can be found in Seldes (1951) and Skornia (1965).

7 For a discussion of these criticisms, see e.g. Beville (1985), Chapters 8 and 9.

6 In search of the audience commodity

1 For a comprehensive analysis of structures, philosophies and practices of advertising in modern consumer culture, see Leiss *et al.* (1986). For historical and theoretical perspectives on the emergence and role of advertising in United States, see e.g. Ewen (1976), Schudson (1984) and Marchand (1985).

2 The final set-up of this system of mutual dependency and distribution of control between networks and advertisers came about by the end of the 1950s. Before that, programmes were generally sponsored and produced by one advertiser, over which the networks had little say. The situation changed at the instigation of the networks, who wanted to keep control over scheduling and programming decisions for themselves. This does not mean however that the advertisers have lost their influence on programming. Overt control has made place for more subtle and less visible forms of interference. See Barnouw (1978) and Boddy (1987).

3 The conceptualization of audience as commodity being evoked here has been the object of heated controversy within the political economy of the commercial television. The so-called 'blind-spot debate' was launched by Smythe (1977). See also, among others, Murdock (1978), Livant (1979) and Jhally and Livant (1986). For an epistemological critique of audience commodity theory, see Allor (1988).

4 Traditionally, it has been conveniently assumed that the audience for a programme is the same for the audience for the commercials inserted in it – an assumption which is reflected in the fact that ratings generally only measure the audience for programmes, not for commercials. Many advertisers now question this assumption; they self-servingly (though often correctly) insist that many viewers do not watch the commercials so that their reach is smaller than reported by the ratings. The measurement of audiences for commercials (rather than programmes) is thus, not surprisingly, a major priority in advertising research circles.

5 For the relation between industry and audience in the early years of American radio and the place of fan mail in the conceptualization of that relation, See Stamps (1979). Fan mail as a source of information about the nature of the audience gradually decreased because of its suspected lack of representativeness. Within the British BBC, too, letters from listeners were originally used

as a means to extract information about the audience. Here too, however, the value of the 'post-bag' as a reflection of public opinion was questioned because it had become apparent that the overwhelming majority of letters came from middle-class writers. This perceived lack of representativeness led to demand for more 'scientific' research. See Silvey (1974: 28–31).

6 The service, called Co-operative Analysis of Broadcasting (CAB), was operative from 1930 until 1946, when it was terminated because competition of private entrepreneurs C. E. Hooper and A. C. Nielsen had become too strong.

7 See Hurwitz (1984) for an account of the role of research in the setting up of the infrastructure of the American broadcasting industry. According to Hurwitz (1984: 212), from the late 1920s onwards researchers have become 'institutional middlemen' between broadcasting and advertising managers, and research 'has come to function as an essential mechanism to maintain equilibrium among ever more integrated institutions'.

7 Streamlining 'television audience'

1 This assumption is reflected in the often heard ideological assertion that ratings are for broadcasting what elections are for politics: a form of mass democracy based on a one-man, one-vote system. The problem with this assertion is its implicit assumption that viewers are free to make their choices on an individual basis. Qualitative, ethnographic research however has indicated that since television is often not watched individually but in family contexts, not all viewers get equal opportunity to watch what they want. In this respect, 'one-man, one-vote' should be taken literally: it is often the father in the family who possesses the power to determine what the entire family should watch. See Lull (1982); Morley (1986).

2 This procedure is not unique to audience measurement, but is common to quantitative social research, which leans heavily on the presupposition that people can be aggregated and divided up in distinct categories, the members of which can be defined in terms of isolatable, measurable attributes. For an excellent discussion of this set of assumptions, see Anderson (1987). See also Taylor (1979).

3 Of course, television producers are generally acutely aware of the fact that they cannot control audience responses to their programmes, although they attempt to anticipate to the heterogeneity of the broadcast audience by constructing polysemic texts, that is, programmes that can be interpreted and enjoyed in multiple ways. See, for an elaboration of this argument, Fiske (1987).

4 Psychographic segmentation does not necessarily have to coincide with demographic segmentation. The VALS (Values and Lifestyle Program) system, for example, divides the American population into nine groups based upon a measurement of their values and lifestyles, not upon fixed demographic variables. The existence of competing segmentation procedures only clarifies the 'fictional' nature of constructing a streamlined representation of the audience. It should also be noted that the drive towards segmentation is generally propelled by a wish to determine audience 'quality', defined as 'attractive and relevant to advertising targets'. However, advertising agencies are often highly sceptical about psychographics, because they often find the data to be too rigid, too simplistic, and too unreliable to be useful as tools for predicting advertising effectiveness. See Beville (1985), Chapter 5. See also Plummer (1972); Wells (1974).

5 It may be illuminating here to evoke the common use of the word 'streamlining' in industrial design. Most elementarily, a streamlined design refers to the smooth cigar shapes primarily associated with aviation technology, a profile for aircraft which presumably serves certain functions such as facilitating speed and maximizing air flow. In a more general sense streamlining denotes smooth, curvilinear form and style – an aesthetic that dominated American industrial design from 1930 to the late 1950s, and that connotes eclectic superficiality (streamlined products accentuated the decorative) and ease of consumption. See Hebdige (1988).

6 Of course, the networks also try to 'predict the unpredictable' (Gitlin 1983) through the pre-testing of programmes and programme concepts. However, despite these research efforts the number of programmes that fail (in terms of ratings success) is enormous. For example, in 1986 only 43 per cent of NBC programme series that were launched a year before remained on the screen because their ratings performance was acceptable. There were years when this figure was even lower. See Stipp (1987) for an overview of programme research in American network television.

7 In more theoretical terms, this means that viewers' identities are to be conceived as temporary 'interdiscursive' constructs, the site of a multiplicity of often contradictory subject positions. See Morley (1980b).

8   The streamlined audience disrupted: impact of the new technologies

1 CBS researcher David Poltrack predicts, quite optimistically, that the figure will stablilize at around 63 per cent by 1995. See Broadcasting (12 December 1988: 49). Other prognoses mention the figures of about 62 per cent in 1990 and 55 per cent in 2000 (Krugman and Rust 1987).

2 As a yardstick for the real size of the audience the results of a large-scale telephone coincidental interview survey were used, in which viewers were asked to which channel they were watching at the moment of the telephone call. The telephone coincidental is a classic measurement technique generally considered to be very accurate and 'realistic' as a consequence of its immediacy, but it is also a very expensive method. It is therefore only used as a validation standard. The method was first developed by C. E. Hooper for radio audience measurement in the 1930s.

3 In the early 1980s the cable industry sponsored a study known as CAMS (Cable Audience Methodological Study) which tested a number of methods to measure cable audiences. The results of this study substantiated the cable companies' concern about the 'unfairness' of Nielsen's diary method, and increased the pressure on Nielsen to do something about it. Similar objections were raised by local independent stations, who also complained that they were shortchanged by the diary. It is doubtful however whether the cable companies and independent stations would have displayed the same concern and frustration about ratings 'misrepresentations' had these been in their favour (i.e. if their share of audience would have been over-estimated). See Beville (1985), Chapter 6.

4 Mehling's rhetorical strategy is rather transparent here: his 'Nielsen family' is a high culture-minded one being humbly tolerant to 'mass taste' – a conversion of the usual attitude towards the mass television audience.

5 See Beville (1985: 111). Other possible sources of bias are, among others, the relatively low response rate (40 to 50 per cent), while those who respond tend to watch slightly more than those who do not respond. Furthermore, 'response fatigue' may affect reporting accuracy, especially during the latter part of the week.

6 Incidentally, the willingness of people to co-operate with consumer marketing surveys, of which audience measurement is an instance, seems to drop consistently over time. In reaction, the market research industry recently launched a campaign called 'Your Opinion Counts Public Education Program', partly funded by the Advertising Research Foundation. See Jaffe (1986).

7 By the mid-1980s, Nielsen reported that 7 per cent of the time people spend watching television is done by playing videotapes, while other data indicated that 20 per cent of all VCR owners rent as many as four or more tapes a month. Lardner (1987) offers a fascinating account of the institutional history of the VCR, including the development of the video rental concept.

8 We should not underestimate the creativity of the industry, however. For example, advertisers have found a way to reach the video audience by packaging their ads with the videocassettes people rent. As a result, measurement of video rental audiences became important for advertisers. So, in 1988 Nielsen introduced its experimental Home Video Index, which is able to tell who is watching which videocassettes and how (e.g., fastforwarding through credits, how many times a tape is watched, and so on). Only specially-coded cassettes can be measured by the new technology (*USA Today* 1988; R. Katz 1989). The video market has also provided a huge new source of revenue for the Hollywood film studios, especially from the sales of film copies to video stores. See Gomery (1988).

9 The opportunity to time shift was Sony's major marketing phrase, coined by chairman Akio Morita himself, by which the Japanese electronics company introduced its Betamax VCR in the American market in the mid-1970s. Sony's advertising campaign triggered a hotly debated legal battle between Sony and Universal, one of the major Hollywood television production studios, over the issue of copyright law. The final outcome of the battle was in favour of Sony and, as a consequence, of viewers. In the words of James Lardner (1987: 93), 'Sony had tapped into a desire which had been gathering force, in a stifled and largely unconscious way, all through the thirty-year history of television'.

10 A 1984 Nielsen survey estimated that about 75 per cent of home taping is for time-shifting purposes (mentioned in Potter *et al.* 1988).

9 The 'people meter' solution

1 See, for a description of the various people meter methodologies, Beville (1986b).

2 Sex and age have traditionally been the most important demographic parameters used in network/advertiser negotiations. The computerized data delivery procedure of the people meter makes far more detailed demographic segmentation possible. In 1987, Nielsen's people meter offered ratings information for 39 demographic classifications, AGB 38. AGB was the first to include income categories in its reports (particularly incomes over $30,000 and $40,000). Furthermore, the people meter services deliver demographic information to the cable networks. This focus on measuring smaller segments of the television audience made an increase of the sample size necessary in order to reduce the effects of sampling error, especially for smaller audience segments (such as audiences for the speciality cable channels). Thus, Nielsen's NTI system made use of a sample of 1700 households, its people meter sample is 4000. See *Broadcasting* (7 September 1987: 37). See also Barnes and Thomson (1988) and Miller (1988).

3 AGB contended that 'compliance rates' in Britain, Germany and Italy, where the firm has experience with its people meter, runs at over 90 per cent.

Incidentally, the 'compliance rate' for the traditional diary only runs at about 55 per cent, according to an Arbitron official cited by Gardner (1984). Beville (1985) estimated the response rate of diaries at 40 to 50 per cent.

4 The networks have been the most vocal in attacking the people meter's alleged lack of accuracy (cf. Poltrack 1988; Rubens 1989), while other branches of the industry – such as the cable networks – have been less critical because they expected to benefit from the new measurement system. For one thing, the people meter offered, for the first time, overnight demographic information about cable audiences, which is seen as a 'tremendous advantage' by the cable companies. (*Broadcasting* 5 September 1988).

5 In fact, the infra-red sensing device is used as a check in case viewers do not push buttons. Furthermore, Percy's people meter is distinctive in that it measures audiences for commercials rather than audiences for programmes. Percy planned to introduce its service nationally, but went out of business because of cash flow problems in the summer of 1988 (*Broadcasting*, 15 August 1988).

6 In Europe, too, the passive people meter idea has caught on in the commercial research industry. The French research agency Motivaction has developed Motivac, an electronic detection system that supposedly can identify individuals by their appearance, their known viewing habits and where they usually sit. Jean-Louis Croquet, head of the agency, intends to enter both the French and the British audience measurement market with the system, which was received with widespread scepticism as to both its technical and financial feasibility. See Kleinman (1989).

10   Revolt of the viewer? The elusive audience

1 However, the idea of the living room as a kind of classroom does play a role in the reformist context of public service broadcasting, as we will see in Part III.

2 Besides, in the competitive world of the television industry there cannot possibly be a consensus about what 'ideal' viewing habits are: what is 'ideal' for (one of) the networks may be not so 'ideal' for the advertisers, or for the cable companies, and so on.

3 That anxiety over the Big Brother threat should have become particularly prominent in relation to the people meter, may be explained by the system's greater emphasis on observation of the individual human body, the sacred site of self in Western culture.

4 While the practice of media and marketing research was quite 'neat, tidy and compartmentalized' in the 1960s and 1970s, recent developments in the research industry are said to be stormy. A host of new data-delivery systems are now being developed, all made possible (as is the case with the people meter) by the current availability of computerized, electronic measurement technology. See McKenna (1988: RC3).

5 The ScanAmerica system was not introduced as a national service until early 1989. It has been tested in 600 homes in Denver since April 1987.

6 As we will see in Part III, however, 'audience appreciation' has been included as a variable in European public service audience measurement services from very early on.

7 Papazian (1986) offers an overview of the then available empirical data on demographic and programmatic differentiations in level of attentiveness (however measured). For example, findings suggest that during prime time, only about 70 per cent of all viewers watch television with full attention (during other parts of the day this is far less), while men are consistently more

attentive than women. Moreover, all surveys have established a significant drop of attentiveness during commercial breaks.

8 The study was part of the huge Report to the Surgeon General's Scientific Advisory Committee on Television and Social Behavior, which was commissioned to establish facts about the effects of television violence. Even in that context, however, Bechtel *et al.*'s project was marginalized. As Willard Rowland (1983: 155) has noted, 'as provocative as this research was, its design violated so many of the normal science requirements for acceptable survey research that it had little impact on the major directions taken by the overall advisory committee program. Indeed this study was permitted only as a way of testing the validity of survey questionnaires. The somewhat radical theoretical implications of its findings were largely overlooked at all levels of review in the project.'

9 How far this paradoxical development can go is suggested by the introduction of SmarTV, a system that consists of a combo VCR, personal computer and artificial intelligence technology. One of the key features of the controversial system, developed by San Francisco-based Metaview Corporation, is that it can automatically delete all commercials if that is what the user wants. (*Variety* 14 March 1989) Such clashes of interest between hardware and software industry branches are similar to those in the music industry, where the unrelenting progress in music recording devices (for example, the DAT recorder and Tandy's THOR recorder, which both enable the consumer to record and rerecord music at compact disc quality) has led the software industries to fight back by taking a hard line over the issue of copyright. In the video business, a similar battle is going on over the issue of what is called 'video piracy'. See also Lardner (1987).

10 Discussion about the 'quality' of contemporary network television is now taking place in the context of growing competition from the cable industry. For example, in the 1988 season network television was perceived to be relying on more explicit sex in its programmes in order to recapture the audience it lost, as well as on reality-based 'tabloid TV' – developments criticized for their lowering standards of quality. See e.g. Cobb (1989).

PART III

11   Normative knowledge: the breakdown of the public service ideal

1 The people meter was pioneered in Europe by Irish Television Audience Measurement and by Telescopie in West Germany, both in 1978.

2 However, for a more cautious view see Morrison (1986).

3 Of course, programming policy can be problematic for commercial television too, but in this context it is always ultimately economic calculations that form the deciding factor for both causing and solving the problems.

4 See Burns (1977) for an in-depth analysis of the organizational culture of the BBC.

12   Britain: the BBC and the loss of the disciplined audience

1 It should be noted that the use of entertainment for educational purposes has not only been a theme in conservative cultural politics. It has also been practised by radical groups, who aimed at raising the consciousness of the popular classes. Think, for example, of the work of Bertold Brecht. See also

the case of VARA, to be discussed in Chapter 13. All these popular educational projects can in fact be seen as part of the same modernist desire for general cultural enlightment.

2 See, for theories of the politics of national culture, Gellner (1983) and B. Anderson (1983).

3 It should be noted that British commercial television has been strictly regulated so far. ITV was granted the monopoly privilege to sell spot advertising time for its revenue, and was at the same time held to comply to rules and regulations concerning programming just as the BBC was. Thus, with the advent of ITV the BBC's 'brute monopoly' (Reith) was subverted and replaced by a 'comfortable duopoly'. Competition then has been a very limited affair in British broadcasting: it is a competition over audience attention, not over advertising revenue. This structure is likely to be fundamentally transformed in the 1990s, as the Thatcher government intends to completely deregulate the television market in Britain. See the Home Office White Paper, *Broadcasting in the '90s: Competition, Choice and Quality* (1988).

4 In the first years of commercial television, figures showed that the BBC lost a lot of its audiences to the new channel. Within the BBC, there was some disagreement about how many per cent of the audience share would be sufficient for the BBC to keep its authority. Some thought 35 to 40 per cent would be enough; others preferred to strive for a 50:50 split between the BBC and ITV.

5 This is the central argument made by Burns (1977) in his study of the development of BBC organizational culture.

6 The BBC even has the official 'duty to study the reactions, needs and interests of the public they serve' in order to provide 'suitable and sufficient means for the representation to the Corporation of public opinion on the programmes broadcast in the Home Services and for consideration within the Corporation of criticism and suggestions so represented', as stated in Article 15 of the BBC Charter. See Home Office (1977).

13   Netherlands: VARA and the loss of the natural audience

1 See, for more general studies of the Dutch system of pillarization, Lijphart (1968) and Stuurman (1983).

2 Given the central tenets of liberalist ideology, with its strong valuation of individualism, it is not surprising that the liberal pillar was the least rigidly organized of the four. The socialist pillar was also less 'total' than the two religious pillars.

3 In terms of overt behaviour (e.g. membership of the organizations concerned), obedience was certainly widespread. It is less sure, however, to what degree people were satisfied or agreed with the official views of their leaders within the pillar. See Akkerman and Stuurman (1985: 16).

4 The pillarized broadcasting system, which became legalized in the Netherlands in 1930 recognized the legitimacy of five private broadcasting organizations, each assumed to be the representatives of the various currents of thought prevailing within the nation. These organizations were AVRO (General Radio Broadcasting Association), which called itself national and neutral but which generally speaking recruited its members among those with a liberal orientation (e.g. entrepreneurs); NCRV (Dutch Orthodox Protestant Broadcasting Association), which represented the orthodox protestants; KRO (Catholic Broadcasting Association), representing the catholics, the socialist VARA (Association of Workers' Radio Amateurs), and finally, the small

VPRO (Liberal Protestant Broadcasting Association), for the liberal protestants.

5 Thus, contrary to most other public broadcasting systems Dutch broadcasting organizations are not charged with the obligation to be 'neutral' or 'balanced' in their provision of information, education and entertainment. On the contrary, showing one's colours serves as the pre-eminent motto. See De Boer (1946) and Bardoel *et al.* (1975).

6 This democratic structure of the association of VARA still exists, and its collective rituals (e.g. meetings to discuss VARA policy and the organization of spring and autumn festivities) are still kept alive by an assorted, ever shrinking and ever ageing group of loyal members (many of whom have been devoted social democrats since the interwar years). Within the organization as a whole, the Association Council, consisting of delegates from the districts, is officially the highest decision-making body. See Sluyser (1965) for a fond and moving ethnographic description of the culture of VARA democracy in the 1930s, based upon his own personal experiences and memories.

7 However, conversations with listeners who were around in the interwar years, carried out in the early 1980s, revealed that they certainly did not only listen to the programmes of their own pillar. See Manschot (1987).

8 Thus the first serious large-scale audience survey, *Radio and Leisure in the Netherlands*, was commissioned by the Minister of Education, Art and Science in 1954.

9 Article 14c of the 1987 Dutch Media Act requires that a broadcasting organization 'represent in her programming a particular . . . social, cultural, religious or spiritual current and to direct its programming to the satisfaction of social, cultural or religious or spiritual needs living within the population'. This article still reflects the traditional 'pillarized' principle.

10 This is, of course, a rather limited and reformist notion of cultural emancipation, based upon the assumption that the working class would gain by becoming equal to the more privileged classes in society. Thus, other, more radical models of cultural politics – in the form of autonomous cultural production, either along the nostalgic lines of the Arts and Craft movement or according to the revolutionary ambitions of modernism, both of which were influential within the Dutch social democratic movement between the two World Wars, were never embraced within VARA. See Weijers (1988).

11 The British original – as well as the satire genre in general – was also very controversial. See Briggs (1985: 336–7). This suggests that the turmoil these programmes generated has international dimensions, and is not so nationally specific as some commentators have implied.

12 For Greene, inclusion of provocative programmes was a logical corollary of his philosophy that the BBC should be a true mirror of all trends in society. See Chapter 12.

13 Many of these programme makers belonged to the New Left, the liberal leftist movement that swept the Western world in the 1960s.

14 As a matter of fact, *Van Onderen* was blandly categorized as 'information' in official VARA discourse, thereby disregarding the radical activist aspect of the philosophy from which the programme evolved (Programma Advies Raad 1973).

15 In 1969 VARA changed its statutes: it loosened its formal ties with the Labour Party and the Social Democratic Trade Union, and decided to broaden its political commitments to all groups on the left. This, of course, was instigated by more general developments within the Left: with the emergence of the New Left and other new social movements, such as feminism. With the change of statutes VARA expressed its wish to serve as a forum for all these groups, but

this 'podium function' never achieved substantive results. See Pennings (1985b).

16 See also De Bock (1983). In this paper De Bock, then head of the Audience Research Department of the Dutch Broadcasting Foundation, proposes market segmentation as a necessary survival instrument for broadcasting organizations. He uses VARA's case as an example.

17 See Cirese (1982) for an illuminating account of Gramsci's complex theory of popular culture. See also Hall (1981).

18 In this sense, Van Dam's discourse reminds us of Laclau's theoretical rejection of the Marxist dogma of the necessary belongingness of certain social elements, e.g. the working class, to certain ideological movements (e.g. socialism). According to Laclau, such belongingness is not a predetermined given, but must be actively articulated in concrete political practice. See Laclau (1977).

19 Thus, it is misleading to suggest that the search for quality does not figure at all in American commercial television. See e.g. Feuer *et al.* (1984). See, on the difficulties with the concept of 'quality', Collins (1989a) and Brunsdon (1990).

14   Repairing the loss: the desire for audience information

1 Silvey's past as an advertising researcher must have played a significant historical role in setting the direction of the development of BBC audience research. Furthermore, he made several trips to the USA where he acquainted himself with American audience measurement systems, although he was very well aware of the limitations brought about by the commercial nature of the American research enterprise.

2 When ITV, the British commercial television institution, was etablished, it set up a completely separate, metered ratings system (TAM). In this respect, the relationship between buyers and sellers of broadcasting time is comparable to that in the United States. For a long time, then, two competing audience measurement operations existed in Britain. The results often conflicted: the findings generated by the BBC system were often favourable to BBC programmes; TAM findings tended to produce estimates of audience size that favoured ITV programmes. These discrepancies led to widespread scepticism about the credibility of the figures in the British press, and spawned extensive methodological discussion. See e.g. Silvey (1974), Chapter 11. In 1981 BBC and ITV embarked on a shared audience measurement system designed to cover the entire field of British broadcasting. This system, using AGB people meter technology, is carried out under the responsibility of an independent body, BARB (Broadcasters Audience Research Board), in which representatives of the BBC, ITV and the advertising community are grouped. See e.g. Fiddick 1989.

3 Metered measurement was set up by STER (On Air Advertising Foundation), an independent organization within the Dutch broadcasting system that sells air time for spot advertising. STER revenues go to the benefit of the public broadcasting organizations and make up about one third of their budget.

4 It concerns the AGB 4900 People Meter.

5 Appreciation is not measured in the case of foreign channels, teletext and VCR use.

6 Among the things studied were the comprehensibility of several BBC programmes. Often, the results were rather unfavourable for the broadcasters, which led Silvey (1974: 142) to comment that 'the findings of the inquiry were received with something less than ecstacy in some quarters'. The BBC also took the initiative to investigate the effects of television on children, which

resulted in Hilde Himmelweit *et al.*'s classic study *Television and the Child* (1958), while the psychologist William Belson was appointed to an inquiry into the effects of television on adults.

7 Personal communication, 8 March 1989.

8 Reported to me by Dick Wensink, VARA researcher, personal communication (15 February 1989).

9 The Swedish Audience and Programme Research Department uses the telephone interview as a method of measuring the audience.

10 This sums up the basic framework of the suggested model, although the model as a whole is more complicated as it also allows for context variables such as the supply of the competition. See Van Cuilenburg and McQuail (1988).

11 According to Dick Wensink and Wim Bekkers, personal communication, 8 March 1989.

12 Wensink, personal communication, 15 February 1989. Nevertheless, interest in pre-testing research is flourishing because pre-testing results do sometimes prove to predict future ratings. For example, VARA decided to schedule the Australian soap opera *Neighbours*, then already hugely popular in Britain, on the basis of satisfying pre-testing results. However, the American experience (where pre-testing has been practised by the commercial networks since the very beginning) has shown that the predictive value of this research instrument is at least limited: programmes that do not do well in pre-testing sessions can become tolerably successful as well, the most famous examples being the situation comedy *All in the Family* and police series *Hill Street Blues*. See Gitlin (1983) and Stipp (1987).

13 The video is a specimen of Collett and Lamb's research of people watching television (who videotaped people in front of the small screen); the (tragic) anecdote was mentioned in Morley (1989).

Conclusions

1 For an historical and sociological analysis of the task of intellectuals as 'interpreters' in (post)modern culture and society, see Bauman (1987).

2 For a methodological critique of this 'finding', see Wober and Gunter (1986).

3 A similarly objectivist and totalizing picture is offered in Barwise and Ehrenberg (1988). It should be noted that these authors have a business school background; it is therefore not surprising that they tend to formulate problems in terms relevant to the business world (advertisers, the marketeers).

4 See, for other critiques of these research traditions, e.g. Elliott (1974); Bybee (1987); Newcomb 1978; Hirsch (1980; 1981).

5 It is interesting to note that Espe and Seiwert (1986) did not find it necessary to paint an equally detailed image of what they call 'information viewers'. In this case, they limit themselves to stating that for this viewer type 'the medium represents a source of political and cultural information, further education, intellectual stimulation and debate' (1986: 321). Why not add to this, for example, the image of the snobbish, hypocritical or elitist television-hater? Is it perhaps because the researchers themselves identify with this 'high quality' viewer type?

6 Thus, although a lot of concern over 'heavy viewing' was related to the presumed harmful effects of watching too much violence on television and so overtly instigated by anti-institutional motives, generally the researchers, certainly in the American context 'were . . . unwittingly co-opted into various economic and political agendas' (Gans 1980: 79). According to Gans, the researchers were not only being used to support the politicians and interest

groups seeking to alter network programming, but were also indirectly involved in the networks' attempt to maintain the status quo. See also Rowland (1983).

7 According to Frissen (1988), this lack of explicit theorization is due to the failure of the researchers concerned to take a critical and conscious stance toward the common sense discourse of public concern about the harmful effects of watching 'too much' television. They have therefore unwarrantedly adopted the terms of that discourse without reflecting on their conceptual validity. Gans (1980: 78) also criticizes the lack of reflection on what he calls 'the metaphysical assumptions of effects research', with its automatic emphasis on 'bad' effects of the media.

8 This is not the place to discuss extensively the methodological implications of this change of perspective. In general, my critique implies a profound questioning of the large-scale, quantitative survey research methods that have been preferred in mainstream communication research, based as it is precisely on the aggregation of data and condensed operationalizations of variables. However, 'quantitative' and 'qualitative' research procedures can – and will – for the time being exist parallel to each other in the social sciences. It is important to develop more careful and theoretically sound conceptions of the relative applicability and limitations of both types of research methods and the kind of data they engender. Bourdieu's (1984) work is an excellent example of the sophisticated use of a combination of survey and ethnographic data. His work also points to the importance of extensive, non-empiricist, theoretically-informed interpretation – and thus, story telling – if one wants to make sense of any kind of data, something which tends to be denied by supporters of positivism. In general, 'quantitative' methods can be seen as relevant for charting general, structural patterns (although, as we have seen, in insensitive hands the patterns found risk to be reified), while 'qualitative' methods are indispensible for understanding forms of cultural meaning and practical consciousness that are hidden behind large-scale patterns. See, for comprehensive treatments of this subject, grounded in explicit theoretical or epistemological considerations, Giddens (1984: 281–347); Sayer (1984); Anderson (1987).

9 See, for a related, poststructuralist critique of psychology's conception of the individual as an integrated subject with a unified identity, Henriques *et al.* (1984).

10 See, for an explication of the importance of 'vagueness' in daily patterns of social interaction, Lindlof and Meyer (1987: 25).

11 Other situation-transcending factors include the traces of cultural positionings and identifications that people 'bring into' and actualize within concrete situations, such as those along the lines of gender, class, ethnicity, generation, and so on, as well as cultural ideologies as to the meaning of television as a social and aesthetic phenomenon. See e.g. my discussion of 'the ideology of mass culture' in Ang (1985a).

12 The limited predictability that sometimes does occur in measured viewing behaviour, allowing for the statistical construction of 'viewing habits', can be explained by the fact that many people, due to the routines in which they have to organize their everyday lives, tend to reproduce similar situations for their recurring television watching practices. Two comments can be made on this. First, these (daily, weekly, and so on) practices are of course never completely similar, (thick) descriptions of each individual situation will certainly reveal subtle differences (the telephone rings, the mood is different, and so on); second, it is fair to expect that when people's living conditions change, they are likely to change their viewing situations as well, thereby altering their 'viewing habits'.

13 As I have pointed out in the Introduction, this change of perspective has already begun to be explored in some recent developments in
audience research, developments that are characterized by a distinctively
ethnographic interest in the social world of actual audiences, in the
contradictory practices and experiences of people living with television.
Ethnography has recently been conceptualized as more than just a research
method, but as a practice of inquiry and writing particularly suitable to do
justice to the complex and dynamic character of contemporary cultural life.
See e.g. Clifford and Marcus (1986); Marcus and Fischer (1986); Van Maanen
(1988).

14 I base my endorsement of relativist pragmatism on the work of Richard Rorty
(1989).

15 In this respect, both the commercial notion of consumer choice and the public
service idea of representational diversity are indispensible values. Richard
Collins (1989a) has usefully noted that while the old public service
broadcasting order was based upon the idea of 'internal' diversity (that is, the
provision of a range of programmes within a limited number of channels run
by institutions given the mandate to do so), the new television landscape opens
up the possibility of extending 'external' diversity (in which a plurality of
channels provides strongly 'branded', single type programming). While there is
no definitive answer to the question of the respective benefits and losses of
both types of regulating of diversity, the new situation does offer more
opportunity of choice and this improvement should not be underestimated,
certainly not in the age of postmodernity, with its orientation toward
increasing individual freedom and cultural pluralism (D. Harvey 1989). As
Collins (1989a: 13) has pointed out in discussing these issues, quoting Brecht,
'the good old things are not always preferable to the bad new ones'.

Bibliography

Akkerman, T. and Stuurman, S. (eds) (1985) *De zondige Riviera van het Katholicisme*, Amsterdam: SUA.

Allen, J. (1983) 'The Social Matrix of Television: Invention in the United States', in E. A. Kaplan (ed.) *Regarding Television*, Frederick, MD: University Publications of America.

Allor, M. (1988) 'Relocating the Site of the Audience', *Critical Studies in Mass Communication* 5, 3: 217–233.

Anderson, B. (1983) *Imagined Communities: Reflections on the Origin and Spread of Nationalism*, London: Verso.

Anderson, J. A. (1987) *Communication Research: Issues and Methods*, New York: McGraw-Hill.

Ang, I. (1985a) *Watching Dallas. Soap Opera and the Melodramatic Imagination*, London: Methuen.

—— (1985b) 'The Battle Between Television and Its Audiences', in P. Drummond and R. Patterson (eds) *Television in Transition*, London: BFI.

—— (1987) 'The Vicissitudes of "Progressive Television"', *New Formations* 2: 91–106.

—— (1988) 'Populair en progressief: een eeuwig dilemma? Zeg 'ns AAA en de VARA', in L. Heinsman and J. Servaes (eds) *Hoe nieuw zijn de nieuwe media?*, Leuven: Arco.

—— (1989) 'Wanted: Audiences. On the Politics of Empirical Audience Studies', in E. Seiter, H. Borchers, G. Kreutzner and E. Warth (eds) *Remote Control: Television, Audiences and Cultural Power*, London and New York: Routledge.

Ang, I. and Tee, E. (1987) 'De kwaliteitsomroep van Marcel van Dam (interview)', *De Groene Amsterdammer,* 13 May.

Anstadt, M. (1976) 'De VARA en het socialisme', *Socialisme en democratie* 33, 2: 67–83.

Arnold, M. (1963 [1867]) *Culture and Anarchy*, Cambridge: Cambridge University Press.

Baker, W. F. (1986) 'Viewpoints', *Television/Radio Age*, 10 November.

Bakker, L. (1964) 'Verslag van een bezoek aan Engeland, met als doel een oriëntatie naar het luister- en kijkonderzoek' ['Report on a visit to England with the aim of orientation of listening and viewing research'], Afdeling Studie en Documentatie, Netherlands Radio Union/Netherlands Television Foundation, Hilversum, March.

Bank, J. (1986) 'Televisie in de jaren zestig [Television in the 1960s]', *Bijdragen en mededelingen betreffende de geschiedenis der Nederlanden* 101, 1: 52–75.

Bardoel, J., Bierhoff, J., Manschot, B. and Vasterman, P. (1975) *Marges in de media*, Baarn: Het Wereldvenster.

Barnes, B. E. and Thomson, L. M. (1988) 'The Impact of Audience Information

Sources On Media Evolution', paper presented at the annual meeting of the International Communication Association, New Orleans, May.

Barnouw, E. (1978) *The Sponsor*, New York: Oxford University Press.

Bartos, R. (1986) 'Archibald Crossley: Father of Broadcast Ratings', *Journal of Advertising Research* 26, 1: 47–49.

Barwise, P. and Ehrenberg, A. (1988) *Television and Its Audience*, London: Sage.

Bauman, Z. (1987) *Legislators and Interpreters*, Oxford: Polity Press.

Bausinger, H. (1984) 'Media, Technology and Daily Life', *Media, Culture and Society* 6, 4: 343–351.

Bechtel, R. B., Achelpohl, C. and Akers, R. (1972) 'Correlates between Observed Behavior and Questionnaire Responses on Television Viewing', in E. Rubinstein, G. Comstock and J. Murray (eds) *Television and Social Behavior. Vol. 4. Television in Day-to-Day Life: Patterns of Use*, Washington, DC: United States Government Printing Office.

Bedell Smith, S. (1985) 'Who's watching TV? It's getting hard to tell', *New York Times*, 6 January.

Bekkers, W. (1988) *25 Years of Audience Measurement in the Netherlands: From Counting to Predicting Audiences?* Audience Research Department, Netherlands Broadcasting Foundation, November.

Beniger, J. R. (1986) *The Control Revolution*, Cambridge, MA and London: Harvard University Press.

Beville, H. M. (1985) *Audience Ratings: Radio, Television, Cable*, Hillsdale, NJ: Lawrence Erlbaum.

—— (1986a) 'People meter will impact all segments of TV industry', *Television/Radio Age*, 27 October.

—— (1986b) 'Industry is only dimly aware of people meter differences', *Television/Radio Age*, 10 November.

Billett, J. (1989) 'The Outmoded Panel Game', *Broadcast*, 2 June.

Billig, M. (1987) *Arguing and Thinking*, Cambridge: Cambridge University Press.

Blanchard, S. and Morley, D. (eds) (1982) *What's This Channel Fo(u)r?*, London: Comedia.

Blumler, J. G. (1986) 'Television in the United States: Funding Sources and Programming Consequences' in J. G. Blumler and T. J. Nossiter (eds) (forthcoming) *Broadcasting Finance in Transition: A Comparative Handbook*, New York and London: Oxford University Press.

Blumler, J. G. and Katz, E. (eds) (1974) *The Uses of Mass Communications*, Beverly Hills, CA: Sage.

Blumler, J. G., Brynin, M. and Nossiter, T. J. (1986) 'Broadcasting Finance and Programme Quality', *European Journal of Communication* 1, 4: 343–64.

Boddy, W. (1987) 'Operation Frontal Lobes versus the Living Room Toy: The Battle over Programme Control in Early Television', *Media, Culture and Society* 9, 4: 347–68.

—— (1990) *Fifties Television: The Industry and its Critics*, Champaign, IL: University of Illinois Press.

Bogart, L. (1956) *The Age of Television*, 3rd edition 1972, New York: Frederick Ungar.

—— (1986) 'Progress in Advertising Research?', *Journal of Advertising Research* 26, 3: 11–18.

Bourdieu, P. (1984) *Distinction*, trans. Richard Nice, Cambridge, MA: Harvard University Press.

Bower, R. T. (1973) *Television and the Public*, New York: Holt, Rinehart and Winston.

Briggs, A. (1961) *The Birth of Broadcasting. The History of Broadcasting in the United Kingdom. Vol. 1*, Oxford: Oxford University Press.
—— (1965) *The Golden Age of Wireless. The History of Broadcasting in the United Kingdom Vol. 2*, Oxford: Oxford University Press.
—— (1985) *The BBC: The First Fifty Years*, Oxford: Oxford University Press.
British Broadcasting Corporation (1961) *BBC Audience Research in the United Kingdom: Methods and Services*, London: British Broadcasting Corporation.
Broadcasting (1984) 'Electronic ratings to be tested in US by British company', 17 September.
—— (1987) '1987 ushers in the people meter era', 5 January.
—— (1987) 'Network researchers rate people meters', 6 April.
—— (1987) 'Tartikoff praises VCR's, pans sweeps', 6 April.
—— (1987) 'BFM conference gets down to the bottom line', 4 May.
—— (1987) 'Television in the Peoplemeter Age', 7 September.
—— (1987) 'Television's Shifting Balance of Power', 12 October .
—— (1988) 'NAB, networks call for study of peoplemeters', 21 March.
—— (1988) 'AGB tells networks it needs contracts to survive', 20 June.
—— (1988) 'Arbitron to go with peoplemeter', 27 June.
—— (1988) 'AGB merges, shuts down US operations', 1 August.
—— (1988) 'Ratings services R. G. Percy and AGB are down, if not out', 15 August.
—— (1988) 'Cable to get peoplemeter demographics ', 5 September.
—— (1988) 'CBS study shows slight decline in three-network viewing through 1995', 12 December.
—— (1988) 'Plotting the future of ratings', 26 December.
Broadcasting Research Unit (1986) *The Public Service Idea in British Broadcasting: Main Principles*, London: Broadcasting Research Unit.
Brown, L. (1971) *Television: The Business Behind the Box*, New York: Harcourt Brace Jovanovich.
Browne, N. (1984) 'The Political Economy of the Television (Super)Text', *Quarterly Review of Film Studies* 9, 3: 174–82.
Brunsdon, C. (1990) 'Problems with Quality', *Screen* 31, 1: 67–90.
Burgelman, J. (1986) 'The Future of Public Service Broadcasting: A Case Study for a "New" Communications Policy', *European Journal of Communication* 1, 2: 173–202.
Burns, T. (1977) *The BBC: Public Institution and Private World*, London and Basingstoke: Macmillan.
Bybee, C. R. (1987) 'Uses and Gratifications Research and the Study of Social Change', in D. L. Paletz (ed.) *Political Communication Research: Approaches, Studies, Assessments*, Norwood, NJ: Ablex.
Cantor, M. M. (1980) *Prime-time Television: Content and Control*, Beverly Hills, CA: Sage.
Cardiff, D. (1980) 'The Serious and the Popular: Aspects of the Evolution of Style in the Radio Talk 1928–1939', *Media, Culture and Society* 2, 1: 29–47.
Cardiff, D. and Scannell, P. (1981) 'Radio in World War II', *The Historical Development of Popular Culture in Britain (2)*, Milton Keynes: The Open University Press.
Carey, J. W. (1989) *Communication as Culture*, Boston: Unwin Hyman.
Carman, J. (1987) 'Networks fight for survival', *San Francisco Chronicle*, 19 September.
Centraal Bureau voor de Statistiek (1954) *Radio en vrijetijdsbesteding*, Utrecht: Centraal Bureau voor de Statistiek.
—— (1962) *Radio, televisie en vrijetijdsbesteding. Herfst 1960*, Zeist: Centraal Bureau voor de Statistiek.

Chaney, D. (1986) 'Audience Research and the BBC in the 1930s: A Mass Medium Comes into Being', in J. Curran, A. Smith and P. Wingate (eds) *Impacts and Influences*, London and New York: Methuen.

Chang, B. G. (1987) 'Deconstructing the Audience: Who Are They and What Do We Know About Them', in M. McLaughlin (ed.) *Communication Yearbook 10*, Beverly Hills, CA: Sage.

Cicourel, A. V. (1981) 'Notes on the Integration of Micro- and Macro-levels of Analysis', in K. Knorr-Cetina and A. V. Cicourel (eds) *Advances in Social Theory and Methodology*, London: Routledge & Kegan Paul.

Cirese, A. M. (1982) 'Gramsci's Observations on Folklore', in A. Showstack Sassoon (ed.) *Approaches to Gramsci*, London: Writers and Readers.

Clifford, J. (1986) 'Introduction: Partial Truths', in J. Clifford and G. E. Marcus (eds) *Writing Culture*, Berkeley, CA: University of California Press.

Clifford, J. and Marcus, G. E. (eds) (1986) *Writing Culture: The Poetics and Politics of Ethnography*, Berkeley, CA: University of California Press.

Cobb, N. (1989) 'The Sex Appeal of Prime Time', *San Francisco Chronicle*, 19 May.

Collett, P. and Lamb, R. (1986) 'Watching People Watching Television', Report to the Independent Broadcasting Authority.

Collins, R. (1989a) 'The White Paper on Broadcasting Policy', *Screen* 30, 1/2: 6–23.

—— (1989b) 'The Language of Advantage: Satellite Television in Western Europe', *Media, Culture and Society* 11, 3: 351–71.

Comstock, G. (1981) 'Television and Its Viewers: What Social Science Sees', G. C. Wilhoit and H. de Bock (eds) *Mass Communication Yearbook, Vol. 1*, Beverly Hills, CA: Sage.

Comstock, G., Chaffee, S., Katzman, N., McCombs, M. and Roberts D. (1978) *Television and Human Behavior*, New York: Columbia University Press.

Connell, I. and Curti, L. (1985) 'Popular Broadcasting in Italy and Britain: Some Problems and Issues', in P. Drummond and R. Paterson (eds) *Television in Transition*, London: BFI.

Cook, W. A. (1988) 'Water Shortages and People Meters', *Journal of Advertising Research* 28, 5: 7–8.

Cronholm, M. (1989) 'Mass Communication Research at Sveriges Radio', *Nordicom Review of Nordic Mass Communication Research* 1: 21–6.

Czitrom, D. (1982) *Media and the American Mind*, Chapell Hill, NC: University of North Carolina Press.

Daudt, H. and Sijes, B. A. (1966) *Beeldreligie* [Religion of the Image], Amsterdam: Polak & Van Gennep.

Davis, B. (1986) 'Single source seen as "new kid on block" in TV audience data', *Television/Radio Age*, 29 September.

De Bock, H. (1974) 'Waarderingsdimensies in het CPO-TV', Netherlands Broadcasting Foundation, Audience Research Department, November.

—— (1983) 'Bij het scheiden van de markt leert men de omroepen kennen', Hilversum: Nederlandse Omroep Stichting.

—— (1984) 'Het E.P.O.S. van het kijkonderzoek', Netherlands Broadcasting Foundation, Audience Research Department, November.

De Boer, J. (1946) *De plaats van de omroep in het openbare leven in Nederland tot 1940*, Ph.D Dissertation, Universiteit van Leiden.

De Boer, J. and Cameron, P. (1955) 'Dutch Radio: The Third Way', *Journalism Quarterly* 32, 1: 62–9.

De Certeau, M. (1984) *The Practice of Everyday Life*, trans. S. Randall, Berkeley, CA: University of California Press.

De Hond, M. (1977a) 'De nieuwe leden van de VARA', internal report.

—— (1977b) 'De VARA en haar toekomstige leden', internal report.

Docherty, D., Morrison, D. and Tracey, M. (1987) *The Last Picture Show?*, London: BFI.

Donlon, B. (1987) 'How will TV's new ratings system rate?', *USA Today*, 15 July.

Douglas, T. (1989) 'TV Researchers Risk Becoming Dictators', *The Independent*, 12 April.

Dreyfus, H. L. and Rabinow, P. (1982) *Michel Foucault: Beyond Structuralism and Hermeneutics*, Chicago: The University of Chicago Press.

Drummond, P. and Paterson, R. (eds) *Television and Its Audience: International Research Perspectives*, London: BFI.

Durand, J. (1988) 'Research Without Frontiers: Towards Europe-wide Television Audience Measurement', *EBU Review* 39, 3: 11–16.

Ehrenberg, A. S. C. and Wakshlag, J. (1987) 'Repeat-viewing with People Meters', *Journal of Advertising Research* 27, 5: 9–13.

Ellemers, J. E. (1979) 'Nederland in de jaren zestig en zeventig', *Sociologische Gids* 26, 6: 429–51.

Elliott, P. (1972) *The Making of a Television Series*, London: Constable.

—— (1974) 'Uses and Gratifications Research: A Critique and a Sociological Alternative', in J. G. Blumler and E. Katz (eds) *The Uses of Mass Communications*, Beverly Hills, CA: Sage.

—— (1977) 'Media Organizations and Occupations: an Overview', in J. Curran, M. Gurevitch and J. Woollacott (eds) *Mass Communication and Society*, London: Edward Arnold.

Ellis, J. (1982) *Visible Fictions*, London: Routledge & Kegan Paul.

—— (1983) 'Channel 4: Working Notes', *Screen* 24, 6: 37–51.

Enzensberger, H. M. (1979) 'Constituents of a Theory of the Media', in H. Newcomb (ed.) *Television: The Critical View*, New York and Oxford: Oxford University Press.

Espe, H. and Seiwert, M. (1986) 'European Television-Viewer Types: A Six Nation Classification by Programme Interests', *European Journal of Communication* 1, 3: 301–25.

Espinosa, P. (1982) 'The Audience in the Text: Ethnographic Observations of a Hollywood Story Conference', *Media, Culture and Society* 4, 1: 77–86.

Ettema, J. S., Whitney, D. C. and Wackman, D. B. (1987) 'Professional Mass Communicators', in S. Chaffee and C. Berger (eds) *Handbook of Communication Science*, Newbury Park, CA: Sage.

Euromedia Research Group (1986) *New Media Politics*, London: Sage.

Ewen, S. (1976) *Captains of Consciousness*, New York: McGraw-Hill.

Feuer, J. (1984) 'MTM Enterprises: An Overview', in J. Feuer, P. Kerr and T. Vahimagi (eds) *MTM 'Quality Television'*, London: BFI.

Feuer, J., Kerr, P. and Vahimagi, T. (ed.) (1984) *MTM 'Quality Television'*, London: BFI.

Feyes, F. (1984) 'Critical Mass Communications Research and Media Effects: The Problem of the Disappearing Audience', *Media, Culture and Society* 6, 3: 219–32.

Fiddick, P. (1989) 'The Ratings Game', *The Listener*, 5 January.

Fielding, N. G. (1989) 'Between Micro and Macro', in N. G. Fielding (ed.) *Actions and Structure: Research Methods and Social Theory*, London: Sage.

Fierman, J. (1985) 'Television Ratings: the British are Coming', *Fortune*, 1 April.

Fiske, J. (1987) *Television Culture*, London: Methuen.

—— (1989) 'Moments of Television: Neither the Text Nor the Audience', in E. Seiter, H. Borchers, G. Kreutzner and E. M. Warth (eds) *Remote Control: Television, Audiences and Cultural Power*, London and New York: Routledge.

Foges, P. (1989) 'Network Blues', *The Listener*, 27 April.

Foucault, M. (1972) *The Archaeology of Knowledge*, trans. A. M. Sheridan Smith, London and New York: Tavistock Publications.
—— (1979) *Discipline and Punish*, trans. Alan Sheridan, Harmondsworth: Penguin.
—— (1980a) *The History of Sexuality. Volume 1: An Introduction*, trans. Robert Hurley, New York: Vintage/Random House.
—— (1980b) *Power/Knowledge*, ed. C. Gordon, New York: Pantheon Books.
—— (1981) 'The Order of Discourse', trans. Ian McLeod, in Robert Young (ed.) *Untying the Text*, London: Routledge & Kegan Paul.
Friedman, W. (1989) 'Watching the Watchers', *Broadcast*, 14 July.
Frissen, V. (1988) 'Towards a Conceptualization of Heavy Viewing', in K. Renckstorf and F. Olderaan (eds) *Communicatiewetenschappelijke Bijdragen 1987–1988*, Nijmegen: Katholieke U. Nijmegen.
Frith, S. (1983) 'The Pleasures of the Hearth: The Making of BBC Light Entertainment', *Formations of Pleasure*, London: Routledge & Kegan Paul.
—— (1987) 'The Industrialization of Popular Music', in J. Lull (ed.) *Popular Music and Communication*, Newbury Park, CA: Sage.
Gans, H. (1957) 'The Creator–Audience Relationship in the Mass Media: An Analysis of Movie Making', in B. Rosenberg and D. M. White (eds) *Mass Culture*, New York: Free Press.
—— (1980) 'The Audience for Television – and in Television Research', in S. B. Withey and R. P. Abeles (eds) *Television and Social Behavior: Beyond Violence and Children*, Hillsdale, NJ: Lawrence Erlbaum Associates.
Gardner, F. (1984) 'Acid test for the people meter', *Marketing & Media Decisions*, April.
Garnham, N. (1983) 'Public Service versus the Market', *Screen* 24, 1: 70–80.
—— (ed.) (1989) 'West European Broadcasting', *Media, Culture & Society* 11, 1.
Gellner, E. (1983) *Nations and Nationalism*, Oxford: Basil Blackwell.
Gephart, R. P. (1988) *Ethnostatistics: Qualitative Foundations for Quantitative Research*, Newbury Park, CA: Sage.
Gerbner, G. (1969) 'Towards "Cultural Indicators": The Analysis of Mass Mediated Public Message systems', *AV Communication Review* 17, 2: 137–48.
Gerbner, G. and Gross, L. (1976) 'The Scary World of TV's Heavy Viewer', *Psychology Today*, April.
Gerbner, G., Gross L., Morgan, M. and Signorielli, N. (1986) 'Living with Television: The Dynamics of the Cultivation Process', in J. Bryant and D. Zillman (eds) *Perspectives on Media Effects*, Hillsdale, NJ: Erlbaum.
Giddens, A. (1984) *The Constitution of Society*, Oxford: Polity Press.
Gitlin, T. (1978) 'Media Sociology: The Dominant Paradigm', *Theory and Society* 6, 2: 205–53.
—— (1983) *Inside Prime Time*, New York: Pantheon.
Gold, L. N. (1988) 'The Evolution of Television Advertising – Sales Measurement: Past, Present and Future', *Journal of Advertising Research* 28, 3: 18–24.
Gomery, D. (1985) 'The Coming of Television and the "Lost" Motion Picture Audience', *Journal of Film and Video* 37, 3: 5–11.
—— (1988) 'Hollywood's Hold on the New Television Technologies', *Screen* 29, 2: 82–8.
—— (1989) 'The Reagan Record', *Screen* 30, 1/2: 92–9.
Goodhardt, G. J., Ehrenberg, A. S. C. and Collins, M. A. (1975) *The Television Audience: Patterns of Viewing*, Westmead: Saxon House.
Gray, A. (1987) 'Behind Closed Doors: Video Recorders in the Home', in H. Baehr and G. Dyer (eds) *Boxed In: Women and Television*, London: Pandora Press.

Greene, W. F. (1988) 'Maybe the Valley of the Shadow isn't So Dark After All', *Journal of Advertising Research* 28, 5: 11–15.

Grossberg, L. (1979) 'Interpreting the "Crisis" of Culture in Communication Theory', *Journal of Communication* 29, 1: 56–68.

—— (1984) 'Strategies of Marxist Cultural Interpretation', *Critical Studies in Mass Communication* 1, 4: 392–421.

—— (1988) 'Wandering Audiences, Nomadic Critics', *Cultural Studies* 2, 3: 377–91.

Gunter, B. and Svennevig, M. (1987) *Behind and in Front of the Screen: Television's Involvement with Family Life*, London and Paris: John Libbey.

Gurevitch, M., Bennett, T., Curran, J. and Woollacott, J. (eds) (1982) *Culture, Society and the Media*, London and New York: Methuen.

Hall, S. (1981) 'Notes on Deconstructing "The Popular"', in R. Samuel (ed.) *People's History and Socialist Theory*, Amsterdam: Van Gennep.

—— (1982) 'The Rediscovery of "Ideology": Return of the Repressed in Media Studies', in M. Gurevitch, T. Bennett, J. Curran and J. Woollacott (eds) *Culture, Society and The Media*, London and New York: Methuen.

—— (1986) 'Introduction', in D. Morley *Family Television*, London: Comedia.

Harré, R. (1981) 'Philosophical Aspects of the Macro-Micro Problem', in K. Knorr-Cetina and A. V. Cicourel (eds) *Advances in Social Theory and Methodology*, Boston, London and Henley: Routledge & Kegan Paul.

Hartley, J. (1987) 'Invisible Fictions: Television Audiences, Paedocracy, Pleasure', *Textual Practice* 1, 2: 121–38.

Harvey, D. (1989) *The Condition of Postmodernity*, Oxford: Basil Blackwell.

Harvey, S. (1989) 'Deregulation, Innovation and Channel Four', *Screen* 30, 1/2: 60–78.

Hebdige, D. (1988) 'Towards a Cartography of Taste 1935–1962', in D. Hebdige (ed.) *Hiding in the Light*, London: Comedia/Routledge.

Henke, L. L. and Donehue, T. R. (1989) 'Functional Displacement of Traditional TV Viewing by VCR Owners', *Journal of Advertising Research* 29, 2: 18–23.

Henriques, J., Hollway, W., Urwin, C., Venn, C. and Walkerdine, V. (1984) *Changing the Subject*, London and New York: Methuen.

Hickey, N. (1984) 'Your People Meter Will Be "Watching" Your Every Move', *TV Guide*, 15 December.

Himmelweit, H. T., Vince, P. and Oppenheim, A. N. (1958) *Television and the Child*, London: Oxford University Press.

Hirsch, P. M. (1972) 'Processing Fads and Fashions: An Organization-Set Analysis of Cultural Industry Systems', *American Journal of Sociology* 77, 4: 639–59.

—— (1980) 'The "Scary World" of the Nonviewer and Other Anomalies. A Reanalysis of Gerbner *et al.*'s Findings on Cultivation Analysis. Part 1', *Communication Research* 7, 3: 403–56.

—— (1981) 'On Not Learning From One's Own Mistakes. A Reanalysis of Gerbner *et al.*'s Findings on Cultivation Analysis', *Communication Research* 8, 1: 3–37.

Home Office (1977) *Report of the Committee on the Future of Broadcasting*, London: Her Majesty's Stationery Office.

—— (1988) *Broadcasting in the '90s: Competition, Choice and Quality*, London: Her Majesty's Stationary Office.

Howard, H. H. and Kievman, M. S. (1983) *Radio and TV Programming*, Columbus, OH: Grid Publishing.

Hurwitz, D. (1984) 'Broadcast Ratings: The Missing Dimension', *Critical Studies in Mass Communication* 1, 2: 205–15.

Jaffe, A.J. (1986) 'ARF at 50; It's been embracing the electronic age', *Television/ Radio Age*, 17 March.

Jensen, E. (1986) 'New Ratings Firm to Heat Up Market', *Electronic Media*, 3 November.

Jensen, K. B. (1986) *Making Sense of the News*, Ahrhus: Ahrhus University Press.

—— (1987) 'Qualitative Audience Research: Towards an Integrative Approach to Reception', *Critical Studies in Mass Communication* 4, 1: 21–36.

Jhally, S. and Livant, B. (1986) 'Watching as Working: The Valorization of Audience Consciousness', *Journal of Communication* 36, 2: 124–43.

Katz, E. (1987) 'Communications Research Since Lazarsfeld', *Public Opinion Quarterly* 51, 4: S25-S45.

Katz, R. (1989) 'Exploring Home Video', *Channels of Communication*, September.

Kleinman, P. (1989) 'Entering count-down', *The Times*, 19 July.

Kloos, A. H. (1978) 'Toespraak van de voorzitter van de VARA voor de vergadering van de verenigingsraad' [Chairman's address to the meeting of the VARA Association Council], 10–11 November.

Kneale, D. (1988) ' "Zapping" of TV ads appears pervasive', *Wall Street Journal*, 25 April.

Knorr-Cetina, K. (1989) 'The Micro-Social Order', in N. F. Fielding (ed.) *Actions and Structure: Research Methods and Social Theory*, London: Sage.

Krugman, D. M. and Rust, R. T. (1987) 'The Impact of Cable Penetration on Network Viewing', *Journal of Advertising Research* 27, 5: 9–13.

Kuhn, R. (ed.) (1985) *The Politics of Broadcasting*, Kent: Croom Helm.

Kumar, K. (1977) 'Holding the Middle Ground: The BBC, the Public and the Professional Broadcaster', in J. Curran, M. Gurevitch and J. Woollacott (eds) *Mass Communication and Society*, London: Edward Arnold.

—— (1986) 'Public Service Broadcasting and the Public Interest', in C. MacCabe and O. Stewart (eds) *The BBC and Public Service Broadcasting*, Manchester: Manchester University Press.

Laclau, E. (1977) *Politics and Ideology in Marxist Theory*, London: New Left Books.

Laclau, E. and Mouffe, C. (1985) *Hegemony and Socialist Strategy*, London: Verso.

Lardner, J. (1987) *Fast Forward. Hollywood, the Japanese and the VCR Wars*, New York: Norton.

Latour, B. (1987) *Science in Action*, Milton Keynes: Open University Press.

Leiss, W., Kline, S. and Jhally, S. (1986) *Social Communication in Advertising*, Toronto: Methuen.

Levinson, R. and Link, W. (1986) *Off Camera*, New York: Plume/New American Library.

Levy, M. R. (1982) 'The Lazarsfeld-Stanton Program Analyzer: An Historical Note', *Journal of Communication* 32, 4: 30–8.

Lewis, L. (ed.) (1990) *The Adoring Audience*, Boston: Unwin Hyman.

Liebes, T. and Katz, E. (1986) 'Patterns of Involvement in Television Fiction: A Comparative Analysis', *European Journal of Communication* 1, 2: 151–71.

Lijphart, A. (1968) *The Politics of Accommodation: Pluralism and Democracy in the Netherlands*, Berkeley, CA: University of California Press.

Lindlof, T. R. (ed.) (1987) *Natural Audiences: Qualitative Research of Media Uses and Effects*, Norwood, NJ: Ablex.

Lindlof, T. R. and Meyer, T. P. (1987) 'Mediated Communication as Ways of Seeing, Acting, and Constructing Culture: The Tools and Foundations of

Qualitative Research', in T. R. Lindlof (ed.) *Natural Audiences: Qualitative Research of Media Uses and Effects*, Norwood, NJ: Ablex.

Livant, B. (1979) 'The Audience Commodity: On the "Blindspot" Debate', *Canadian Journal of Political and Social Theory* 3, 91–106.

Livingston, V. (1986) 'Statistical skirmish: Nielsen cable stats vex cable net execs', *Television/Radio Age*, 17 March.

Lovell, T. (1980) *Pictures of Reality*, London: BFI.

Lu, D. and Kiewit, D. A. (1987) 'Passive People Meters: A First Step ', *Journal of Advertising Research* 27, 3: 9–14.

Lull, J. (1980) 'The Social Uses of Television', *Human Communication Research* 6, 3: 197–209.

—— (1982) 'How Families Select TV Programmes: A Mass Observational Study', *Journal of Broadcasting* 26, 2: 801–11.

—— (ed.) (1988a) *World Families Watch Television*, Newbury Park,CA: Sage.

—— (1988b) 'The Audience as Nuisance', *Critical Studies in Mass Communication* 5, 3: 239–42.

McCain, T. (1985) 'The Invisible Influence: European Audience Research', *Intermedia* 13, 4/5: 74–8.

MacDonell, D. (1986) *Theories of Discourse*, Oxford: Basil Blackwell.

McKenna, W. J. (1988) 'The Future of Electronic Measurement Technology in US Media Research', *Journal of Advertising Research* 28, 3: RC3-RC7.

McQuail, D. (1969) 'Uncertainty About the Audience and the Organization of Mass communication', in A. Halmos (ed.) *The Sociology of Mass Communicators*, Keele: University of Keele.

—— (1987) *Mass Communication Theory: An Introduction*, London: Sage.

Madge, T. (1989) *Beyond the BBC: Broadcasters and the Public in the 1980s*, Houndsmills, Basingstoke and London.

Manschot, B. (1987) 'Televisie: tussen afstomping en plezier', in T. Van der Kamp and H. Krijnen (eds) *Dagelijks leven in Nederland*, Amsterdam: De Populier.

—— (1988) 'Publieke omroep en programmastrategie', in L. Heinsman and J. Servaes (eds) *Hoe nieuw zijn de nieuwe media?*, Leuven: Acco.

Marchand, R. (1985) *Advertising the American Dream*, Berkeley, CA: University of California Press.

Marcus, G. E. and Fischer, M. M. J. (1986) *Anthropology as Cultural Critique*, Chicago and London: University of Chicago Press.

Marton, A. (1989) 'Ad Makers Zap Back', *Channels of Communication*, September.

Meehan, E. (1984) 'Ratings and the Institutional Approach: A Third Answer to the Commodity Question', *Critical Studies in Mass Communication* 1, 2: 216–25.

Mehling, H. (1962) *The Great Time-Killer*, Cleveland, OH: The World Publishing Co.

Metz, C. (1975) 'The Imaginary Signifier', *Screen* 16, 2: 14–76.

Miller, C. (1989) 'Subconscious', *The Listener*, 24 August.

Miller, P. V. (1988) 'People Meters: Thoughts on the Evolution of A New Measurement Technology', paper presented at the annual meeting of the International Communication Association, New Orleans, May.

Mingo, J. (1983) *The Official Couch Potato Handbook*, Santa Barbara, CA: Capra Press.

Mingo, J., Armstrong, R. and Dodge, A. (1985) *The Couch Potato Guide to Life*, New York: Avon Books.

Mollema, G. and Voskuil, B. (1989) 'De Methode Van Dam (interview)', *Nieuwe Revu*, 30 March.

Morgan, J. (1986) 'The BBC and the Concept of Public Service Broadcasting', in C. MacCabe and O. Stewart (eds) *The BBC and Public Service Broadcasting*, Manchester: Manchester University Press.

Morley, D. (1980a) *The 'Nationwide' Audience*, London: BFI.

—— (1980b) 'Texts, Readers, Subjects', in S. Hall, D. Hobson, A. Lowe and P. Willis (eds) *Culture, Media, Language*, London: Hutchinson.

—— (1986) *Family Television: Cultural Power and Domestic Leisure*, London: Comedia.

—— (1989) 'Changing Paradigms in Audience Studies', in E. Seiter, H. Borchers, G. Kreutzner and E. M. Warth (eds) *Remote Control: Television Audiences and Cultural Power*, London and New York: Routledge.

Morrison, D. (1986) *Invisible Citizens. British Public Opinion and the Future of Broadcasting*, London and Paris: John Libbey.

Murdock, G. (1978) 'Blindspots about Western Marxism: A Reply to Dallas Smythe', *Canadian Journal of Political and Social Theory* 2, 109–19.

—— (1990) 'Television and Citizenship: In Defence of Public Broadcasting', in A. Tomlinson (ed.) *Consumption, Identity, Style,* London and New York: Comedia/Routledge.

Newcomb, H. (1978) 'Assessing the Violence Profile Studies of Gerbner and Gross: A Humanistic Critique and Suggestion', *Communication Research* 5, 3: 64–82.

Newcomb, H. and Alley, R. S. (1983) *The Producer's Medium*, New York: Oxford University Press.

Nightingale, V. (1986) 'What's Happening to Audience Research?', *Media Information Australia* February, 39: 18–22.

NOS (1989) *Experiences with the PeopleMeter in the Netherlands*, Hilversum: Netherlands Broadcasting Foundation, Audience Research Department.

Outhwaite, W. (1987) *New Philosophies of Social Science*, Houndsmills: Macmillan.

Papazian, E. (ed.) (1986) *TV Dimensions '86*, New York: Media Dynamics Inc.

Pauka, T. (1974) 'De televisie is een ongemakkelijk zitmeubel', *Massacommunicatie* 2, 2: 72–85.

Pekurny, R. (1982) 'Coping with Television Production', in J. S. Ettema and D. C. Whitney (eds) *Individuals in Mass Media Organizations: Creativity and Constraint*, Newbury Park, CA: Sage.

Pennings, P. (1985a) 'Identiteitskonstrukties in de jaren zestig', unpublished report, Vakgroep Collectief Politiek Gedrag, University of Amsterdam.

—— (1985b) 'De strijd om de identiteit, 1970–1976', unpublished report, Vakgroep Collectief Politiek Gedrag, University of Amsterdam.

Peters, J. D. (1986) 'Institutional Sources of Intellectual Poverty in Communication Research', *Communication Research* 13, 4: 527–59.

—— (1988) 'Information: Notes Toward a Critical History', *Journal of Communication Inquiry* 12, 2: 9–23.

Plummer, J. (1972) 'Life Style Patterns', *Journal of Broadcasting* 16, 1: 79–89.

Poltrack, D. (1988) 'Living With People Meters', *Journal of Advertising Research* 28, 3: RC8-RC10.

Potter, J. and Wetherell, M. (1987) *Discourse and Social Psychology*, London: Sage.

Potter, W. J., Forrest, E., Sapolsky, B. S. and Ware, W. (1988) 'Segmenting VCR Owners', *Journal of Advertising Research* 28, 3: 29–39.

Programma Advies Raad (1973) 'Advies over de Van Onderen-programma's', Internal report, VARA, 8 May.

Radway, J. (1988) 'Reception Study: Ethnography and the Problems of Dispersed Audiences and Nomadic Subjects', *Cultural Studies* 2, 3: 359–76.

Rengelink, J. W. (1954) 'Het omroepbestel. Autocratische of democratische cultuurvorming?', *Socialisme en democratie*, 11, 5: 311–18.

Richeri, G. (1985) 'Television from Service to Business: European Tendencies and the Italian Case', in P. Drummond and R. Paterson (eds) *Television in Transition*, London: BFI.

Rojek, C. (1985) *Capitalism and Leisure Theory*, London and New York: Tavistock.

Rolland, A. (1989) 'Norwegian Broadcasting and Mass Communication Research', *Nordicom Review of Nordic Mass Communication Research* 1: 15–19.

Rorty, R. (1989) *Contingency, Irony, and Solidarity*, Cambridge: Cambridge University Press.

Rose, R. (1989) *Ordinary People in Public Policy*, London: Sage.

Rosengren, K. E., Wenner, L. A. and Palmgreen, P. (eds) (1985) *Media Gratifications Research*, Beverly Hills, CA: Sage.

Rosenthal, E. M. (1987) 'VCRs having more impact on network viewing, negotiation', *Television/Radio Age*, 25 May.

Ross, C. (1988) 'Viewers Tuning Out of the Networks', *San Francisco Chronicle*, 22 April.

Rowland Jr., W. D. (1983) *The Politics of TV Violence*, Beverly Hills, CA: Sage.

Rubens, W. S. (1984) 'High-Tech Audience Measurement for New-Tech Audiences', *Critical Studies in Mass Communication* 1, 2: 195–205.

—— (1989) 'We Don't Care About Research Quality Anymore', *Journal of Advertising Research* 29, 1: RC3–RC6.

Saarloos, J. (1989) 'Programme Appreciation and Audience Measurement: The Dutch Way', paper presented at the 121st ESOMAR Seminar on Broadcasting Research: Experiences and Strategies, January.

Said, E. (1985) *Orientalism*, London: Penguin.

San Francisco Chronicle (1987) 'First People Meter Ratings Confirm Fears', 17 August.

—— (1989) 'New "People Meter" Device Spies on TV Ratings Families', 1 June.

Sayer, A. (1984) *Method in Social Science*, London: Hutchinson.

Scannell, P. (1988) 'Radio Times: The Temporal Arrangement of Broadcasting in the Modern World', in P. Drummond and R. Paterson (eds) *Television and its Audience*, London: BFI.

Scannell, P. and Cardiff, D. (1982) 'Serving the Nation: Public Service Broadcasting before the War', in B. Waites, T. Bennett and G. Martin (eds) *Popular Culture: Past and Present*, London: Croom Helm.

Schaafsma, H. (1965) *Beeldperspectieven*, Amsterdam: Wetenschappelijke Uitgeverij.

Schiavone, N. P. (1988) 'Lessons From the Radio Research Experience For All Electronic Media', *Journal of Advertising Research* 28, 3: RC11–RC15.

Schlesinger, P. (1987) *Putting 'Reality' Together: BBC News*, 1st edition 1978, London: Routledge.

Schudson, M. (1984) *Advertising: The Uneasy Persuasion*, New York: Basic Books.

Seiter, E., Borchers, H., Kreutzner, G. and Warth, E. (eds) (1989) *Remote Control: Television, Audiences and Cultural Power*, London and New York: Routledge.

Seldes, G. (1951) *The Great Audience*, New York: Viking.

Sendall, B. (1982) *Independent Television in Britain. Vol 1. Origin and Foundation, 1946–62*, London and Basingstoke: Macmillan.

Sepstrup, P. (1986) 'The Electronic Dilemma of Television Advertising', *European Journal of Communication* 1, 4: 383–405.

Silverstone, R. (1989) 'Let us then Return to the Murmuring of Everyday Practices: A Note on Michel de Certeau, Television and Everyday Life', *Theory, Culture & Society* 6, 1: 77–94.
—— (1990) 'Television and Everyday Life: Towards an Anthropology of the Television Audience', in M. Ferguson (ed.) *Public Communication: The New Imperatives*, London: Sage.
Silvey, R. (1974) *Who's Listening? The Story of BBC Audience Research*, London: Allen & Unwin.
Sims, J. B. (1989) 'VCR Viewing Patterns: An Electronic and Passive Investigation', *Journal of Advertising Research* 29, 2: 11–17.
Skornia, H. J. (1965) *Television and Society*, New York: McGraw-Hill.
Sluyser, M. (1965) *Een klein mannetje met een klein potloodje*, Amsterdam: Arbeiderspers.
Smith, A. (1986) 'Licence and Liberty: Public Service Broadcasting in Britain', in C. MacCabe and O. Stewart (eds) *The BBC and Public Service Broadcasting*, Manchester: Manchester University Press.
Smythe, D. (1977) 'Communications: Blindspot of Western Marxism', *Canadian Journal of Political and Social Theory* 1, 3: 1–27.
Soong, R. (1988) 'The Statistical Reliability of People Meter Ratings', *Journal of Advertising Research* 28, 1: 50–6.
Spigel, L. (1988) 'Installing the TV Set: The Social Construction of Television's Place in the American home', Ph.D. dissertation, Los Angeles: University of California.
Stamps, C.H. (1979) *The Concept of the Mass Audience in American Broadcasting*, New York: Arno Press.
Steiner, G.A. (1963) *The People Look at Television*, New York: Knopf.
Stipp, H. (1987) 'Programmforschung für amerikanisches Network-Fernsehen am Beispiel NBC', *Media Perspectiven* 6: 388–97.
Stoddard Jr., L. R. (1988) 'The History of People Meters: How We Got To Where We Are (And Why)', *Journal of Advertising Research* 28, 5: RC10–RC12.
Streeter, T. (1987) 'The Cable Fable Revisited: Discourse, Policy and the Making of Cable Television', *Critical Studies in Mass Communication* 4, 3: 174–200.
Stuurman, S. (1983) *Verzuiling, kapitalisme en patriarchaat*, Nijmegen: SUN.
Svendsen, E. N. (1989) 'Media Research at Denmark's Radio', *Nordicom Review of Nordic Mass Communication Research* 1: 1–8.
Swierstra, N. (1975) *Geboorte en opkomst van de V.A.R.A.*, Hilversum: VARA.
Taylor, C. (1979) 'Interpretation and the Sciences of Man', in P. Rabinow and W. M. Sullivan (eds) *Interpretive Social Science*, Berkeley, CA: University of California Press.
Television Audience Assessment (1984) *Program Impact and Program Appeal: Qualitative Ratings and Commercial Effectiveness*, Boston: Television Audience Assessment, Inc.
Traub, J. (1985) 'The World According to Nielsen', *Channels of Communication*, January/February.
Tunstall, J. (1977) *The Media are American*, New York: Columbia University Press.
Turow, J. (1982) 'Pressure Groups and Television Entertainment', in W. D. Rowland Jr. and B. Watkins (eds) *Interpreting Television: Current Research Perspectives*, Beverly Hills, CA: Sage.
TV World (1987) 'The US is Watching', September.
Tyler, S. A. (1986) 'Post-Modern Ethnography: From Document of the Occult to Occult Document', in J. Clifford and G. E. Marcus (eds) *Writing Culture*, Berkeley, CA: University of California Press.

Tyler Eastman, S., Head, S. W. and Klein, L. (1981) *Broadcast Programming: Strategies for Winning Television and Radio Audiences*, Belmont, CA.: Wadsworth Publishing Co.
—— (1985) *Broadcast/Cable Programming: Strategies and Practices*, Belmont, CA: Wadsworth Publishing Co.
Unger, R. M. (1987) *False Necessity*, Cambridge: Cambridge University Press.
USA Today (1988) 'Nielsen will keep watch of videos', 19 August.
Van Cuilenburg, J. J. and McQuail, D. (1988) 'Data voor beleid. Suggesties voor het Nederlandse kijk- en luisteronderzoek. Een gevraagd advies', Amsterdam: Stichting Het Persinstituut, May.
Van Dam, M. (1987) 'Productformule en werkwijze', internal report, VARA, 15 September.
Van den Heuvel, H. (1976) *National of verzuild*, Baarn: Ambo.
Van den Heuvel, A. (1982) 'Prioriteiten 1983', note to VARA management, 5 August.
Van der Gaag, A. (1989) 'Television Research – International Symposium (1)', *Adformatie*, 26 October.
Van Dijk, T.A. (ed.) (1985) *Handbook of Discourse Analysis*, London: Academic Press. .
Van Maanen, J. (1988) *Tales of the Field*, Chicago and London: University of Chicago Press.
Van Wijk, H. (1978) 'De VARA in 1978 en daarna', internal report, VARA, 13 February.
VARA (1983a) *Zorg om de cultuur* [Care for Culture], Hilversum: VARA.
—— (1983b) 'Concept Totaalplan', 24 June.
—— (1984) 'De VARA in Perspectief, beleidsplan 1984–1989', September.
—— (1987) 'Jaarverslag' [Annual Report], Hilversum: VARA.
VARA Gids (1969) 'Verruiming van de doelstelling, wijziging van de statuten', 22 February.
Variety (1989) 'Just what tv's been waiting for: a gizmo that purges commercials', 14 March.
Verstraeten, H. (1988) 'Commercial Television and Public Broadcasting in Belgium: The Tension Between the Economic and the Political Dimension', in P. Drummond and R. Paterson (eds) *Television and Its Audience: International Research Perspectives*, London: BFI.
Waters, H. and Uehling, M. (1985) 'Tuning In on the Viewer', *Newsweek*, 4 March.
Weijers, I. (1988) 'Van ons en voor iedereen, het dilemma van een moderne rode omroep', in M. Krop, M. Ros, S. Stuiveling and B. Tromp (eds) *Het negende jaarboek voor het democratisch socialisme*, Amsterdam: De Arbeiderspers/ Wiardi Beckman Stichting.
Wells, W. D. (1974) *Life Style and Psychographics*, Chicago: American Marketing Association.
Werkgroep Luister- en Kijkonderzoek (1963) 'Report to the NRU and NTS Administrations', 6 November.
White, H. (1978) *Tropics of Discourse*, Baltimore, MD: Johns Hopkins University Press.
Wigbold, H. (1979) 'Holland: The Shaky Pillars of Hilversum', in A. Smith (ed.) *Television and Political Life*, London: Macmillan.
Wilensky, H. L. (1967) *Organizational Intelligence*, New York and London: Basic Books.
Williams, R. (1961) *Culture and Society*, Harmondsworth: Penguin.
—— (1974) *Television: Technology and Cultural Form*, London: Fontana/Collins.
—— (1976) *Communications*, Harmondsworth: Penguin Books.

Wilner, P. (1987) 'Are new forces imposing changes in web TV strategy?', *Television/Radio Age*, 27 April.

Wober, J. M. and Gunter, B. (1986) 'Television Audience Research at Britain's Independent Broadcasting Authority, 1974–1984', *Journal of Broadcasting and Electronic Media* 30, 1: 15–31.

Index